# RAMALA

*A School on Earth*
*teaching*
*The Truth of The Heavens*

# THE WISDOM

## of

# RAMALA

SAFFRON WALDEN
THE C. W. DANIEL COMPANY LIMITED

First published in Great Britain in 1986 by
The C. W. Daniel Company Limited
1 Church Path, Saffron Walden
Essex, England

ISBN 0 85435 185 X

Set in 10 pt Times
by MS Typesetting, Castle Camps, Cambridge
and printed by Hillman Printers (Frome) Ltd, Frome, Somerset

*'Though you may possess all the Knowledge in the World, without the Wisdom to use it, it is as nothing.'*

*The Ramala Source*

## DEDICATION

We dedicate this book to the Source of all Wisdom and to all those who serve that Source.

## ACKNOWLEDGEMENT

We would like to express our gratitude to all those who have given so generously of themselves in order to make this book possible. Its production has truly been a combined effort, with many individuals contributing in thought, word and deed. To all of them we would like to say a heartfelt 'Thank you'.

# CONTENTS

# FOREWORD
## by
## Sir George Trevelyan

If rational materialism were the only truth, then the prospects for Humanity are indeed bleak. Let us eat, drink and be merry for tomorrow we die — by the million! But there emerges in our time the holistic world-view, which brings a supreme hope in our age of turmoil. We rediscover what the Ancient Wisdom knew — that the Universe is Mind, that life in all its diversity is an intricate Oneness, that the Earth is truly an integral being, a living creature of which Humanity is the potential brain and nervous system, that ethereal space is an ocean of life and intelligence and that the human mind can unite with higher Mind and draw knowledge direct from the spiritual world.

So Humanity sets forth on a path of exploration in consciousness, first to transform the self — that one point in the Universe for which we are really responsible — and then to work out the implications of the truth that Humanity is itself One Organism, of which each of us is a cell. Contact with Higher Intelligence is then seen as of paramount importance and this book should help to establish its validity, for it is certainly a fine contribution to the new vision and should arouse much interest in Britain and America and indeed around the world.

The 'author' remains anonymous, for the whole volume consists of teachings given through him as channel, during group meditation at Chalice Hill House, in the holy centre of Glastonbury. This is a sequel to *The Revelation of Ramala* published in 1978 and received in the same way through inner attunement to the Masters of Wisdom.

Of course in such communications we must 'test the spirits' and use our judgement and intuition to sense their validity. But in this time of tension, when the rational intellect alone seems quite inadequate to cope with the planetary problems we have created, then contact with our higher self and with the discarnate Masters of the Spiritual Hierarchy can bring a fresh light and hope into our thinking. Here is a factor wholly ignored in our usual politics, economics and even ecology. We are ignorant of our chief allies who can help in the redemption of the planet.

The emergence of the holistic and spiritual world-view brings a supreme hope for our time. We simply must come to terms with the fact that the Universe is spirit, a living Oneness of Mind to which we can innerly attune for guidance. This present volume is an example of a really clear channel surrendered to the thought of advanced beings from the Hierarchy. These chapters should be read with an open mind and judged on their value in throwing fresh light on our human situation. The book should convince many people that communication with the Higher Worlds is valid and, indeed, invaluable.

In this great transition period into a new Age, when the cleansing of our polluted planet will take place, it is of supreme importance that we all learn, according to our capacity, to attune to the living Powers of the Light. For it appears that a veritable force-field of Light on high solar frequency is at this time being flooded into the material plane, raising the vibratory rate and opening consciousness towards fourth dimensional vision. We must come to terms with this factor, which is vital for our survival. And we shall find that the redeeming power in this force-field is Love.

So I urge you to read this book and sense the depth of wisdom behind the communications. Also appreciate the deep concern of the Masters in the spirit world, in their support of Humanity, as we pass through the period of change into the New Dawn.

# INTRODUCTION

We live in a World in crisis. No matter what our race, colour or creed, no matter whether we dwell in a land of plenty or a land of poverty, no matter whether we live under a government of democracy or a government of autocracy, the Human Race as a whole is fast approaching a moment of decision. We will either have to recognise the divinity of our being or else die. We will either have to recognise that as a Race we are one, no matter what our political, financial or sociological conditioning, or else accept that the divisiveness and separation that exist today will continue to grow at an ever increasing rate until East faces West and North faces South in a conflict to end all conflicts. Humanity, therefore, has to choose between Darkness and Light, between self-centredness and God-centredness. We either have to purify ourselves of our own choice or else be purified in the cosmic fire of a nuclear holocaust.

Since the Ramala teachings were first published over fifteen years ago few would deny that our World has become a more dangerous place. Whilst on the one hand it can be said that a small number of people are emerging to ground and demonstrate a new understanding of life and to bear witness to a new race of Humanity, on the other hand the vast mass of Humanity continues in the pattern of its forbears, a pattern of self-centredness and self-possession rather than of wholeness, or holiness, and sharing. Let us therefore recognise that what we are witnessing is the descent of Humanity, at an ever increasing rate, into Darkness. No matter what its technological and material advances Humanity has lost its soul, its God-centredness. Here in the West, especially, we worship not God but Mammon. We are, therefore, fast approaching a moment of planetary crisis, an event which will signify the ending of an Age, the ending of a pattern, a time which is sometimes called Armageddon, the Apocalypse, the Cataclysm or the Day of Judgement. The Ramala teachings should be seen in this context, namely, that we, as individuals, will soon have to decide where we stand. This is our supreme moment of choice — either to recognise or to deny our spiritual birthright. Each one of us will have to choose and to demonstrate by thought, word and deed whether or not we are ready to participate in the Golden Age of Aquarius, the millennium of Peace and Plenty.

The Ramala Teachers often use the analogy of a lifeboat to describe the purpose of the Ramala Centre and its teachings. They say that the Earth can be likened to a ship on which Humanity is sailing. At present the ship of Earth is sailing through relatively calm waters and even though storms can be seen ahead no-one is particularly interested in building lifeboats or practising lifeboat drills. But when the ship does sail into stormy weather then Humanity will rapidly become interested in the lifeboats, and should the ship of Earth appear to be foundering then many will rush to the safety of these lifeboats. The Ramala Centre therefore is but one of many centres preparing a lifeboat — not a physical lifeboat but a lifeboat of consciousness, as did the prophet Noah before the last great planetary upheaval six thousand years ago. For what was the Ark but a lifeboat, a lifeboat of human consciousness. The purpose of the Ramala teachings is to help Humanity to prepare for this great moment of transformation and transmutation so that we may be ready for the Golden Age that is to come.

It was in the Spring of 1970 that the Ramala teachings were first made available to the general public. Over the years, as their popularity has grown, pamphlets have given way to booklets and then to a book, *The Revelation of Ramala*, first published in April 1978. This book has now been reprinted four times and has also been published in the Dutch, German, Spanish and Scandinavian languages. In 1982 selected teachings were also made available on tape cassettes which have proved to be very popular. Now, three years later, comes the second book containing over thirty of the more recent teachings. This book must be seen as a continuation by the Ramala Teachers of their efforts to help in the transformation of human consciousness. Many of the subjects discussed in earlier teachings are developed and expanded upon.

In particular those teachings which in the past have aroused conflict or have been open to misinterpretation are restated and the spiritual principles behind them more carefully explained.

It is significant, however, that throughout the time that the teachings have been received never once have the Ramala Teachers felt the need to correct anything that has been said or to retract any of their prophecies. Indeed, several of their predictions have already been proved to be correct. The source has been consistent both in its content and its presentation. There has never been any feeling of compulsion or imposition of authority on the part of the Ramala Teachers. They only speak when they are spoken to. They respond only to our soul murmurings, never to our personality desires. They use the channel only for teaching and counselling, never to satisfy personal curiosity. They are concerned with the universal rather than the individual. As many as ten different beings have spoken through the Ramala channel but the bulk of the teachings have been given by just three Teachers. Who they are they will not say, except to describe themselves as belonging to a Spiritual Hierarchy, on a higher plane of existence, responsible for helping Humanity through this time of crisis. It is evident, however, that these Teachers speak through channels all over the World and this is born out by the remarkable similarity of the teachings received through channels living in countries as far apart as India, Australia and the U.S.A.

How are the teachings received? Usually a group of up to twelve people meet in the Ramala sanctuary, known as the Sanctuary of the Holy Grail. After a period of meditation, when the energy has been built up between David and Ann, the husband and wife team who form the channel and who always sit facing each other, one of the Ramala Teachers overshadows David and speaks through him to give the talk. At all times David is fully conscious of what is being said. He likens the experience to standing behind someone who is giving a talk yet being able to hear the words before they are actually spoken. The subject matter of the teachings is nearly always a response to some question that has arisen during recent days or because someone in the meditation group is in need of counselling on some problem that they are facing. The talk normally lasts for twenty to thirty minutes and then the Teacher withdraws and David's personal guide appears to answer any questions that may have arisen from the talk. If the

Ramala Teachers sometimes appear to be remote and impersonal then David's guide, known as Zen Tao, is the very opposite. He has a wonderful and distinctive personality with a delightful sense of humour. He has endeared himself to literally hundreds of seekers. In the questions and answers that follow most of the talks in this book, Z.T. is the abbreviation for Zen Tao, David's guide who answers the questions put to the channel. Because Zen Tao is very close to his instrument and has himself experienced several recent incarnations on the Earth he is well qualified to link the World Visible and the World Invisible. He is often able to translate the spiritual concepts behind the Ramala teachings into a more practical and human standpoint. He is aware, only too well, of our human weaknesses and failings and of the limitations imposed on us by the physical body in which we dwell. At all times, though, he takes great care to ensure that he is not regarded as an authority and does not become a crutch on which we lean. He is always saying that his purpose is not to answer our questions but to get *us* to answer our own questions.

We therefore introduce this book to you by saying, as would our Teachers, that it should not be regarded as an authority. It should not be thought of as a bible, as a book of religious dogma. Its true purpose is that of being a mirror, to awaken in the reader his or her own spiritual knowingness. There exists the trinity of belief, knowledge and knowingness or spiritual insight, and of these three spiritual knowingness is the source to which we must turn if we are to successfully face the trials and tribulations of physical life. It is only when we have established that link with our divine spirit that we can be at one with the flow of all life, that we can understand the true nature of the tragic events happening in our World. It is only too obvious that events are now happening at a rate faster than Humanity can either control or understand. Humanity, in the form of its religions and its sciences, can no longer explain the true nature of life. It is only too apparent that Humanity is no longer controlling World events either natural or human. Humanity is now being controlled by World events. Many people, therefore, are seeking a new understanding, a new perspective on the reality of physical life, but it is difficult to achieve this in the World in which we live today, a World where almost every child is conditioned from the cradle to accept the authority of the past. It is here, surely, that the Teachers from the

Higher Planes of life can help us, for they can present a holistic viewpoint of our World, they can give us fresh insight into the true nature of our physical existence. Above all, by their emphasis on the universal rather than the individual, they can help us to see that the Human Race is one, dwelling on one planet under one God. We do not have to agree with their understanding of life and death, of the World Visible and the World Invisible, but we must surely listen in humility to what they have to say.

As with the first book, so *The Wisdom of Ramala* is published anonymously. This is not done out of false modesty or from a desire to avoid contact with the general public, but simply to make it clear that the instruments are not the source of the teachings. Indeed, they themselves are still struggling to exemplify the point of consciousness of the teachings, to ground the wisdom of the Ramala Teachers in their own lives. The teachings should stand or fall by themselves. There is no glamour, no reputation, no recommendation attached to them. It is for you the reader to decide. What is truth for one person may not be for another. If the teachings bring forth a spark of recognition from within you then accept them into your being, but if they clash with your understanding of life then place them aside for the time being. Dip into the book at will. Do not feel that you have to read it from cover to cover. Take from it as you are so inspired, recognising that for some it may be just a single seed form.

The teachings have been presented in the chronological order in which they were received. The first to the last embraces a period of four years. They have been selected, from several hundred teachings received, on a purely subjective basis. Many have been edited and condensed but always with strict regard to the original meaning. Inevitably the personality and the soul consciousness of the instrument is imprinted on the teachings, for in this form of communication the Spiritual Hierarchy has to work through the mind of the instrument concerned. Nevertheless, over the years, as trust has been established, so it has become possible for the Teachers to express concepts of life with which the instrument does not agree or else has not yet grown to understand. We humbly offer the Ramala teachings to you, the reader, in the spirit of love with which they were given to us. Our earnest desire is that they will act as the spark which will ignite the flames of your own intuition and so will help you to develop your own personal and unique link with your Creator.

RAMALA
Glastonbury 1985

# EDITOR'S NOTES
## ON
## THE WISDOM OF RAMALA

Since the publication of *The Revelation of Ramala* in 1978 there has been a great deal of feedback to the Ramala Centre concerning the book and, in particular, on the way the teachings were presented. In *The Wisdom of Ramala* we have tried to embody several of the suggestions put to us by our readers and to present the teachings in a more universal form.

Language, of course, can be a great obstacle in any form of communication. The meaning and interpretation of any particular word is never universal. In the first book the Ramala Teachers talked of 'Man' and 'Mankind', although meaning both man and woman, and referred to God as 'Him'. Although they themselves are very universal they are forced to use the instrument's language, the language of a patriarchal society. Many women, quite naturally, find this objectionable and so the Teachers have willingly changed their vocabulary. Man and Mankind have now been replaced by the word Humanity and God, being neither male nor female, is referred to as It. Although this may sound very impersonal it does remove the accusation of sexism! Where Man or Woman is used it now refers only to either the male or the female of the species. Numerous other small changes in vocabulary have been made which the reader will discover for himself or herself. The intention always is to be universal rather than individual, to include rather than exclude, and if there are words remaining which give offence we would only say that it is the fault of the instrument's vocabulary, not the Teacher's point of consciousness.

One criticism that was made of the first book was that it was too didactic and that the teachers appeared to talk *at* people rather than *with* them. In practice nothing could be further from the truth and it was obviously a mistake on our part to omit the many questions and answers that came after each lecture. In this book, therefore, we have published a selection of the questions and answers that came after many of the lectures so that the reader can see that there is indeed an open-mindedness and a willingness on the part of the Ramala Teachers to explain and discuss. They have always welcomed the challenge of debate.

Finally, as mentioned elsewhere, the abbreviation Z.T. used in the questions and answers stands for Zen Tao, the name of David's guide, for it is he who answers all the questions put to the Ramala source after each talk. Even through the restricted medium of channelling one cannot fail to be impressed by his open-mindedness and tolerance, by his love and humility, and if this book does nothing else than to introduce him to a wider audience of seekers it will have served its purpose well.

# THE
# RAMALA
# CENTRE

It was in the Spring of 1975 that David and Ann, the founders of Ramala (pronounced Rahmahlah), came to live in Glastonbury. How they came to find and purchase Chalice Hill House is a story in itself but sufficient to say that their inner guidance told them that this old manor house was destined to be the place where Ramala would put down its roots and grow. Over the intervening years many people from all over the World have come and helped them to renovate the house and to turn it into a place of beauty and peace. At the same time that all this work was being carried out on an outer, physical level, so on an inner level, too, creation was taking place. Through the channellings and meditations, through both group and personal experiences, a wonderful energy began to grow. Today the Ramala Centre is a power point where weary pilgrims can come and recharge their spiritual batteries.

The Ramala Centre is now able to offer spiritually minded people, both individuals and small groups, an opportunity to stay at Chalice Hill House either to tap into the Ramala point of consciousness through its teachings and day-to-day living or else to experience the energy of the power centre of Glastonbury, the ancient Avalon. Guests stay on a Bed and Breakfast basis, with evening meal by arrangement. Anyone wishing to stay at the Centre should write for our brochure which provides information on our facilities and current room rates. Donations of stamps are always appreciated. The essential qualifications for all who stay at the Centre are a willingness to serve, the ability to be flexible and open to the moment and a respect for the principles and rhythms of the Centre.

The Ramala sanctuary, situated in the grounds of the house, reflects the nature of the spirit of Ramala — universality. No matter what your race, colour or creed you will find no conflict here. All are welcome to express their understanding of life and whilst in return we offer the Ramala teachings there is no imposition in this matter. We have no desire to convert and only speak of these things when spoken to. During the last year over three thousand people have visited the Centre and therefore reservations or appointments are essential so that visitors can be accommodated without disturbing the work of the Centre. The Centre provides a comprehensive guest information service both on Ramala and on the legends and traditions of Glastonbury, including an audio-visual presentation and lectures on cassette and video tapes, together with articles of interest written by the Centre. The Ramala Centre is happy to host small workshops or conferences given by other groups provided the subject matter has empathy with the Ramala teachings.

We hope that, should you feel the need to make closer contact with Ramala, we will be able to welcome you to Chalice Hill House and that your experience will be a rewarding one both for you, the Centre and the planet.

The Ramala Centre,
Chalice Hill House,
Dod Lane,
Glastonbury,
Somerset BA6 8BZ,
England.

## ARTIST'S NOTES ON THE BOOK COVER

Visual symbols, no matter how universally recognisable they are, must ultimately be rendered and viewed in individual terms. They suggest concepts resulting from experiences which, to a degree, unfold uniquely to us as individuals. The symbols on the cover of *The Wisdom of Ramala* are the result of concepts partially formed during my stay at the Ramala Centre, Chalice Hill House, Glastonbury, where the material for this book was channelled.

The central image, the chalice, symbolizes the search for truth. At the top centre of the chalice is a circle with a cross through it. The circle, God, the cross, Christ, together represent that part in each of us which is directly of God — the Christ Consciousness. It is shown in an emerging, not yet fully formed, state. The dove is of the Heavens, the serpent of the Earth. Together they represent the awakening of the Earth and those who dwell on the Earth through the influences of those beyond the Earthly plane. The Sun, active, the Moon, passive, depict the forces or energies balancing and working throughout the system. At the base of the chalice are the red/orange flames which purify and refine the physical, the violet flames which purify and refine the consciousness.

Below the flames is the twelve pointed star of Ramala with six male (purple) and six female (gold) points. Within the centre of the star the new world is emerging from the old dying world through a trial or purging by fire. Below the star are two bands of the colour spectrum representing all energy: on the left, in its raw or initial form, on the right, order emerging through time (the wave). The female/unicorn figure represents wisdom or understanding, the male/lion figure strength and commitment. They are joined at the chalice in the search for truth. Beyond these figures is space, not a void but teeming with creative energies. In the lower right hand corner is a black flower, my personal symbol, which recognizes that God is the creator and that we are part of God.

David Maclagan,
Harrison Hot Springs,
British Columbia,
Canada.

# THE NEW AGE

I wonder, as you hear my words, if on a physical level you are aware of the responsibilities that have been placed upon the shoulders of all evolved souls at this most critical time in the Earth's evolution. I wonder if you are aware in your innermost beings of the reality of the present world situation and of the choices which Humanity faces at this time. Yes, a new Age is dawning, but many other Ages have come and gone. You yourselves are aware of the events of the Piscean Age and know how its evolutionary cycle has unfolded. You are aware of the human progress that has been achieved but, equally so, you can recognise the errors that have been made. You can see how Humanity has strayed from its destiny path leading to this moment of world crisis which you face today. What, therefore, is so significant about this new Age? Why is this Aquarian Cycle so much more important for the path of human evolution than any other Age, than even the last Piscean Age which witnessed the grounding of the Christ energy?

I will begin by asking you to visualise a ceremony of the ancient Druids, as they met to celebrate the summer solstice. Standing in their circles of stone they would wait expectantly for the sun to rise. They would know the direction and time of its rising, and as they stood in the morning twilight, eyes fixed on the marker stone, so they would be aware of the first rays of light as the sun began to rise towards the visible horizon. You, today, can be compared to those Druids, and the sun is but a symbol of the new Age. At this time you are experiencing the twilight of the Aquarian Age. You cannot see the Age for it has not yet risen above the visible horizon but, like those Druids, you wait in anticipation for it. You cannot yet see its power and its light. You cannot yet know of the path of its evolutionary cycle. You cannot

1

yet know, unless you are a soul of the highest consciousness, of the picture that this Aquarian Cycle will paint on the Earth.

Now there are some today who say that they know these facts and, because of this, they are misleading many people by defining the new Age according to their limited vision. It is for this reason that I speak now to all evolved souls on the plane of Earth at this time. Recognise that you are part of a select band of beings who come on the Earth to initiate and transmute, to help the Earth move forward from one cycle to another. You have experienced this event in many lives, in many cycles, and therefore you feel within you a sense of anticipation, the same as you would await the birth of a baby. You know that the seed has been sown, that the baby has formed itself, that the Age is about to dawn, and that at the correct moment it will come into life and will be touched by the same cosmic breath that awakens a baby to life. You all know that the new Age is soon to dawn. You have within your soul-consciousness the knowledge of the part that you have to play in that birth, the individual responsibilities that you have come to fulfil, for you are the midwives of the Aquarian Age. Although the cosmic energy pattern is present, it still requires individual human activity to ground that cycle to come, in just the same way as the Nazarene grounded the Christ Energy two thousand years ago. It needed his physical presence on the Earth in order to become manifest.

But as we of the Spiritual Hierarchy look down on the Earth at this time we see everywhere that many souls of aged evolution are being misled. It is inevitable, at such a critical time in the Earth's evolution, that the Forces of Darkness should be present just as much as the Forces of Light. Therefore as you strive to ground the energies of the new Age recognise that what you create now, what you bring into physical manifestation, will attract corresponding energies in the Universe as a whole. Hence the Forces of Darkness would like nothing better at this time than to subvert the path of the Aquarian cycle, for this cycle is destined to be the greatest cycle in Humanity's evolutionary path. It will surpass even the evolutionary cycle of Atlantis. Many of you lived in that cycle and have returned now, as part of the karmic pattern for which you are responsible, to prepare the way for the re-emergence of the Atlantean energy. Recognise, therefore, that much of the evil that was present in Atlantis is coming to the surface again. As you look at the planet today, as you observe the quickening of the Earth's vibration and note the increase in the frequency of natural disasters, the increase in Humanity's violence, in its self-centredness, in its arrogance, so you cannot but fail to recognise that you are approaching a time of decision. You are approaching a time when Humanity, both individually and collectively, must decide on a path of action.

To you, perhaps, the concept of Armageddon is frightening. It signifies the release of energies beyond the control of Humanity, but if Humanity did but know it, it rarely controls its environment. Because of its great intellectual progress Humanity has been led into believing that it is the master of its fate, that it is the master of the physical World, that Humanity alone decides the path upon which it walks. But those of you who are aware of the God in all things, who recognise that the Divine Plan alone manifests on this Earth, know in your heart that the cycle which is now beginning was planned aeons of time ago. It has been seen on other levels and has been prophesied by many beings. It is a necessary path of evolution for this Earth. You are here, therefore, as witnesses to that path of evolution. Within your innermost beings is the knowledge of what is to come. It may not be with you on a conscious level, on a level which you can pull down into everyday physical reality, but within your heart is the knowledge of what is to come and the part that you must play in it.

It is, therefore, of the utmost importance at this time that those of you who have come to herald this new Age, who have come to birth this new child, should be true to yourselves, should be true to the spirit within you. You should strive at all times for purity of thought, word and deed, for as you create now so you are creating for the new Age, you are preparing the ground for the new Age seeds that will come. As the sun, symbolising this new Age, rises above the visible horizon, and as you greet it as did the Druids of old, let us hope that you will be able to say that the ground has been properly cultivated and that the souls for which you are responsible have been trained and made aware of their responsibilities. We, for our part, pray that as the light of that sun, as the light of the Age, comes down and the seeds begin to shoot, you will be able to look back and say "I have been worthy of the trust that has been placed in me".

3

Q: Could you be more specific about the nature of life in the new Age. We have so very little to go on.

ZT: I will answer that question by giving you the analogy of Leonardo da Vinci and his aeroplane. You will remember that five hundred years ago Leonardo da Vinci, through his intuitive senses, drew an aeroplane. That was almost four hundred years before the first aeroplane actually manifested in physical reality on the Earth. Now for Leonardo da Vinci to see that aeroplane it was already in existence on another level but even he, and I don't know if any of you have ever seen his simplistic drawing of an aeroplane, would not have been able to grasp, shall we say, the complexity of the aviation world today as represented by the supersonic aeroplane called Concorde. Now your idea of the new Age is similar to the little aeroplane that Leonardo da Vinci drew. Not one of you can conceive of the magnificence of the new Age. You all have, to varying degrees, a little idea within your consciousness of what the new Age represents, but that is all. It is just a line drawing not in the least bit representing the full development of the Aquarian Age.

As I look at the thought forms emanating from you now as you think of the new Age I can discern the esoteric principle of the Age that is dawning. But you, obviously, are not concerned with that esoteric truth at this time. What you are tapping into is the particular aspect of the Age which appeals to you, for you are all individuals and, as individuals, you all have responsibilities for your own particular aspect of the new Age. However you are all tapping into the initial stages of the Aquarian Age, to what is to happen within the next three hundred years. At this moment none of you are seeing beyond that time, and that is only natural because you will, of course, all be incarnating on the Earth again within that period. You will then have to harvest the seeds that you are sowing now.

The Age that is now dawning is, in truth, beyond your comprehension. It will manifest changes on the Earth of which, even in your wildest dreams, you can barely conceive. It will see a new race of Humanity on the Earth. You may find it hard to believe this, but in the imminent re-emergence of the Christ Energy you will be able to see the life cycle of the Aquarian Age. It is an esoteric fact that in

4

the life of the Master, or Masters, who initiate an Age you may see the destiny of the Age that is to come. So as you look at the life of Jesus, he who was overshadowed by the Christ Energy, you may see in his life, and especially in the years of his ministry, the whole evolutionary cycle of the Piscean Age. That, of course, is why people talk of a violent ending to the Piscean Age, why they compare the crucifixion of that Master with the crucifixion of Humanity that is to take place. So, in the not too distant future, in the lives of the beings who will ground the Christ Energy, you may see the evolutionary cycle of the Aquarian Age. They will herald the most significant evolutionary change that has ever taken place on the plane of Earth.

There are souls of great evolution incarnating on the Earth at this time. Some of them have not been present on the Earth for over ten thousand years. However they are incarnating into an environment which they find hard to understand. Your world today is so out of balance that it is almost impossible for an evolved child to find the harmony necessary for spiritual growth. It is therefore imperative that an environment be created where these great souls can manifest their true wisdom and potential, and so allow them to be the heralders of the new Age.

Q: It is so interesting to see how children respond to the right environment. I was watching my son this afternoon listening to a meditation tape. He was absolutely enthralled by it and even commented on how much he enjoyed it when he went to bed. It just shows that if they are exposed to new concepts and ideas they are like little sponges and absorb everything.

ZT: Think back to your own Piscean childhoods and to the way in which you were birthed. Think back to the restrictions which were placed upon you and which perhaps even now you are only just beginning to overthrow and to recognise as false. Those restrictions have confined you to certain paths, to certain ways of life. Let us resolve that our Aquarian children shall be allowed to grow in freedom.

# THE NATURE OF SUFFERING

You are all aware of what it is to suffer, for you yourselves have all suffered, on many levels, to varying degrees. You are aware both of how you as an individual have suffered and of how your family and the World as a whole have suffered. There are therefore two kinds of suffering. There is the perceived suffering when you as an individual see others undergoing their trials and tribulations, their suffering, and there is the suffering which you as an individual experience because of your own actions. It is essential that we comprehend the significance between these two forms of suffering, for they are not the same.

Many people today believe that all suffering can be externalised. They can place the responsibility for their suffering on God, the government, their job or some other person. Let us begin, therefore, by looking at the relationship between God and suffering, for if we understand that relationship we can apply that understanding to all the lesser examples. The question is often posed, both consciously and unconsciously, that if God is a God of love, how then can that God permit suffering? The answer is, of course, that God does permit suffering for suffering is a refining process on the soul's path of evolution. Suffering should not be seen as a punishment visited upon a wayward child by a dominant parent. Suffering is something which both individuals, groups and nations attract unto themselves. It is usually the result of what they have done, of the seeds that they have sown, both in this and previous lives. Although the power that you call God could alleviate that suffering if It so wished, It does not, because It too is ruled by the Laws of the Universe, Laws such as the Law of Cause and Effect and the Law of Equalisation. Therefore, in Its wisdom, your God sees the purpose of suffering. It sees the need for individuals to come to terms with what they have attracted and brought down upon themselves.

7

It is difficult, if your consciousness cannot accept the concept of reincarnation, of life after life after life, to see how suffering can be regarded as an evolutionary process. For if you lead only one life and then perish forever, and if you have suffered deeply and grievously in that one life, then how can there be justice in that? Truly, if that was the case, then life would not be just. But those of you who have walked a little further along the evolutionary path than most of Humanity are aware that you bring into being with you in your physical body all that you have created in other lives, on other levels of existence beyond the physical plane of Earth. You bring with you not only your spiritual wisdom, but also the sins of the past, the lessons you have not learnt, the karma you owe both to yourself and to others. So as you advance through the life which you now lead you will automatically attract unto yourself the lessons which you have chosen to learn, the karma you have chosen to transmute.

If there is one point which I would like to emphasise now, it is this: that suffering is chosen by yourself. It is not given to you by your Creator as a punishment. It is chosen by you, willingly, as a lesson to learn, as a lesson which your soul needs at this particular point in its evolution. Therefore, when you who live in England at this time observe the suffering of other countries, of other races, as they conflict with each other, you must realise that those countries and races are learning a lesson in which you have no part, for you have come to learn a different lesson, a different aspect of evolution. You can observe the suffering of others but you must not become one with it. Recognise that the suffering is part of their lesson. You may express compassion for them, you may offer help when it is sought, but there is little that you can do to ease their suffering, their trials, their tribulations, for that is something which they as individuals have to resolve. You in your wisdom might see the resolution of their problem, the answer that must come about, but you cannot impose that answer upon them. They must bring it forth from within themselves in order to end their suffering.

As you look around the World today you can observe the quickening of the planet, the fact that Armageddon is approaching. Because of this, suffering will abound and multiply all over the planet. No one can avoid it. You, as individuals, must come to terms with that. You must not allow the suffering which this great evolutionary step forward will create to swamp you. It may seem to you that I am inviting you to be hard-hearted, to shut your eyes to the suffering of others, but I am not. Yes, you may have eyes for them. Yes, you may have compassion for them, but do not let the lessons of other people, do not let the karma of other nations, become your karma. You can, of course, take on that burden if you so choose. That is your birthright. But is it the destiny of your choosing? It is so easy to externalise your own suffering, your own lessons, your own evolutionary path, onto the suffering of others, onto the lessons that you have already learnt, because you do not want to face your own path, your own struggle. There are many today who side-track their evolutionary path by placing themselves on the paths of others.

As individuals you are all going to suffer. The basic cause of all suffering is ignorance. There is no need to suffer, for where there is Light, where there is Truth, where the Love of your Creator is present, there can be no suffering. Suffering can exist only in Darkness. It cannot exist in Light. So when you, as an individual, think that you are suffering, recognise that it is because you have not come to terms with yourself as an individual. You have not balanced yourself with the surroundings in which you live, you have not merged your soul, your spiritual wisdom and knowledge, with the physical evolutionary path that you have chosen.

There is no need for suffering. With the understanding of suffering comes the removal of pain, both physical, emotional and spiritual. It is a hard lesson to comprehend, but it is true. If you think back in your life to when you have suffered you will discover that that suffering was born out of a separation between yourself and your Creator. Suffering only occurs when you lose trust in Its Plan, in Its Perfection, in Its total Being within which you live, move and have your being. When you have fear you are not in touch with your Creator. When you have extreme emotion you are not in touch with your Creator. At such times you will suffer. It is in the harmonisation of one's being with the Universe of which you are all a part that there comes an end to suffering.

So as you progress through the years to come, as you face your lessons in life, some painful, some less painful, when you think that you are suffering, look at yourself. Look at that part of you which is suffering. Is it the soul or is it the ego, the personality self? Even the Master Jesus upon the cross suffered. But what was the nature of his suffering? It was not for himself. It was for the World which he was soon to leave, the World which had apparently ignored his message and act of being. He who was overshadowed by the Christ, who had come to lead the World into the Piscean Age, was about to be crucified and the suffering that he felt was the suffering of an evolved soul for a less evolved Earth. It came from his understanding of what the Earth would have to go through. He saw what was to come. That was the nature of his suffering. So when you as individuals suffer, think of that example. Think not of yourselves but of the Earth, for when the Earth as a whole suffers then truly you will suffer as well.

## QUESTIONS AND ANSWERS

Q:   Suffering to me means pain, physical pain, and you cannot say that we do not experience physical pain.

ZT:   There are many forms of suffering. Some obviously involve pain, and when I talk of pain I am talking of physical, emotional and spiritual pain. Believe it or not, the easiest pain to bear of those three is physical pain. So what we are talking about is that eventually one learns not so much to overcome pain but to come to terms with it because one can see a meaning and a purpose in that pain. What is difficult to handle is when one experiences pain for no apparent purpose. If there is a purpose and meaning for the pain, for example when in childbirth, then one comes to terms with that pain and can see it as an evolving process.

When you come to deal with emotional and spiritual pain that is something entirely different. Physical pain is something you can understand, but how do you come to terms with emotional pain, shall we say when your husband or your wife dies and you are left grieving at the loss. Then let us consider the next degree which is spiritual pain. Suppose that you were to die at an early age of a heart attack through abusing your physical body by wrong eating and wrong living and you left behind a wife and young children. From the higher planes of life you would then witness your family living in great difficulties and although you would want to help them you could do nothing about it. That would cause you spiritual pain. That sort of pain is very difficult to come to terms with, but it is something you will all have to face one day.

10

Q: My husband is dying of cancer. It seems to me that his suffering has a far wider implication. There are many more people involved than just him. Is it not a lesson for all of us?

ZT: A popular misconception is that only bad people suffer and that good people are protected from suffering by their good behaviour. That is nonsense. Very often the good suffer for the bad! It is often the case that the good offer to demonstrate great suffering in order to show Humanity not only the nature of their being but also to teach Humanity of the true nature of physical, emotional and spiritual life. Young children, especially children under the age of twelve, who experience death or a high level of suffering, are very often great souls who have come on the Earth to help Humanity, to make Humanity aware of the gift of life, of the real value of one's physical body and of one's emotional and spiritual stability.

The concept that you are not your physical body is one that is difficult to come to terms with. Your body is like a car in which you drive for a short time. What is evolving is not the car, which is gradually wearing out as the mileage gets higher and higher, but the spirit within that car. That is what is learning. That is what is evolving. You must never lose touch with that fact. What you take with you when you die is not the car but the learning whilst driving that car.

It is very difficult to say that I am not my body when one has a painful toothache, because at that stage you are fully aware of your body. But all that your body is doing is communicating with you. What has happened is that your body was talking to you long before the pain but you would not listen to it. Eventually, the only way your body could make you listen was to scream, and when the body screams that is pain. At that stage there is little that you can do except listen to the screaming. That is the purpose of physical pain. It concentrates your energy on one particular aspect.

Q: Is there any pain on the higher levels of life?

ZT: Yes, there is pain on all levels of life, since there are lessons to be learnt on every level. You are forever evolving, having to come to terms with new aspects of your being and that, usually, involves suffering. But you do not have to suffer.

Q: Surely that is a contradiction?

ZT: Let me explain it to you in this way. There are some boys in a

11

classroom who are being taught mathematics. If they pay attention to the teacher they will learn the subject matter according to their natural ability. But if one of them was to misbehave in the classroom, was to try to distract the other pupils and did not concentrate on the lessons, then at the end of the term he will not have learnt much about mathematics, and when there is an exam, he will fail. Now the learning for that boy starts to become unpleasant because he either has to learn at twice the rate he did before in order to make up what he has missed, or else because he cannot progress any further with that class he has to leave it and return to a lower class. So by his own actions he has made the learning process more difficult. It is the same with suffering. Suffering is brought about by your own actions. Your Creator does not impose the suffering. Having said that I must also say that there will be a few times in your life when you will have to suffer, when you will have to come to terms with a particular emotion or lesson as part of your evolving evolutionary pattern. But that will be on very few occasions.

Q: I have always understood that it is up to me whether I suffer or not. If my mother dies I can choose whether or not to make a big thing out of it, to increase my natural suffering, or to see her death in the bigger picture and release it.

ZT: That is only partly correct. If your mother dies and you believe that she has gone from you forever, then that loss would probably lead to suffering. But if, on the other hand, you knew that, although dead, she was even closer to you and could talk to you more meaningfully than she did before, then where would be that loss? You would not suffer in the least. So our understanding, our point of evolution, determines whether or not we suffer. As was said earlier, where there is Light and Truth there can be no suffering. Suffering can exist only where there is ignorance. So the next time you are suffering, try to look behind the physical, factual evidence and see an understanding and a reason for it.

Q: That is difficult to do at the moment of suffering! My greatest suffering has always been through guilt, for example, when my dog died, but it was also a great learning experience because it made me aware that I would never again be caught having not done something that I wished I had done.

ZT: So what you now recognise, in hindsight, is that your suffering

12

was in effect a great evolutionary lesson which has changed your attitude to life. Although you suffered at the time, perhaps through ignorance, the lesson of that suffering has produced a great evolutionary step forward.

Q: Yes, I would agree with that. If you are suffering very profoundly on a physical level and totally accept that suffering and the purpose of it, will that suffering then be removed?
ZT: Yes, although I must also say that if one is suffering for other people to learn then it will remain until those people have learnt their lesson.

Q: Which, as you say, almost always goes back to previous lives?
ZT: Almost always. It is difficult to explain the relationship of time to soul evolution because you cannot conceive of anything beyond your physical time. But if you take any of the great flash-points of this world, no matter whether it be the Middle East, Ireland or India, then the people who are involved in those clashes have been incarnating in those countries for life after life after life. They have been continually wronging each other life after life. Therefore whilst you might feel compassion for them, what you also have to understand is that the resolution of that problem lies within their own hands. That is something with which they have to come to terms. How, therefore, are they to bring about change? Simply by looking anew, by looking through the eyes of their Creator instead of through their individual biassed eyes. They have to recognise the whole before the individual, and the whole is not their country but the planet.

# THE ENERGY OF CREATION

If I was to ask most people on the Earth today how they would define the energy of creation they would, perhaps, smile knowingly at me and say that it was the energy of the sexual act. But we of the Spiritual Hierarchy, who dwell on the higher planes of life looking down on the Earth, would give a very different answer, for we would say that the energy of creation was love. Humanity has divorced love from the sexual act and it is this misconception which more than anything else symbolises the problems now facing it. I would go even further and would say, because I can see the planes both above and below the physical plane of life, that it is the misuse of the sexual act which hastens Humanity towards a cataclysmic upheaval. There is no more pressing problem that faces Humanity at this time than the understanding of the sexual act and what lies behind it on the higher levels of life. For if Humanity does not control the World population, and limit the influx of new souls, the presence of all those young energies on the crowded plane of Earth will lead to an imbalance that will destroy this planet.

The energy of creation is a pure energy which emanates from our Creator and, because of this, the principle of creation is the same no matter whether one talks of the birth of a planet or the birth of a baby. It is only the degree of manifestation that varies according to the vibratory rate of the being that is creating. It is that vibratory rate, that point of consciousness, which decides the nature and the form of conception and birth. The basic principle remains the same no matter whether one is an interplanetary or a human being. One creates in the image of one's God, exercising the gift of creation given to one by one's God. One creates in Its image using the energy of Its love. As you look at the visible Universe through your telescopes and see the many galaxies that have been created, as you look up at the night sky and see the stars in their appointed place,

15

as you observe the order of even your own planetary system, so you can see there the perfection of divine creation. In just the same way Humanity should be able to look at the perfection of its own creations. That is the awesome nature of the responsibility that has been placed in your hands by your Creator.

If you look in a dictionary at the meaning of the word 'sex' you will see that it is defined quite simply as male and female or positive and negative. Furthermore, if you look at the meaning of the word 'sexual' you will see that it simply means pertaining to male or to female. But in the World in which you live today do not those words have so much more connotation? Does not a large part of your daily living revolve around those two words? Do they not reflect the most energy absorbing aspect of your physical being? This is because the nature of life on the Earth today has been distorted beyond all recognition. The result of this is that the souls of the Aquarian Age incarnating into physical life at this time have to overcome a great obstacle. They have to rediscover the true nature of the creative energy before they themselves create. They have to reject the sexual conditioning of the World in which they find themselves and recognise that the nature of sexuality has become so distorted that they are not seeing a true picture.

The sexual act is an act of creation and, as is the case with any creative act, when it is performed you create on many levels of life. You create on the physical level in the way of which you are well aware, but you also create on levels above and below the physical. The motivation of your body, mind and spirit at the moment of that act of creation will decide the nature of what you create. As gods in the making you were created in the image of your God. You were given the divine gift of free choice and the priceless right of self-creation or self-reproduction. You must therefore be responsible, just as your Creator is, for everything that you have created. Every single time you perform the sexual act, even if you are not creating babies on the physical level, you are creating spirit babies and spirit thought-forms on either the higher or lower levels of life. You create on many different planes of life. Just as you should take responsibility for what you have created on the physical plane, as a mother and father take care of their baby, so you must take responsibility for what you have created on the other planes of life.

Every time you perform the sexual act you are creating responsibilities and burdens for yourself. On the physical plane of life you know only too well that when you create a baby you are also creating a lifetime's responsibility. For twenty years you are tied to that being until it has established its point of consciousness on the Earth. From the moment of birth until it can stand on its spiritual feet at the age of twenty-one you are responsible for nurturing that being. Deny that responsibility and you create karma for yourself for lives to come. Deny that responsibility on the higher or lower levels of life and you do just the same. You burden yourself down for many lives to come. You cannot deny responsibility for what you have created and if what you have created, in your earthly sense, goes astray in the World and performs evil then you are responsible for that evil too. Let me give you an example. A thought-form which you create in a moment of lust is picked up by one of your less-evolved brothers. He, in his turn, imitates that thought-form and creates in lust himself from which comes a child. You are equally responsible for that child. You are therefore tied to that spirit for many lives, until such time as the responsibility for its point of evolution has been balanced according to the Laws of Karma. That is the true nature of the responsibility for the creative energy.

Now I say this not to make you afraid of the energy of creation but so that you may understand it more fully, for you have come on the Earth to learn to be a Master of creation. You first have to learn to control your physical body, your thoughts and emotions, to master these and to place yourself on the path of initiation. Then you have to learn to master the energy of creation. You can create on many levels and in many ways as I have said. If you are a Master, then like Jesus, you can create in physical form at your will. You can multiply the loaves and fishes. You can resurrect or recreate life. You can control all physical matter. This is as nothing. All of you are walking the path to that knowledge. That is the nature of the power which you seek and which one day you will have to master.

At this moment in time all of you are seeking to master a low level of creative energy. You are seeking to understand physical creativity. That understanding is distorted by the World in which you live, for the World in which you live is governed by sexual energy, by the force of human sexuality. Young people today growing to physical maturity have little idea of the correct use of sexual energy. They do not understand its nature and what it seeks to do.

17

Let me state clearly now that the sexual act was intended solely for the procreation of the species. That is its sole purpose and function and if you are at all honest with yourselves you will know that to be true. Today, however, the sexual act has become synonymous with the pursuit of pleasure, but a pleasure which can never be satiated.

Consider the young men and women of today as they go around having sexual relationships with different people, constantly seeking a sexual fulfilment which ever evades them. They change their partners, they change their sexual habits, they change their social environment, constantly seeking the illusion of the perfect sexual relationship. But even if they were to find this great pleasure which they so desperately seek, does it signify the ending of the search for them, the finding of their destined partner? No! That is never the case, for such people are constantly searching, looking outwards, looking even beyond the bonds of marriage, for a sexual pleasure that does not exist except in their own thoughts.

Today sex has changed the traditional path of human evolution. The search for sexual pleasure, the ecstasy of the perfect orgasm, has replaced spiritual ecstasy. Whereas the wise beings of old would seek spiritual ecstasy, people today seek sexual ecstasy. You might not think that they are the same, but truly they are. Today millions of souls are being seduced from the path of spiritual evolution. They are being side-tracked from their destiny paths for many years in a fruitless search for an illusion, whereas if they had but followed the path of love, the creative energy of the Cosmos, they would have so easily obtained what they really sought.

It is the pursuit and understanding of love, the creative energy of the Cosmos, that will give you the ecstasy that you seek. You cannot have ecstasy without love. You cannot obtain love from sex. You cannot obtain love even from the creation of a child. Love must come first. Any time you have to ask somebody if they want sexual intercourse you should not be doing it. Any time you have to pursue someone to obtain sexual intercourse you should not be doing it. For it is the bonding of souls on a higher level of life that leads to the true act of sexual creation. It should take place without need of thought. Where thought intrudes with its desire for pleasure, when sexual satisfaction becomes the primary goal, then love is not present. It is the ego that seeks pleasure, not the soul, and when one creates with this motivation one is burdening oneself down for lives to come.

The young people of today face a difficult task. They have to ask themselves if there can be a form of human relationship different to that which the World demonstrates today. Can one live without sex in the sense that your World uses the word? Can one live without the constant need for obtaining sexual pleasure? Have you ever asked yourself those questions? Have you ever considered the possibility that the act of love does not require the act of sexual completion and, indeed, that when you create through perfect love in imitation of your Creator that no sexual act is necessary at all? That is how your Creator creates — through the perfect breath. You are condemned to create through your sexual organs. You are limited in your point of expression by that fact, but recognise that it is only a limitation. You must seek the path beyond it. For most people that moment is many lives and many cycles down the path of evolution, but it is a limitation that you will eventually overcome.

So I ask the young people of today to consider these questions. It is possible, if one is in perfect harmony and balance, to live without the sexual act. Recognise that the energy which is used in that act is a creative energy and can be redirected to create in other ways. Within marriage, as I have said, the sexual act was intended solely for the creation of destined children, that is children who chose to come through their parents before they even incarnated into physical matter. It is therefore a matter of cosmic creation. When a child is destined there is no need to perform the sexual act every day for a month to ensure conception. The energy of love between the parents will decide the correct time and the correct place without them even being aware of it. For creation, although Humanity does not realise it, is not solely within the province of human will.

The energy of creation, then, is yours to use, to use positively or to waste, to use for good or for evil, for construction or for destruction. Even on the physical level you can see the nature of its power. You can witness the jealousies, the hatreds, the divisions, the destruction it can produce. Likewise you can see the constructive side: children born out of perfect harmony and love, carrying forward the evolutionary cycle of the Human Race. Every time that you perform the sexual act consider what forms you are creating. Are you creating selfishly or selflessly, are you creating for your own pleasure or are you creating for the evolution of the Cosmos? Are you creating an energy which when you die and return to the higher planes of life you will be happy to acknowledge as your child, and take responsibility for, as is your birthright? Or will you, perhaps, when you meet that energy after your death fail to recognise that it is your creation, and therefore your responsibility, and wish to disown it? That choice is created every time you perform the sexual act, so consider carefully.

Your world today desperately needs people who will use the act of creation with responsibility, who will use that energy wisely, not only to ensure harmony in their own evolutionary pattern but to bring balance to the World as a whole. They must exemplify the correct use of the sexual energy so that the children of the Aquarian Age may be helped into an understanding of the true relationship of male and female, of positive and negative, and of the correct use of the act of creation. It is a great responsibility that has been placed upon the shoulders of a few evolved souls for if they fail then that misuse of the sexual act will destroy not only them but the World in which they live. We who look from the higher planes of life can see this so clearly. Positive creation means a positive World, a positive Cosmos. Negative creation means a negative World, a cataclysmic destruction. That is the importance of the energy of creation.


## QUESTIONS AND ANSWERS


Q: I would like to ask what part marriage and the marriage blessing play in the creative act. Does it matter if two people choose to create a child without being married? Does it matter if a child is illegitimate? Should one have a blessing on one's union before creating a child?

ZT: As always, you need to look at the motivation behind the marriage. It is not just a question as to whether or not people are conforming with the social or moral values of the society in which they live. You can have two people who, shall we say, unite themselves in their own form of marriage service but nevertheless invoke a divine blessing on their union. When they create a child in that union they are, perhaps, creating in the spirit that the Master talked about. Equally so, you can have two people who marry in a church, who make their vows but have no intention of keeping them, who do not even recognise the sanctity of the vows they have taken. When they create a child within that marriage, whilst this might satisfy the moral values of the society in which they live, for the child is legitimate, that child can be a wrong creation and may even bring about the destruction of their marriage.

By invoking a divine blessing on a marriage you are asking that every creation of that union, on every level of being, not just the physical, should be at one with your Creator's will and purpose. You are asking that you should be at one with the energy of creation at all times, recognising it as a gift from your Creator. Therefore invoking the blessing of your Creator on your marriage is an important act, for it signifies a recognition of your part in the divine scheme of things and asks that you be directed to use the energy of creation with responsibility.

Q:   Where does homosexuality which is so prevalent today come into this? Is a sexual relationship between members of the same sex a creative act as you define it?
ZT:   Sexual intercourse between two men or two women is not an act of creation. It is not a correct use of the creative energy. It is an abuse. It is a use of the energy for personal pleasure. It is a use of the energy for egotistical ends, regardless of the physical cost, and no good thing will ever come from it on any level. Having said that, let me make it quite clear that a loving relationship between two men or two women can be a positive and creative union on many levels. Remember the story of David and Jonathan in the Bible.

Q:   Is contraception wrong? It does, after all, prevent unwanted children, but does it not also prevent destined children from coming on the Earth? Also, if the World does not practise contraception are we not going to overpopulate and destroy our planet?
ZT:   Contraception is necessary only because of Humanity's misuse of the sexual act. If Humanity used the sexual act with correct motivation, if it understood the true nature of physical conception, there would be no need for contraception. Conception is not just due to the union of the male and female reproductive cells. There is also a cosmic act of union taking place and if you recognise that fact then you will begin to understand how conception occurs. Evolved souls agree on the higher levels of life before they even incarnate to allow a child to come through them on the physical

plane. Sometimes that agreement is made two or three thousand years before the birth. So the responsibility for having a destined child is known and recognised for a long time. Evolved souls nearly always honour that agreement, although they may limit the occasions on which the child can come through them, because they are aware of the destiny of the child coming through them and its impact upon the World. This would have been the case of Mary and Joseph with the Master Jesus. Humanity has to learn to trust its Creator and to create in Its image according to Its divine Will and Plan.

Do you really control your physical destiny? Do you really control when you have your children? To a small degree you do, but only to a very small degree. You can choose to say "No" to your children, destined or otherwise, just as you can choose to say "No" to many other things, but thereafter the pressures of life will always be reminding you of the promises that you made until you honour them.

I myself do not believe that there are many evolved souls waiting to come through to the Earth who cannot get through to this plane of life because of the use of contraception. There may be a very few, but at a time like this, when it is so important to have the right souls upon the plane of Earth, all those who are meant to be here will be here.

Q: You have talked about sex being used either for creation or for pleasure, but you haven't talked about sex as an act of love. Why cannot one make love for love's sake?

ZT: How does one make love for the sake of love? Love is not a romantic, storybook ideal. It is the energy of your Creator pulsating through you. When you are in tune with that energy you are in love. When you are fulfilling your Creator's will for you, when you are acting selflessly, you are in love. Love is not something that can be planned and created. You cannot say that we will make love tonight or tomorrow. That is not love. Love is something far higher than that. Love is a spontaneous act of creation. You can make love to fulfil the principle of love only in the sense that you are responding to the energy of your Creator, not to your own desires or pleasures. It is the love of creation that creates the desire for sex. It is not the other way around. To make love with someone seeking love is seeking an illusion and you will never find it. Love is. Love never will be and never has been. It is now. It is the joy of the moment. You cannot seek it. It seeks you. When you read in the romantic novels of people making love, that is not the love of creation, that is the love of the ego. When the I is present so is desire. True love is an act of cosmic creativity not of human frailty.

Q: How can you be sure that you will have a destined child. Cannot any soul slip in if it is given the opportunity?
ZT: When you are in tune with the Universe, when you are acting only from your highest centre and with the highest motivation you can only attract the highest to you. That is the Law of the Universe. Right action produces the right things in your life because you are in harmony with life and everything around you. Right enforces right. Conversely it is only wrong action that produces wrong things in your life, when you create from your lower centres. The nature of creation is controlled by your behaviour in thought, word and deed.

Q: Young people today find it difficult to cope with all the sexual energy present in our society. There is so much pressure to behave like everyone else and experiment sexually before marriage. What advice can you give?
ZT: Society does not compel, only impel. It is surely a measure of your society today that if you are a virgin when you marry you are thought to be abnormal, whereas two centuries ago you were thought to be abnormal if you were not a virgin. You have lost the understanding of the virgin principle, of what it is to be a virgin, and I use that principle for both male and female. To be a virgin is to be pure in thought, word and deed, is to channel the creative energy correctly. In the days of old, patriarchal tradition believed that a women should be a virgin so that she would be pure for her husband and sire only his children. That belief was based on the ancient virgin principle of purity, that one should remain pure until the correctly motivated act of creation. Amazingly enough, this principle applies equally to the male although this fact seems to have been lost over the years! The original concept of men and women not having sexual relations until they were married was not just because of social morality, it was to preserve one's purity for the act that mattered most, the act of creation. If you have made a

hundred attempts at creation before you produce your own child, where lies the purity of your creation.

Now society will not change overnight. What we of the Spiritual Hierarchy are trying to do is to lead young people into an understanding of what is really involved in the sexual act, to make them think for themselves and to realise that one can be in society without actually following all the customs of society. It is possible to be a virgin and have a happy life! Once the energy of sexual creativity has been aroused and initiated it can transform your life. Consider what would happen if you, an unmarried girl, were to find yourself pregnant by a boy whom you neither love nor respect. What would you do? Have an abortion, marry him or become a single parent family? Either way your life is affected. The child who is coming into incarnation is affected. Your parents' life is affected. Your boyfriend's life is affected. Your friends and society around you are affected and so on. The ripples on the pond spread out. Multiply that one ripple by millions and you can see why the World is in the state that it is today.

I too have lived on the plane of Earth and I know the pressures under which you all live. You have to come to terms with your physical body, with its needs and desires. You have to contend with your lusts. We all have them. Even the greatest Masters that ever walked this Earth have had them. They were just as you. But why were they different from you? Because they did not respond automatically to them, because they did not blindly follow the impulses of their bodies, of their desires. They would consciously seek to align themselves with the force of creation and would try to harmonise with it, and if the thought, the desire, the act, was not at one with that creative force then they would not create it. They were the masters of their bodies.

Q: What about people who don't marry, who share life as partners together without recourse to the sexual act?
ZT: There are many experiences of life that can be obtained from such partnerships. There is nothing wrong in going through life in such partnerships. Indeed, the evolutionary cycle encourages them. One can be a friend, one can live with someone without automatically becoming involved in sexual activity. You can give to each other in many fields. The union of male and female is a valuable source of creativity, in many important aspects of life.

The creative energy of the one sparks off the other and out of the two comes 'the child', to form the trinity of creation.

Q: It seems to me therefore that there are many possibilities to be explored in male/female relationships of which we know very little today. It seems to me that sex has destroyed so many possibilities.

ZT: I would agree with that. In the field of human relations great developments can be made especially in the area of male/female relationship without sexual involvement. There is so much pleasure to be obtained from union on many other levels.

Q: It seems to me that it is only in a really balanced, loving relationship that a woman can say "No" to the sexual act and be respected for her decision.

ZT: Woman may find this hard to accept, but a large part of the blame for the present state of human sexuality lies with her and not with Man, for it is she who has fallen from her pedestal and by degrading the sexual act has degraded Man's opinion of her. She has lost her purity. She has not upheld her divine responsibility for right creation. It is Woman who conceives and bears the child. She is the womb of creation. What greater praise or honour can the Lords of Creation give to her! Every woman can say "No", not for herself but for Creation. Woman has great innate wisdom. She can read a man better than any book. She knows when a man does or does not love her. She is all seeing, all wise. She should not bow to other pressures. There are many paths of creativity waiting to be explored by the young couples of today.

Q: The trouble today is that because people associate love with the sexual act they feel insecure unless they commit the sexual act. They feel that their partner doesn't love them. They feel that the sexual act is a necessary bonding.

ZT: If that is so, then they are not in love.

Q: So are you saying that people who are in love in the true sense of the word do not need to commit the sexual act unless they are to conceive a child?

ZT: Love is a selfless emotion. By its very expression it allows

25

you to see in your partner the highest potential that you would wish for them on this Earth. You love them not for what you need from them, not for what they can give you, but for what they are. Such a love does not need to be supported by the sexual act; especially if one of the partners is an unwilling participant. If I could leave you all with one thought, it would be that it is not sex that makes the world go round. It is love.

# AWARENESS OR EXPERIENCE

It has been said that the plane of Earth can be likened to a school, a school through which Humanity passes on the upward spiral of its evolutionary path. This, of course, is a very crude analogy. Moreover your understanding of what constitutes a school is based on your own personal experience of schools and of the educational systems which exist in your world today and is, therefore, far removed from the real nature of the School of Life on this Earth. Indeed, if your schools were truly modelled on the School of Life as it manifests on the Earth how great would be the transformation in the products of those schools! However, for the purpose of our talk, I would ask you to accept that the plane of Earth is a school and that you, as individuals, go to that school to learn the lessons of life as they manifest on the Earth. You incarnate into a physical body, guided by your spirit, with its memory, the soul, prepared for the lessons that you are to face on the plane of Earth. You decide the nature and the place of your being, the nature and the place of your class-room.

Now at this particular time in the evolutionary cycle of the Earth you are under the influence of the planet Saturn, the Saturnine or the Satanic influence. That influence is not the force of evil that some religions would have you believe. It is a testing influence. You willingly submit yourselves to that planetary influence in order to be tested and the nature of that test is that you have to make a choice. It is for that reason that your Creator has given you the divine gift of free choice so that you may exercise that choice when tested. It is how you make that choice that produces growth and evolution. Throughout your lives you are continually exercising your free choice as you are subjected to the testing influence. Indeed your spirit demands such tests as you walk along your destined path. Sometimes the tests are large, sometimes they are small.

All are important, however, for even a small test ignored or postponed will soon grow into a bigger one. Tests have to be recognised as such, and faced, and when faced one should remember that one has the duality of life to handle them in order to bring forth the trinity of creativity — the solution.

The essence of Humanity's vibration on the Earth at this moment is that it grounds itself through the duality of positive-negative, yin-yang, male-female, intellect-intuition. In the field of testing this duality can be described as experience and awareness. The very nature of the tests you face will decide the balance of this duality, for just as you cannot say that male is right and female is wrong, that intellect is right and intuition is wrong, so there is no right or wrong in the way that you face and solve your tests. Where Humanity goes so wrong today in the solving of its problems is in establishing the correct balance of the positive and the negative, of the male and the female. Whilst there are some tests that require intellect more than intuition in order to solve them, so there will be others that require intuition more than intellect. Some will completely demand intellect, others will completely demand intuition. Some tests you will solve only through experience, others you will solve only through awareness. What you have to decide is the balance between the two.

Now your intellect, your physical brain, is the sum total of all your Earthly experiences in your present life. It links you to the life you lead. It grounds you to the social customs and traditions of the society in which you have incarnated. Your intuition, on the other hand, knows nothing of this present life. It does not possess the experience of intellect. It possesses only the wisdom of past lives. Therefore if the test which you face demands a knowledge of present life, inevitably the balance must swing more towards intellect and experience, modified to a certain extent by your inner wisdom, to help you reach your decision. Equally so you will face some tests which you cannot solve with intellect, if only because you have never experienced such a situation before in this life. Inevitably therefore you will then have to rely mainly on intuition and awareness, to summon up that still, quiet voice within and to listen to the wisdom that you have gained through your experiences in past lives. You will have to fall back on that priceless wisdom which you have gleaned through pain and ecstasy, through joy and sadness, as you have incarnated in innumerable bodies in innumerable lives. That wisdom will help you to face the tests which you now have to face.

If you have been faced with a test and have not handled it correctly for your point of soul consciousness — and I wish to stress for your point of soul consciousness — then that test will be repeated at another time, in another life, to enable you to experience the necessary learning experience. Therefore when you face a test in this life your intuitive processes will sometimes recall past life experiences when you faced a similar test. This often results in a heightening of the emotions and senses as you face the test again in this life. Obviously, though, the nature of the test is modified by the society and by the evolutionary consciousness of the World in which you now live.

The balance between intellect and intuition, experience and awareness is always variable. What you have to decide is the nature of that balance. This decision cannot be made intellectually but rather by being completely open to the problem. Do not think that any test is purely an Earthly thing, relating only to the physical life around you. Every test comes from Spirit, is of Spirit, for you are surrounded and enveloped by Spirit. You are powered by the energy of your Creator which envelops, motivates and creates all things. You are a spirit living within Spirit, you are a living part of that Spirit. Therefore all things are spiritual from the highest to the lowest, from what you call the most holy to what you call the most evil, everything is a part of Spirit. It is Spirit which tests you at all times.

Recognise that not only are you always being tested but that tests are a natural part of the growing, evolutionary process. Recognise that a test is an opportunity to grasp, not something to be avoided. Recognise that a test taken and solved opens the door to a new understanding of life, to a greater perfection of your physical being, both now and in the future. Tests therefore demand your total understanding and commitment. Now do not think that life is a constant test. Your life is obviously full of continual decision making, but the tests that come along are nearly always separated by periods of rest, a time for demonstrating what you have learned from the last test and, of course, preparing for the next test, for that is the nature of the life that you lead on Earth. So face your tests with hope. Face your tests with courage. Face your tests with understanding and acceptance. Know that there is no such thing as failure as there is in your Earthly schools, only opportunities for learning. Even if you make what for your point of consciousness is a wrong decision, remember that that is not wrong for evermore, for you will simply face that test again and again until the lesson is learned. Remember that some of you have experienced many lives just facing the same test, the *same* test, and what I am talking about now is the facing of deep soul patterns, deep soul commitments and understandings, not the trivia of physical life but the very essence of the Universe, for you are all gods in the making.

So as you face your tests remember the balance of the positive and the negative, the intellect and the intuition. Remember that you can learn either through experience or through awareness. Sometimes you must learn through experience. Sometimes you can learn only through awareness. Remember, though, that the intuitive awareness will always take preference over the intellectual experience, for the force of intuition is the force of God moving through you. Intuitive awareness flows from the Divine whereas the force of experience is that which you have created through your own intellect. The balance must, of course, always be there but be aware of the centre which is making the choice. Wise is the person who learns through awareness in preference to experience, for he or she will learn faster and with less pain. Wise is the person who can learn from another person's experience through an awareness of that experience. Wise is the person who can learn from another country's experience through an awareness of that experience. Wise is the person who can learn from another planet's experience through an awareness of that experience.

Remember these things as you face your tests. Remember the choice which lies before you. Remember that you are spiritual beings surrounded by Spirit, guided by Spirit. Therefore invoke that Spirit. Invoke the true nature of your being and be tested. Rejoice in the testing as it is an initiation of love given to you by your Creator for your own evolution and upliftment. Recognise that test as an act of love, as an act of divine evolution, in this school of love.

Q: I can see the advantages of learning through awareness rather than experience. I know that I can learn from another person's experience without having to go through it myself, but what if there is nobody around who is facing the particular test that I am facing?

ZT: Obviously, as you progress up the scale of human evolution there are less people around you facing tests similar to yours and so there are less people to learn from. Inevitably, therefore, evolved souls usually have to learn through their own experience rather than from the experiences of others. Nevertheless you would be surprised just how many people you can learn from if only you were to look more carefully!

Q: I met someone recently who was facing a test similar to me, about whether or not to leave his job and become a spiritual teacher, but he was told what to do by his guidance. Can we be told if we do not know?

ZT: I would think that his test was different to yours because it is one thing to be told what to do and it is quite another thing to make up your own mind what to do. Obviously if you are told what to do then much of the learning experience has been removed since you have not discovered for yourself. If you are faced with a test that you have not faced before, in this life anyway, it is obvious that intellect or experience is of no use to you, and when I say of no use to you I mean only in the decision making, because obviously you have to use your intellect to manifest your decision on the plane of Earth, to meet your Earthly commitments. Such a test has been demanded by the force of Spirit and so Spirit will help you as you face your test, but ultimately it is you that has to decide what to do.

Q: Obviously I have to decide first of all if the decision to give up my job and become a spiritual teacher is a correct one. Is not that true?

ZT: As I see it you have to consider two aspects. Firstly, is this the right move for you, does it flow with your destiny and by your destiny I mean not just yours but your family's as well, for no man is an island? Secondly, if it is right for your destiny then is it the right time in your destiny to do this, is it the right time for you to remove yourself from physical commitment into spiritual commitment? There is a time for everyone to renounce physical commitment and to enter into spiritual commitment, a time when you know that you no longer have to take care of your physical needs because those needs will automatically be met by the force of Spirit. Of course you have to accept that the force of Spirit might do this in a way that you as an individual neither desire nor seek, but commitment means that you are happy to accept that.

Q:   I work on universal feed-back and if the Universe gives me a very definite, positive affirmation then I proceed onwards because the physical and the spiritual are the same thing when it comes down to reality. Is that not correct?
ZT:   Of course the Universe will feed back to you, but what we are talking about here is commitment. You are not changing your role in life simply because you want to. You are changing because you are committed to a new role in life, mentally, emotionally and above all spiritually. It is difficult to explain the difference between physical and spiritual commitment to one who has known only physical commitment, but when you commit yourself spiritually to the path of life it means that you are willingly submitting yourself to your Creator's will, in a sense suppressing your own will to fulfil Its will through your being.

If you commit yourself to Spirit, and I mean this not in the sense of committing yourself to a religion but of truly committing yourself to Spirit, if you agree, because of your point of consciousness, whilst recognising your own individuality, to place yourself in the service of your Creator then you have reached a significant step on the path of Mastership. However it is imperative that you understand the nature of that step for once you have taken it there can be no turning back, there can be no changing of your mind. Once you have made that decision there can be no denial. Once you have put yourself forward for the test it must be taken.

To serve your Creator will involve sacrifice. It will involve suffering. Look at the disciples of Jesus. Would it be any different in the World today? To serve your Creator will involve isolation. It will mean being alone. It will mean walking alone. Remember the disciples of Jesus. It will mean going where you are not wanted, going where you are unloved and having the finger of scorn pointed at you, but being impervious to all these things because you know you are fulfilling the will and the purpose of God. It could even mean sacrificing your life to fulfil that will. I say this not to deter you, not to frighten you, simply to make you aware of the true nature of the commitment. It is a great step to take. I wish to draw a distinction between the step of simply acknowledging the presence and the will of God in all things, and trying to follow it, and the step of actually being at one with the will of your Creator in every aspect of your life, a step which implies the surrender of your own desires, needs and wants and, above all, the total acceptance of that surrender.

# GUIDANCE

I wonder why you think that you need guidance and why, in particular, that you should seek guidance through mediumship. Why should you, incarnate beings on the plane of Earth, equipped with your physical senses, living in the reality of physical life, seek guidance from me, a discarnate being living in a realm beyond your comprehension, far removed from the physical plane of Earth? What is it that I can give you which will help you to walk your path in life? Perhaps you seek this form of guidance because not being in touch with your own inner voice, with your own spiritual guidance, you are grateful to be able to listen to any other source which is accessible to you. Moreover this form of guidance requires no effort or concentration on your part, for you just sit back, relax and listen. In a sense, everything is done for you. The harder way would be for you to obtain the guidance that you need through your own divine channel.

I, for my part, am very conscious of the responsibility of giving guidance, for I am responsible for what I say until the end of time. I am karmically responsible not only for what I say to you but for what you do because of it. It is essential, therefore, in any interchange between the planes of life such as this that you are aware of this responsibility. Indeed, it is vital when you seek guidance in this way that first and foremost you establish that the spirit which is giving the guidance to you is, at the very least, the equal of yours in spiritual consciousness and, desirably, more evolved; for any guidance given to you by a less evolved spirit is worthless. How then are you to assess the vibratory note of the spirit being that gives guidance to you except by the right practice of what that spirit being says and by continually checking that guidance both with your own inner feelings and with the World around you, for what is the World around you but your Creator talking to you.

35

Do you not also consider it strange that you should listen to the guidance of one far removed from your plane of life and yet accept what that spirit being says without even being aware of the personality or the form of the being who speaks to you? But such is the nature of life on the Earth today, where intellect rules over intuition, that this form of guidance is sought by many who are trying to understand what is happening on this planet. You have often used this form of guidance in previous lives. For you it is an accepted form of communication, one which you have relied on in the past and will use again in the future. You accept guidance as your birthright.

I will begin by saying that it is essential in this form of guidance that you understand that I would never tell you what to do. I would never say that you should take a certain course of action, that you should walk along a certain path. That is not my purpose in talking to you. Any guidance which does this should be treated with the utmost caution. The essence of guidance is that it helps you to reach your own decisions, not that you accept its decisions and implement them in blind trust. That is not guidance. If I take away your choice, if I remove your lessons in life, the obstacles which you face on your evolutionary path, then I am removing your learning experiences and no good will come from that. I seek to guide you. I seek to teach you. I seek to help you to evolve your point of consciousness. But you must do the work; I cannot do it for you. I am simply the spark that awakens within your own consciousness what you already know to be true.

But why do people seek guidance? For some it is the path of laziness. How easy it is to ask someone else to solve your problems and to have them tell you how, or when, to do something rather than you discovering for yourself. When one has lived for a long time in the illusion of one's personality, denying the wisdom of one's soul, one comes to a point in time when one is truly lost, when one has walked so far along that path of illusion that one can no longer see the reality of life around one. Only at that time does one acknowledge that something is wrong and seek help. But you have to face the karmic responsibility for being in that situation, a situation of your own causing. That learning experience is vital to the soul. To remove that lesson is to destroy the very purpose of the soul being here on the plane of Earth.

Others seek guidance because they have come to a point in their lives when they simply cannot see the direction to take, because they are faced with a major decision such as whether or not to marry, whether or not to emigrate to another country, whether or not to give up their jobs. They have become so confused by their own thoughts and fears, by the well-meaning advice of their friends, that they can no longer see the wood for the trees. But why, for so important a decision as this, should you look outwards for guidance, for who really can advise you since you are a unique being, unique in the whole Cosmos? There is no other being in the whole Cosmos who vibrates on your frequency, who possesses exactly the same point of soul knowledge and wisdom that you do, who operates on your unique vibratory note. Who then can give you guidance as to the path that you should take?

There is only one being in the whole World who truly knows you and what you should be doing. That being is your Creator. Your Creator knows not only the destiny of your present incarnation but also your past and your future ones, not only the destiny of your family and your friends but also the destiny of the planet on which you now dwell. We of the Spiritual Hierarchy, the Creator's servants on the higher planes of life, have cognizance of that destiny for on our level of life there is truly no time. There is no past: there is no present: there is no future. All is one and so we see clearly in the wholeness of being that which you face as a moment in time. It is purely from this viewpoint that we are able to give guidance for we can see clearly the path on which your soul is set. Therefore the guidance that we give is to your soul, not to your personality. We are not interested in the facets of your personality which manifest now, have manifested in the past or will manifest in the future. We talk only to the soul, to that spark of spirit which is eternal, which is beyond physical flesh, which is linked even now to us on the higher planes of life.

Guidance: to act as a guide, to show the way, to point the way, to demonstrate the way. There are many who incarnate on the plane of Earth and give guidance through the very act of their being, great Masters such as the Nazarene, the Buddha. That is the reality of guidance. Through their lives, through their individual demonstrations, they provide guidance to Humanity. See in the lives of such Masters the guidance which you seek. See in the paths that they walked, in the revelation of their minds, what is the reality of physical life. Observe your fellow human beings who are all divine sparks of Spirit, observe the physical World around you and see how they respond to your thoughts, words and deeds for they are the mirror of your being. There is the guidance that you seek. You have no need to seek guidance of us when around you is the guidance of your Creator: the manifest World and the beings of spirit upon it. That form of guidance has always been and will always be available to you. As you come into contact with the Kingdoms of this Earth, not just the Human but the Animal, the Vegetable and the Mineral as well, you sound your note which brings forth a response from those Kingdoms which confirms or denies the rightness of your actions. There are those, of course, who cannot or do not want to see and for them there are other forms of guidance available, one of which we are using now. But, as I said before, that guidance is to the soul, not to the personality.

Among young people today there are many who seek guidance because they are truly lost in the World in which they find themselves. Why should this be so, for they are the sons and daughters of this World. They chose to incarnate into it. Indeed they had to struggle on the higher planes of life for the very right to incarnate on the Earth at this critical time, for there are many thousands of souls who desire to incarnate on the Earth at this time to experience the great changes that are now manifesting, to witness the transition of the Ages and the rebirth of the planet. Therefore these young people must recognise that they are here of their own choice, because of their souls' understanding of what the Earth and the Universe have to teach them. If they chose to be here, why therefore are they lost? Why do the Earth and the Universe not reveal to them the direction and the path that they must take?

For the most part it is because the young today do not listen either to the Earth or to the Universe. They listen only to themselves. They listen to the illusions and the thought-forms that they have accumulated, to what they have established as truth. They have closed their ears to the source that could reveal to them what is the true reality of life on this Earth. The nature of the educational system through which they have progressed is such that they have always been taught to look outwards for information and instruction. Only on very rare occasions have their intuitive channels been cultivated and allowed to come into play. Only on very rare occasions have they been called upon to be creative, to

38

bring forth from within themselves what they hold to be sacred. Indeed, have they as individuals ever considered what they do hold to be sacred, what they hold to be of the God-head?

Today you live in a world which is based on technology. You live in a world in which technology has been developed regardless of human considerations. There has been little control over the scientific advances that have been made. The result is that advanced technology is here without the wisdom to use it. Yes, a machine can replace a hundred men and women, but what of those hundred men and women? What are they to do? The essence of life is work: creative industry, the exercise of the talents which Humanity has been given by its Creator. These talents must be exercised or they atrophy and will eventually wither and die. When these talents are lost there is an apparent loss of direction and purpose and people seek desperately to establish motivation for their lives. Many people today are losing their divine talents either because they do not or cannot practise them or because they have lost the will to work. They have grown up in a society where work is not an essential part of living.

Now work is the means by which you manifest the spirit of your Creator. Work is the means by which you manifest the power of your own spirit. In everything that you do in your work either through thought, word or deed you are creating on this plane of Earth either for good or for evil. That choice is always present. You are but channels of divine energy. It is for you to use and direct that energy. That is the lesson of life. However, because of the so-called Welfare State which exists in many countries of the Western World, a belief has grown up that if one is provided for by the State then there is no need to work. That is not so. The Welfare State as it exists today is corrupting people for it is removing the lesson of the incentive and the desirability of work, of work not for money's sake but of work for work's sake.

You should work as if your life depended upon it for, truly, it does. How you work now decides the nature of the life that you will experience in the future. The work that you do now is spiritual energy to be stored up and repaid in the years to come. It is, so to speak, spiritual potential that you have established. Until you have worked and established that potential then energy cannot flow to you from Above. You have to earn energy before it is given to you. If you would seek to advance in one particular field then maybe

39

you must work very hard in an entirely different field in order to be worthy of receiving that gift from Above. Inspiration does not fall like rain from the skies. It has to be earned. It has to be earned through right demonstration, through work. When that has been achieved then the inspiration flows down and you will see the direction that you should take and begin to understand the destiny that lies before you.

There is great uncertainty amongst the young people of today because of the nature of the Age. Many of them are very old souls. Some of them have not incarnated on the Earth for thousands of years and they return now to an Age that is witnessing the break-up of a civilisation, an Age where moral and spiritual values are almost totally disregarded. Moreover, their understanding of the true nature of physical life is constantly being denigrated by those in authority if only because that authority is being challenged. Inevitably young people will be in conflict with authority, for their understanding of the true nature of life will differ from authority's. But that is why the young people are here. They are here to transform the World. They are here to bring the Piscean into the Aquarian Age.

What the young people of today consider as the reality of life will be very different from the past. The way in which they wish to lead their lives, the way in which they behave morally, socially and politically will be very different from the past. Do not be afraid of such changes. Do not be afraid of such diversity. It is what the young people have come to ground and demonstrate. But this new understanding must be made manifest, demonstrated through work, through right practice, through mixing with both the older and the younger generations. Remember that the children of the young people of today will look to them for a demonstration of Aquarian principles. They have great responsibility in this respect for they are parenting a new Age.

We of the Spiritual Hierarchy, therefore, are drawing close to the Earth at this time to guide Humanity into that understanding of life. We seek to show you in moments such as these that there is a vast source of wisdom into which you can, and must, tap and that there is an intuitive channel already present within you to that wisdom. We seek to show you that there is a divine source of power and energy beyond the physical plane of Earth which truly controls the destiny of this Earth and all upon it down to the smallest

40

element of life. The God-head is all around you. God is present in every aspect of every being, in every element, in every atom of matter that exists in your World. Every time you handle that matter you are handling your God. Every time you work with that matter you are working with your God. As you work so the destiny of the Universe will be revealed to you. The understanding which you now perceive but dimly, will grow into a physical reality and you will have fulfilled what you came to fulfil: to be the founders of the Aquarian Age. That is your guidance.

## QUESTIONS AND ANSWERS

Q: We seem to have been travelling a great deal recently. Do you feel that this is right for us or should we be settling down more now that we are married?

ZT: It depends on the reason why you are travelling. There are some people who travel to avoid permanence and will forever travel. There are others who travel to find permanence. There must always be a reason for travelling otherwise it becomes a form of escapism. You should travel only when there is a need for travel, when you can see because of the feedback from the World around you, because of the opportunities that come to you, that you should travel. You must be careful that you do not travel to pass the time, as a pastime, for travelling can be a very tiring business which completely saps the energy of your being.

When you travel what are you really doing? You are moving the very roots of your being, you are changing the vibrations of the ground on which you reside, the aura of the place in which you live. You are crossing lines of force, lines of power. You are uprooting yourself and then having to settle and acclimatise in a new place. Look at the example of Nature. When you move a plant from one part of the garden to another the plant does not like it. It takes time to settle again and to be itself. It is the same with human beings even if you do not realise it.

Q: Do you feel that I should stay and try to settle here or should I move out of the area to a place less demanding of a new marriage than Glastonbury.

41

ZT:   I think that for a short time it would be good for you to stay in this area. It would be good for you and your wife to spend some time harmonising yourselves together and acquiring an understanding of what is involved in marriage, in the union of two beings on a common path, and coming to terms with that reality. You must decide what work you are going to do, both individually and collectively, and how you are going to use your energies to achieve that objective. You must bring down through your own channels what work you are really meant to do. That knowledge lies within your souls. After you have done all this then I feel that there will be a move, but that move will be for a positive reason, to do something together which you both want to do.

Q:   I feel that I am about to experience a big change in my life. Can you tell me why I should feel this?
ZT:   There are many forms of change taking place at this time. There is planetary change, the movement from one Age to another. There is change on the spiral of evolution as the vibratory rate of the Earth quickens. All this is felt not only by you but also by those beings who dwell above and below the plane of Earth. There are, of course, many lesser degrees of change which filter down to you from the larger changes. At present there is a great release of energy taking place upon the planet and because of this a new understanding is growing of the direction that life is going to take. Two years ago most people could not conceive of what was going to happen to this planet and to life upon it, but now, due to this release of new energies, many are beginning to see clearly the path on which this world is set and what, as individuals, they must do in order to be at one with it.

   Change occurs naturally in the cycles of life. As you move from one physical cycle to the next, every ten years, so there is change. There is a new facet of your being to explore and to master. A new cycle of energy opens within your body. Life involves constant change, every minute of the day. What you are now you will not be a second later. You accept most forms of change very happily but there are some forms which you do not like, which cause concern and irritation mainly because you cannot understand the reasons for the change or because they present a challenge for you to master. It is this change which catches the attention, on which you focus.

Normally change of this nature is occasioned by aspects of your being which you still have to master. This means that the World around you becomes a mirror, reflects your imperfections and demands change saying that you cannot continue in the same mould, in the same pattern, that you must change so as to be in harmony with the vibratory note of the World around you. If you do not change, then the challenge becomes more and more demanding and attracts more and more of your attention. The change that you feel is a sign that some aspects of your being have to change to be more in harmony with the World around you.

Q:  Is there any guidance you could give me as I come to work at the Ramala Centre?
ZT:  When one joins a Centre such as this you must be aware that there are many complex spirals of energy present, not only those of its founders and the Angel of Ramala but also those of the other people who live and work here, of the people who come and stay here, of the people who visit here. It is important, therefore, that you realise the nature of those energies and learn how to balance yourself with them. You must learn the balance between your own individuality, your own spiritual desires, and the desires of the entity that is Ramala and of what takes place here. By all means serve Ramala. That is why you are here. But also be aware of your own spiritual destiny and birthright. Recognise that you are contributing to the energy that is Ramala and that what you do in thought, word and deed is of vital importance to the energy that exists and is being generated here. Seek perfection in everything that you do, not only for yourself but for that greater energy. Be aware that just as a bricklayer puts individual bricks into a wall and builds a great edifice so you too are putting bricks of energy into a centre which many people will tap into not only in this year but in the years to come. You are building for future generations as well as for yourself. That is the nature of the sacrifice of being here.

Q:  There is someone where I work who is always criticising either me or the people who work with me. I get quite negative about him. How should I handle this criticism?
ZT:  When someone criticises you, what really is that person doing? Are they pointing out a fault in your being or a fault in their own being? Why is it that in general we do not like to be criticised?

43

Why do we usually regard criticism as a bad thing? What right have we to criticise anybody? What good is served by criticism? As you can see, we could spend a whole evening discussing criticism but I know that you want a quick answer.

Criticism can be either constructive or destructive. You should remember that fact the next time you feel the need to criticise. Destructive criticism is worthless. But what if people criticise you? They criticised Galileo because he said the Earth was round and that the planet moved around the Sun. He was right, but the people of his time did not think so. All that you can do when you are criticised is to honestly examine in your meditation the criticism that is given and then either accept or reject it. What is important, though, is that you then release it. What you must not do is to allow that criticism to become a burden which you carry around. Criticism must be handled when it comes. On the very day it is given you must decide honestly whether it is true or false. If it is true then profit from it. Allow it to be a mirror to your personality self and then modify that personality. If it is wrong, then reject it and send it back to the person who gave it to you with love.

Do not be afraid of criticism. It can be a great learning experience, for you can only see yourselves when you look in a mirror and most of you do not like doing that. So be open to criticism. Indeed, if you are to walk a path different from society you must expect it and, perhaps, be thankful that with the criticism do not come stones!

# AN EASTER MESSAGE: DEATH

It is the time of Easter. I am going to speak to you twice during this celebration, firstly about death and then about resurrection. Closely associated with both these subjects is the nature of sacrifice and how sacrifice affects both death and resurrection. We therefore have the trinity of our Easter celebration: death, resurrection and sacrifice.

These three elements are, of course, embodied in the Christian dogma of Easter which is centred around the Master Jesus. However I do not wish to consider only that aspect of Easter for, as I have mentioned on previous occasions, Christian dogma has distorted the true meaning of Easter. Easter is a celebration far older than the Christian Church. In ancient times Easter was associated with the worship of the Goddess, Mother Earth, and was always celebrated at the passing of a moon cycle. The Christian Church chose to celebrate Easter at this time in order to associate the death of Jesus, and the meaning which was held to be present in his death, with that ancient Earth festival. Therefore let us look at Easter in a pre-Christian context, remembering that Christianity reveals but one aspect of the real meaning of Easter.

Today is Good Friday and, as Christians, you recognise the death of a great soul, the Master Jesus. But what really is death? At this very moment you perhaps think of death as the ending of physical life but, truly, that is not the whole meaning of death. Have you ever considered that as you sit here now you are dead to the past. You cannot relive it. You are also dead to the future and, indeed, if you were to die soon after this moment in time there would be no future at all. Therefore you can live *only* in the present. At all other times you are dead. If only Humanity would grasp this understanding of life and death it would indeed put death in its correct perspective. It would see death not as a thing to fear,

45

not as a thing for which to wait agonisingly but, truly, as something that you experience every second, every minute, every hour of the day. You die to the second that has just passed. You cannot relive it. You can only remember it. That memory is not the reality of what took place in that second, only what your brain has chosen to remember. Therefore if you live in that past minute, in that past hour, in that past day, you are living an illusion of life, for you are living in death.

Death, therefore, has to be considered in relation to the whole meaning of life and resurrection should be seen as the arising from death. Why is Humanity, for the most part, so afraid of death? If there is one thing of which you can be certain in this life it is that you will die, and you have all died so many, many times, not only in past lives but also in this present life. You can perhaps remember those moments when you have died, when physical living has slipped from your being. You can also recall moments of great stress and conflict in this life when you were faced with great problems, when the world closed in on you and you 'died'. But you survived. You rose again. You passed from that moment of death into resurrection. The message of Easter is that death is not an ending but a beginning.

As the flowers in your garden grow again after the death of winter and bring forth their beauty, fragrance and colour, as they bloom to reveal the secrets they have held within their innermost beings throughout the winter, so they demonstrate life beginning again. In Nature, if you did but recognise it, you have the greatest example of your Creator present on the Earth today, for there you can see the natural will of your Creator displayed for you. The person who understands Nature and the birth and death cycle of that Kingdom truly understands the evolutionary pattern of this Earth and of Humanity upon it.

The seed of a flower grows and comes forth out of the darkness. Within it is the consciousness, the wisdom of its being which will blossom in the light of the sun. A flower manifests not for the sake of the flower, not for the sake of the human being who planted it, but for the World as a whole. A flower does not bloom for itself. A tree does not bud to please Humanity. They come forth in response to the energy of their Creator, to follow the will of their Creator, to bring forth life on the physical plane of Earth.

You come from darkness in a similar fashion. You grow from a seed just like that flower. After physical birth you gradually reveal from within your being the nature of your point of consciousness and spiritual evolution. You bring forth the nature of your being not for yourself, not for your family, not for the country in which you live, but for the whole Cosmos. You are a pinprick of light within a Universe of light, yet you manifest your light for the whole Universe. That is the essence of your human responsibility as you live on the plane of Earth.

As you live your life on the Earth you are constantly changing and evolving. You are forever facing tests, challenges and problems. You come into contact with your fellow human beings and you conflict, and from that conflict comes evolution. When the water of life flows over the rocks of Earth there is turbulence, the water becomes ruffled and parted. That is the nature of human life: Humanity flows like the water of life and the separation opens up the consciousness of Humanity to learning.

But what of death? Are you alive or are you dead? I say this to you seriously. Are you truly alive at this moment in time? Are you listening to me or are you living in the past or in the future? Are you dead to me, or are you dead to the past and the future — as you should be? So much of Humanity today lives either in the past or in the future. They are dead to life. That is the meaning of Good Friday. Death to the past. Death to the future. Alive to the moment. When the Master Jesus was crucified on that fateful Good Friday he was not dying, he was living and that act of living resulted for him in a transition from one plane of life to another. He passed from his physical body into one of his higher bodies. He did not die. Because he was living in the moment he was living in consciousness and therefore that moment of transition created no pain, no conflict, no loss of being. It was a transition just as if you walked from one side of the street to the other. When there is total consciousness in the moment there can be no death, no fear of death, no running one's life based on a false understanding of what death is or is not.

So for the Master Jesus there was no fear. He knew that death awaited him. Furthermore he knew the time of his death, which is something which most of you do not know for you are not yet of the consciousness to be responsible for such knowledge. Because you do not yet understand the nature and the meaning of death you may not know the time of your own death. That knowledge is hidden from you. But as the moment of your death approaches you will gradually become aware of it. Before the actual moment of the death of your physical body you will know it, sometimes hours, sometimes days, and for those few evolved ones, perhaps even a month before it happens. You will know within the innermost part of your being that death is coming, that the transition from the physical to a higher level awaits you. Death therefore is not something to be feared. It is a transition from one act of consciousness to another. You will die to your physical life and be alive to the next moment of your being on whatever plane you dwell.

Good Friday, for Christians, is marked by the emotion of grief. They express sorrow that the Master Jesus died. But he was not dying on that cross, he was living and, furthermore, he was living in the consciousness of what he was doing. For the very act of his dying was a sacrifice, a sacrifice not for himself, not for the Jewish race, but for the World as a whole. Two thousand years later you who look back on that sacrifice may see what has resulted from it. You have the perspective of time to recognise the real nature of what he did and why he did it. However, I would ask you to place yourselves in the shoes of that Master as he was about to die. He would know that he was to die, but he would have no fear of death. What, therefore, could cause anguish to arise within his consciousness? Why should he feel at the last moment, perhaps, that there was no purpose in his sacrifice? Only because he could not see on the physical level that the nature of his sacrifice would bring about the evolutionary change that has come to pass over the last two thousand years. That was a test which he, even at his level of being, had to face.

There are many of us who would sacrifice our lives if we could see purpose in that sacrifice. If in the field of battle you give away your life to save another then that has purpose and meaning. If you die to further some great evolutionary leap forward, if you sacrifice your life to perfect some technological achievement which will benefit Humanity, then that sacrifice too has purpose and meaning. You can see a reason for surrendering your life. But what if no purpose is presented to you? What if you are being asked to sacrifice your life just in the name of your Creator? That is the test that the Master Jesus faced, for his Creator had asked that to fulfil Its plan his life should be sacrificed at that time. The reason for that sacrifice was not known. It was sufficient that it had been demanded.

48

That is the kind of love which we are talking about at Easter. That a person such as the Master Jesus, because of his at-oneness and his love for the Creator of us all, could sacrifice his life in such a way even though he could not see the purpose of that sacrifice. That is the sacrifice which you should all remember at this time: the giving of yourselves to the love of your Creator, the recognition that that force which gave you life, which allows you to manifest as you do now on the physical plane of Earth, ultimately controls the nature of your being down to the very moment when you lose your own identity as individuals once more. It is how you recognise that link, how you see your Creator, how you love that Being, that reveals the vibratory note of your consciousness.

How do you love a Creator Whom you apparently cannot see, with Whom you apparently cannot communicate, Whom you can only worship in ignorance? The answer is very simple: your God is all around you. The person who sits beside you now is a part of your God. If you cannot love that person and if you cannot love yourself then you have no love for your Creator. That is something which you have to learn and the learning of that knowledge is achieved through dying, through dying to the past and through living in the moment, through living life as it was meant to be lived — in balance and harmony, in right relationship with your fellow human beings and with the other Kingdoms of Matter on this Earth.

Do not be afraid of death. It is a signpost of evolution. Do not be afraid of death, for it signifies only the death of that which is past. Death is the heralder of life. Death is the heralder of resurrection. Remember that out of the ashes rises forth the new. Out of the old body comes forth the more splendiferous new; the new level, the new being, the new person. At Easter you are being asked to release the old in death, to release it joyfully, to see why it must be released so that the new can come forth.

As the buds come forth in the spring time to reveal once more the life-force of the tree, so that is what you must do at this time through prayer and meditation. By going deep within yourselves you can come forth with the knowledge of the seed within that is so dear to you, the spirit that is a part of your Creator. That soul knowledge is available to you and to you alone. Your responsibility is, like the flower, to bring it forth and to display it for all to see, so that in the seeing of it all those around will recognise their Creator and bring forth that seed in themselves. So perfect your flower, perfect your being. Release your fragrance, your scent, to the Cosmos. Share it with the World around you and you will reveal and discover the love of your Creator.

## QUESTIONS AND ANSWERS

Q: The speaker said that the essence of Easter is pre-Christian and yet much of the talk tonight has been about Jesus and Christianity. Why is this so?

ZT: We recognise that you have all been brought up in the Christian tradition and so the purpose of tonight's talk was to get you to see that the Christian Church, no matter which sect you belong to particularly, does not represent the total understanding of Easter. Indeed that Church reflects only a small, a limited aspect of it. By focussing the ceremony of Easter on one man it is doing both that man and his Creator a disservice. But that is the nature of the Christian religion and why it has only a limited appeal. We are inviting you to look beyond the Christian interpretation to the greater meaning of Easter.

What is significant, as the first speaker said, is that the celebration of Easter is consecrated at this time of the year. Easter brings life and death into focus and that is what I would like you all to do: during the next three days, each of you, within your own heart, consider life and death and come to an understanding of it.

Unless you are approaching seventy years old, or feel you are about to die, you do not normally concern yourselves with death. Death is rather like the dust on the floor which you sweep under the carpet. You hope that it will stay there and not become visible again. That is because you look at death only from the viewpoint of the ending of physical life, so if you do not think that you are near the end of your physical life death has no meaning. That is why so many young people, if they die a violent death, say in an accident or in a war, can become lost souls, for they arrive on the other side of life totally unprepared. You must remember that the consciousness which you have now goes over with you to the other planes of life. You take with you all that you now think and believe, and you will arrive on the other side of life with that

50

consciousness. How much better, therefore, to understand death and not to be lost, to arrive on the other side of life fully aware of the transition and of what has happened. You can prepare for that transition by living and dying to each minute, each day, each year.

Q: How do you die on a higher level of life?
ZT: That is an interesting question! How do you think we die on the astral or the higher planes of life, because we do?

Q: Do you get reborn onto the physical plane of Earth again?
ZT: Yes! What a death!

# AN EASTER MESSAGE: RESURRECTION

As I said to you three days ago, when I spoke on death, I do not intend to limit tonight's talk on resurrection to just the Christian viewpoint. But as you are Christians, as you do live in a Christian society and as today, Easter Sunday, is the highpoint of the Christian calendar, let us begin by briefly considering the resurrection of the Master Jesus.

How strange it is that a Church which holds the resurrection of human life as the basic tenet of its belief should be unable to explain to its followers what exactly takes place in that act of resurrection, what scientific laws are involved, what facets of cosmic understanding are being demonstrated. Resurrection is something which the Christian Church accepts, and worships, blindly. But, truly, like everything else which takes place on this physical plane of life there is a scientific or a cosmic law behind that happening.

You may compare the resurrection of Jesus with the resurrection of King Arthur, for both are similar, and I talk now not of the Arthur of the sixth century but of the archetypal Arthur, the Sun God of the older dispensation. In both cases there is a story which suggests that the body was removed from the physical plane of life and was carried off to another realm, there to await a suitable moment for its return. There are other recorded instances throughout history where great beings are deemed to have performed this act and you can discover them for yourselves if you care to investigate further.

It is difficult for you today to understand the restructuring of physical matter, for you do not understand the cosmic laws involved. Indeed, even the greatest and wisest of you today, when you die, are not capable of restructuring your bodies and resurrecting them as did the Master Jesus and the archetypal Arthur. The reason for this is very simple; the bodies of those great Masters are not like

53

the bodies which you inhabit. You will never be able to resurrect your bodies in their present form, but the bodies of those great Masters contained certain elements which come from beyond the physical plane of Earth.

Your physical bodies are made completely from the matter of the Goddess, Mother Earth. Their bodies were made up for the most part from the matter of Mother Earth but they also contained certain cosmic elements which are kept in secret places on the Earth and are used by the great Masters in the construction of their bodies. Their bodies are finer, they vibrate to a higher note than yours, and therefore after death, after the release of physical life, they are able through transmutation and the understanding of cosmic law to increase the vibratory rate of their bodies and to transport them from the physical place of death. These special elements, if I may call them as such, are capable of being removed from the physical body and are kept in waiting for the return of any great being who wishes to incarnate and use them again. Therefore when the Master Jesus died, certain elements of his body were removed from the physical plane of life and even now are stored, if I may use that expression, awaiting the next cosmic being who wishes to use them to manifest on the plane of Earth.

However what I am concerned with now is the principle of resurrection, its deeper meaning for you, as individuals, as you lead your everyday lives. Just as the story of Arthur is a parable from which you can take inspiration, so the story of Jesus and his death can also be regarded as a parable from which you may learn certain cosmic laws and obtain an understanding of life and death and of your purpose on Earth. Resurrection literally means the rising again of the spirit, not necessarily from the dead, the rising again, the release of the spirit, for that surely is the force which brings about the resurrection. If you are dead you cannot control your physical body and its movements: there has to be a force outside the body which can bring about the resurrection. That force is the force of spirit. You tend to think of resurrection as a movement from life to death and thence to another form of life again, but if you actually lived on one of the higher planes of life, and 'died' on that plane, you could be resurrected on the physical plane of Earth! So the movement from one plane to another is but a form through which the resurrection takes place. You resurrect onto the plane of Earth and you resurrect onto the higher planes of life after physical death.

So resurrection is a changing of structure, an act of metamorphosis, like the caterpillar becoming the butterfly, a coming forth again in a new dimension, in a new form to fulfil a new purpose. It can, and indeed often does, involve movement between the planes of life, but the form of resurrection of which I wish to talk now is the one which you may experience whilst you live on the physical plane of life. How many of you have considered resurrection not as a once and only mystical event at the end of your physical life, but as something which can happen every day of your physical lives? As I said earlier, death is but the release of yesterday, the release of tomorrow. To live in the moment is life, to live out of the moment is death, and from living in the moment comes the opportunity for resurrection. For if one lives in the moment, if one has disowned death, if one is not a part of it, of living in the past or living in the future, then that moment will act as a mirror to the spirit which lies within, the spirit which we have already identified as the source of resurrection.

Your spirit contains within it, like the seed of Nature, the quintessence of your whole being, the spiritual wisdom which you have accrued over thousands of lives on many planes of existence. That seed is lying there dormant, waiting for the moment to be awakened into physical consciousness. You can awaken that seed whenever you desire. That decision lies with you. Do not think that because you have chosen the aspect of spirit that you now manifest that this aspect is fixed and cannot be changed. Do not think that the physical shape which you now inhabit is the perfection of your present being and is immutable. It is not. It merely represents the aspect of spirit that you have chosen to demonstrate and ground upon the plane of Earth at this time. If that aspect is mastered then a change will be necessary, indeed, will be inevitable. Throughout your physical lives on Earth you are always changing, sometimes in small amounts, at other times, in the face of challenge and crisis, in large amounts. But at all times be aware that you are changing.

With every change comes the emergence of a new aspect of spirit. The spirit resurrects the body, casts off the old and creates the new. That which you have been is not what you will be. Now that does not necessarily mean that you will be what you think you will be, for the thought-forms which you create during your physical living, your dreams, your desires, your ideals, are not the reality. If you define yourselves according to those thought-forms, the creation of

55

the ego, the lower personality, then you will limit the real aspect of your being. That is what people do today. They are unaware of the quality of spirit which lies within them and of what can, and should, be released to make them cosmic beings on Earth. That was the mission of the Christ. When you are Christed you release from within yourselves an energy with which you can create at will upon the plane of Earth.

Easter Sunday, therefore, represents an invitation to change, to change according to the true nature of your being, to resurrect the new form within. You are met today in the sign of Aquarius in the Glastonbury Zodiac, the symbol of which is the phoenix. The phoenix symbolises the rising of the new from the ashes of the old. There has to be the destruction of the old before the new can arise. The new cannot arise while the old is present. The nature of the release of the old is the act of sacrifice. As I said earlier, the trinity of death, resurrection and sacrifice form the path of your spiritual progress on Earth. You will die and resurrect many times. Involved in that is the act of sacrifice which is the essential lesson of this planet: Sacrificial Service in Love. Sacrifice using the power of love, the power of your Creator.

The nature of sacrifice is that you have to release. You have to release the individuality, you have to release the ego, that it may burn in the fire so that the new form may come forth. This, for you who are essentially physical human beings, is a great sacrifice, for it means the release of physical matter. It means the recognition of the fact that you are not a being of this planet, that you are not held by the chains of matter and that when you die you are simply releasing the physical and going to the true dwelling place of your being. What you are being asked to do, then, is to release physical matter on a day-to-day basis. Something which you will have to do anyway when you die, you must do daily, as a matter of spiritual practice. Now that does not mean that you need not be responsible for physical matter, that you can ignore the reality of physical life. No, it means simply that you are not bound by physical matter, that it is not the primary force which controls your destiny, which moves your spiritual being, for you are beings of spirit. You have travelled the depths of space. You have lived on planets and planes beyond your comprehension. This Earth is but a passing stage on the eternal path of your spiritual evolution. To be restricted by physical matter is to deny your divinity. You only permit it to happen because you do not realise the true nature of your beings.

So sacrifice involves the release of physical matter and once you have learned to release it, as did the Master Jesus, then you too will be resurrected. You will change form, you will release new energy, you will experience a new dimension of life. The primary lesson of the Master Jesus, the essence of his whole life, was in the nature of his death. That is why the Christian religion holds onto it. Resurrection: the fact that one does not die, that one is not forever encased in form, fixed in shape, the fact that there is always another life, another form, another shape, another purpose, another level of being. You are cosmic beings who have eternal life. You dwell for the most part beyond the realm of Earth and after your physical death you will return to higher and more familiar realms.

Do not allow yourselves, as cosmic beings, to be limited by the physical. Be the masters of it. That is the lesson which you have come to learn: to be the masters of the physical plane and you master that plane by sacrificial service, by the act of giving, by the act of releasing. You have to release the old in order to obtain the new. You have to release the old individualised thought-forms to obtain the new and until you release the old, like the phoenix of Aquarius, the new cannot come forth. This, for you who are grounded in physical thought and memory, is a difficult thing to do, for if you live totally on the physical plane and are content to be limited by it, how can you release the old form? If the physical plane is everything to you, to release it is death. Then so be it. Face that death. Release it and await the new.

That, above all, is the message of Easter. Release the old. Await the new. Do not try to create the new. Do not seek it, for it is already there within you. It will reveal itself to you. New concepts, new ideals, new expressions of your being will manifest. That which before you thought you could not do, you will now do with ease. That which before you could not express or understand, you will now see with clarity. All that lies within you. The message of Easter is the resurrection: the resurrection of spirit, the release of the old, the birth of the new. As with the Master Jesus it may involve pain, it may involve suffering, it may involve death, but what is that but a transition. If you recognise that transition and accept it joyfully for what it is, a passage into light, then you will look forward to that moment when you truly obtain your resurrection.

Q:   Could you tell me more about this act of releasing?
ZT:   Perhaps you should first begin to understand what it is that you are trying to hold on to. Perhaps you should first discover what it is in your being that creates the individualised character and form that you regard as yourself. Only then can you see if you are ready to release it. Can you, as an individual, deny what you are today? Can you say that the image that you have created of yourself is unimportant and that, if necessary, you could release that image, turn around and walk forth in a new direction to fulfil a new purpose?

The trouble with Humanity today is that because you live in a world of thought, where the intuitive channel has been blocked for so long, where science and technology are regarded as God, you think that the World is defined by that science and that technology. You have become crystallised in thought and that crystallisation has become your limitation. If you think about it, the great philosophers and scientists of this Earth, those who ground new concepts on the Earth, nearly always reject that crystallisation. They always look beyond it. They always say that what you hold to be truth, I do not, that what you hold to be the limitation of a certain object, I do not. So what you hold to be the definition of yourself, I do not. Always there is something new to be discovered. No truth on the face of this Earth is ever infinite or absolute. So you must recognise that what you manifest is but a very, very small part of your total being. How are you to discover that being but by releasing the old.

If you believe in reincarnation, if you know it to be a fact of cosmic law, then you will recognise just how many thousands of lives you have lived. Now consider just how much wisdom you have learnt in your present life so far, and remember that most of you have not yet reached 55, the age when you begin to collect and assess the wisdom of your living. Now if you multiply that wisdom by the factor of, shall we say, the ten thousand lives that you have lived, you will begin to appreciate the amount of wisdom that is stored away within your soul waiting to be tapped into and used, waiting to be released on the plane of Earth. That is what you have to bring forth. There is no problem, no test, that you face on this Earth which you have not got the wisdom to solve in an instant.

Q: The teachings that have come through are so beautiful, but I feel such guilt sometimes at not being able to achieve the ideals presented to us.

ZT: Guilt, of course, is a difficult emotion to analyse. There are many forms of guilt. You know what is possible. You know what can be achieved. When you hear messages such as this, when you read inspirational books or listen to people discussing on a soul level, then you grasp a concept of what could be. But what could be is not what is. Between them lies a vast gulf and in that gulf lies the feeling of guilt, or remorse, because if that is possible, then why is one not achieving it? If one could be doing something, then why is one not doing it?

Why does one feel this guilt? Because one is not releasing, because one is not giving up, because one is not prepared to bridge that gulf. I am not talking now of you as an individual, but of Humanity as a whole. If Humanity will not sacrifice then it will not bridge that gulf between what is and what could be. The guilt of Humanity is the sum total of the guilt of the individuals concerned. So if each one of you, as an individual, would renounce your guilt and would be what you feel you could be now, then you would uplift this plane of Earth.

Q: I only feel guilty about something which has passed and which I know I cannot change. I don't feel guilty in the situation when I know I can change something.

ZT: Why do you feel guilt about something you cannot change?

Q: Because I just wish, looking back in retrospect, that I had acted in a different way and had not caused a certain event to happen.

ZT: So you could have changed it if you had wished?

Q: Yes. I feel guilty about anything that I cannot change in this lifetime. But I don't feel guilt for the future because I can do something about it.

ZT: In essence, guilt for the future and guilt for the past are both wasted emotions. Guilt drains the soul. So let us concentrate on the present. If you sit here tonight and because of what has been said feel guilt, feel remorse, then now is the time to stoke up the fire and prepare to burn the old, to become the phoenix. It is an amazing thing, but even though you hold onto the old so desperately, rather like some people hold onto life, when you finally release it and like the butterfly emerge from the cocoon in your new body after metamorphosis, you wonder why you held onto the old for so long!

Q: The speaker was saying that crystallised thought-forms block our intuitive channel and prevent us from experiencing our true selves. Would it be a good idea, then, first to achieve mastery of thought-forms and then to seek the intuitive force? Also, what is the language of intuition? How do we listen to it?
ZT: That is a good question. Let us first consider what is the language of intuition, or more importantly, what is the means of communication of intuition.

Q: Is it an energy?
ZT: Yes. An energy is the means of communication. But what sort of an energy? It has nothing whatever to do with thought. It comes from an entirely different source. Whilst it might be expressed in thought, thought comes after the energy. So what is the energy?

Q: Is it love?
ZT: Yes. Love is the energy of intuition and when I say love, I do not mean the ego love of most human beings, I mean divine love, the life-force of our Creator, the love which flows through us all. So the language of intuition is love, received and given freely both from above and from below. If you are to receive that energy, which has nothing to do with thought, you must be open to love. You must be receptive to it. That love is manifested not only by you but by everyone around you expressing their love. Intuition can be sparked off by your fellow human beings.

So a person that is intuitive is a person who is in love. Is it not curious how always in the romantic stories it is the ladies who fall in love. Men always seem to experience the emotion of love to a lesser extent, with not quite the same grand passion of the ladies. This reflects the nature of Woman's role in the cosmic pattern of life as the intuitive channel. Men, of course, do possess an intuitive channel and use it to varying degrees, but it does not approach the great intuitive channel of the prophetess or the priestess.

60

Q: Is getting rid of contrived thought-forms what you mean by release?

ZT: Yes. You must release the thought-forms of the World that you have created and allow love to communicate with you. Love really is like the sun. If you pull back the curtains of your thought-forms then the sunlight can illuminate the darkness of your being. If you build up a picture of yourself in your own mind, that picture is not really a true one because it has been created by the thoughts that you have of yourself. So when someone comes along and holds a mirror before you, you do not like it, or rather you do not like the person who holds the mirror. What is a mirror but the people around you in the way they think, speak and behave? They are a mirror to your being. So what you have to do is release the old, all the thought-forms you have accrued up to now.

Let us suppose that before you came into this room you had a quarrel with someone. If, as you leave this room, you were to meet that person again, what would you do? You would see that person with the eyes of memory and immediately you would remember all the thought-forms you had had of them, all the incidents that had taken place between you. The result is that like two armies you would take up your entrenched positions and immediately would carry on from where you left off. But if you did not look with the eyes of memory but instead greeted them as you would do a complete stranger, your reaction would be completely different.

Why, therefore, do you hold onto your old thought-forms? Firstly, because for the most part when conflict occurs you do not resolve it. If you have an argument with somebody, rather than resolving that argument and ending it, you part still in conflict and so you carry on the argument for hours and hours afterwards, trying to justify your position even though the other person is not there. The result of this is that when you do meet that person again the same process takes place. Sometimes an argument can go on for days, even for years. So an argument should be resolved at the moment that it occurs. It has then gone for ever. Secondly, you must realise the limitations of thought and see that thought is not the only channel of communication. There is another channel open to you. If you cannot communicate by thought, then perhaps you can communicate by love. There are some people with whom you can only communicate by thought, but equally so there are many with whom you can communicate by love.

61

Q: You say that the lesson of this planet is Sacrificial Service in Love. During his ministry the Master Jesus demonstrated some very unearthly qualities. Were not those demonstrations just as important as his sacrificial service part? Surely he was beyond the limitations of matter at that point?

ZT: The Master Jesus had no need to return to the plane of Earth, to go back to school. He returned not for himself but for Humanity as a whole, to further the evolution of the Earth plane. He sacrificed himself for the good of the whole. You must also understand that just as it takes time for a child to grow to adulthood, so a Master has to prepare himself in order to manifest his consciousness on the Earth plane. Even the greatest Master has to grow to physical, mental and spiritual maturity before he or she is truly capable of being of service. This was true of the Master Jesus.

His period of preparation was three cycles, or thirty years. When you think of the powers that he then possessed, he could have ruled the World. There was no being that could have touched him. He need not have died unless he chose to die. Certainly, if he could resurrect his body after death, if he could walk on the water, change water into wine, raise the dead, what else could he not have done? What else did he do of which you are not aware today? He could have ruled the whole Earth and this indeed was one of the temptations that was put before him to prove that he was ready to be of service. Think of the sacrifice of having all those powers, of being able to raise the level of Humanity at a stroke, and yet not doing it because he saw that individuals must be responsible for their own evolution.

So the Master Jesus was sacrificing on many levels, but the essence of his sacrifice was service for, after all, what was his ministry but total service. He lived solely for the people around him and for the World which he served, but through that sacrifice came the great resurrection which we remember today.

# WOMAN: THE FEMININE ENERGY OF CREATION

As the Age of Pisces dies and Piscean ideas fade away, as the Aquarian Age comes into being, so you are experiencing a period of apparent chaos whilst the old gives way to the new, whilst the energies and impulses of the new Age begin to ground themselves upon the plane of Earth. Piscean concepts and characteristics are fading away, lacking the energy and vitality to keep them going, for they have come to the end of their time. Many people, therefore, are seeking a new understanding of the meaning and purpose of life and nowhere is this more apparent than in the feminine energy of Creation — Woman.

As you look around your World today you can see everywhere that Woman is striking out in new directions and is seeking new purpose in her being. She is trying to establish a new pattern of living, a new way of life, a new identity. She is striving to ground a spiritual quality which has not yet manifested on the plane of Earth. Let us therefore very quickly examine the nature of Woman in the past and, in particular, see where her energy is going now and what will be her purpose in the New Age.

Throughout the Piscean Age the World has been under the domination of patriarchal energy, the male aspect of Creation. This patriarchal domination was, however, part of the divine plan for human evolution. For the women who have experienced this domination there has been a painful lesson to learn, a point of consciousness to comprehend, but it was only possible for Man to rise to the dominant position that he has held because Woman had failed in her divine role. For if Man and Woman were both truly manifesting their divine energy then the male would balance the female on the scales of life and both would live and evolve in harmony. It is only when one of them is out of balance, when the energy of creation is unequal, that such a domination becomes possible. There have, of course, been Ages when Man was under the domination of matriarchal energy, the female aspect of Creation, due to Man's failure to manifest his divine birthright. The evolutionary spiral demands that both Man and Woman experience such a lesson in order to perfect their beings.

When we look at the struggle between Man and Woman today as she strives to gain her freedom, to achieve the equality of the sexes, we can see that the present increase in the divorce rate has come about directly because of that struggle. This has resulted in many broken marriages, many broken homes and, as a result, many unbalanced children, which in turn is leading to an unbalanced World. If Woman is really to have the freedom that she seeks there must also come a recognition from within her of her personal responsibility for creation. She must recognise the divine source of her creativity, of whence it came, and the true nature of her unique responsibility for motherhood and children. If the repressive discipline of the patriarchal society is to be removed then there must come a self-perpetuating, a self-motivating discipline from within Woman herself, both to balance the male energy and to replace the discipline which has gone. One cannot pull down without replacing. One cannot destroy a discipline without having personal responsibility to replace it. Woman should realise that it was only her fall from grace many, many centuries ago that led to the necessity for such a discipline and resulted in this cycle of patriarchal domination.

We are now reaching the end of that patriarchal cycle and a time when equality will once again be granted. It will be granted not only because of the striving of Woman seeking that equality but because the time is now right for that equality to come into being. The lesson of the past cycle has been learnt on the plane of Earth. Now is the time, at this the dawning of the Aquarian Age, for the male and the female energies to begin to live in perfect harmony and balance. This, therefore, calls for an awareness, a perception by both sides of life: the male for the female and the female for the male. They should recognise each other as divine sparks of the duality of creation, each placed on the plane of Earth by their Creator to ground the cosmic nature of Its Being. There can be no comparison between the two. Each is unique. Each grounds a divine aspect which the other does not possess, for there is no duplication in creation on this plane of life.

64

The feminine energy now grounding itself upon the Earth, and remember that this feminine energy comes from a Divine Source, touches both Man and Woman. Obviously it has a greater effect on the female than the male and it is this which is bringing forth all these changes. It is bringing forth changes because Woman is beginning once more to recognise the true nature of her being. She is growing into a true understanding of her responsibility towards the male of the species as the other half of creation, her responsibility towards marriage, her responsibility towards birth and the education of children, her responsibility towards the grounding of the female aspect of creation on the plane of Earth. If Woman is to achieve all of this then she has to climb back onto her pedestal, where she originally was in past Ages, to become once more the Goddess, the female aspect of the divinity manifesting on the Earth.

Is it not strange that in the days of old it was always the man who sought the hand of the woman? The man was always considered to be the suitor asking the woman for her hand in marriage. Why should this be so? It was because in the days of old it was recognised that Woman was the wisdom aspect. It was she who knew whether a suitor was right or wrong for her. The male, with his emphasis on intellect, did not usually possess her wisdom. It was the woman who would say yes or no according to the force of divine intuition that flowed through her. She would know in her heart of the man who was destined to be her partner and so could respond to that suit from the male. The wisdom of our Creator, the force of God in motion, runs most strongly through the feminine aspect of creation. That is the real nature of Woman's responsibility. That is what the male aspect must recognise, accept and, above all, respect.

In recent centuries feminine energy has been severely restricted, indeed even persecuted and banned from the face of the Earth, but Woman is now once more resurrecting the true aspect of herself and is manifesting it in the World today. She is revealing a concept of creation far removed from the one which has become established as reality during the past century. The aspect that you see manifesting today as the feminist movement is, in part, a revolt against the suppression of the true role of Woman. Nevertheless, Women's Liberation, as it is sometimes called, is but only one small part of this movement. Yes, Woman must be liberated, but what will she do after she has become liberated? To be free is one thing, but with that freedom comes the responsibility for right thought, right speech and right action.

You are approaching the time when the feminine aspect of creation is to be given its freedom, when the cycle of patriarchal oppression will cease. Woman will then respond to the energies flowing down through her and will begin to create upon the Earth once more according to her own consciousness and her own feminine energy. She will therefore manifest many new ideas, many new aspects of creation, not only in relation to the family unit, to marriage, birth and death, but also to the whole creative structure of Humanity, to the arts, to science, to politics and, above all, to that which you call religion, the spiritual guidance of Humanity. The World is in the state that it is today mainly because Woman's spiritual guidance does not manifest on the Earth.

In the Aquarian Age Woman will be faced with a great responsibility. She truly is being offered the choice, and the chance, of saving or damning the World, for the World has fallen from grace because Woman in the past has fallen from her pedestal. The choice once more is being offered to her to climb back onto that pedestal and to receive, ground and manifest the wisdom of her Creator, to be an example for all to see, in fact, to become once more the goddess. Much that is wrong in the World today only exists because Woman does not manifest that which she knows within her to be Truth. She hides and covers up her innermost feelings. She denies what she knows to be true for fear of offending either the society in which she lives or the male of the species. Woman must ground and manifest that which she intuitively feels within her. It may be very different to that which has been. Then so be it.

However Woman must be sure that what she grounds is not just a reaction against the past but is indeed the flow of the divine through her. Everything that has been grounded in the past is not necessarily a bad and corrupt practice to be discarded just because there has been a cycle of patriarchal domination. Humanity, after all, has been evolving for thousands of years and has just experienced the lesson of the Piscean point of evolution and consciousness. Much can be learned from that. Humanity is now going to modify that pattern and ground the energies of the Aquarian Age, which are even now becoming discernible. Some of you may have a little idea of what is going to happen, but you cannot see the complete picture.

Women today are the mothers of the Aquarian Age. It is their children who will ground and manifest this energy. These new feminine souls will be unlike Woman today. They will differ from Woman today in both thought, word and deed. Some of their philosophies and ideas will appear outrageous even to the trend-setters of today, but that is the way it should be for a new aspect of being has to manifest itself upon the plane of Earth. It must come. Woman must ground it. Woman must exhibit the purity of her being. She must once more stand on her pedestal. She must learn to say no. She must learn to uphold the truth and to shun that which is evil and false. She must learn to speak out against that which degrades the Goddess in all things. She must learn to uphold that which is of the Divine, for by doing so she will indeed save the World. Woman has the potential to save the World where Man has failed. Man would destroy it, Man maybe will destroy it, but Woman can save it. Wisdom will always have pre-eminence over Power. Power will always respect Wisdom when it is grounded and manifested in perfection.

However, there are those today amongst Woman who, sometimes with the best of intentions, are degrading the female of the species by their behaviour in thought, word and deed. Those who are involved with pornography, for example, are destroying the purity of the Goddess. I therefore ask all those women to consider very carefully exactly what they are doing. Ask yourselves "Is what you are doing for the benefit of the Divine or for Man, for the benefit of your Creator or for the male aspect of creation?". You should honour and obey not the male but your Creator. Your link is with the Godhead. Your responsibility, your karma, is with that great Force. You must be true to it at all times.

As the energies of the Aquarian cycle begin to flow down Woman will begin to ground and manifest many new aspects of life, but her responsibilities in the family as the mother, as the cornerstone of family life, will of course remain, for she is still the conceiver and the carrier. She still gives birth to the child. That is a great and honourable duty. It is one which the Creator specifically gave to her in preference to Man. Women are the mothers of creation. They are the physical womb of creation itself and that responsibility for birth and motherhood is paramount. If they fail in that

67

duty then they are failing Creation. If they fail their children then they have failed the Cosmos.

There will be many women in the new Age who will not have children. Woman will grow into an understanding that she can create with her feminine energy without actually conceiving and giving birth. In the Age to come Woman will become more selective about marriage and conception, which will not become automatic functions of her being. She will be free to create in many other fields of life. Remember that even whilst a woman is creating a child within her womb she can still create on other levels that are just as important, for she dwells on many planes of existence even whilst in her physical body. When her child has grown to adulthood then she can once more pick up the mantle of her cosmic responsibility and fulfil the true nature of her being. But she must always discharge her divine responsibility for her child to the utmost of her ability, for in the understanding of that act of motherhood, in the feeling of compassion and joy for that creation of her God, is the greatest evolutionary opportunity for learning that she will ever experience.

Woman possesses the creative energy of the God-head within her physical being. She is the womb of Creation. She therefore controls the flow of energy into this World. If the World is not as she would wish it then she has no one to blame but herself, for she is the source of all physical creation. She is the source of all that has been and ever will be on this plane of Earth. Through her womb comes every human form that will ever manifest on the physical plane. What a responsibility! Consider it wisely. Remember that she has also been given an intuitive channel to her Creator to exercise that responsibility. May she use it. Woman, listen with your heart and so fulfil the will of your Creator.

## QUESTIONS AND ANSWERS

Q:  Do you feel that marriage and the concept of the individual family unit will continue in the New Age?
ZT:  The family unit has existed since the beginning of time, born out of the need for the male and the female to come together to create and then to nurture a child. In human societies the nature of

the family unit varies, depending upon the cultural traditions of the society in which people live, its understanding of marriage and, more importantly, on the point of consciousness of the people concerned. That will always be so. One's concept of marriage is dictated by one's point of consciousness. You will find that evolved people, people of high consciousness, no matter what their religion, their race or their country, indeed their planet, would demonstrate the same understanding and responsibility towards the family unit because of their point of consciousness. Therefore it is one's spiritual consciousness that decides one's concept of the family unit.

It would seem to me, however, that the mother and the father who are aware of the responsibility of creation and of what is involved in the conception, birth and raising of a child would wish their child to be brought up in their auras, in their understanding of life, if only because of the simple fact that the child chose them, before it even incarnated, to be its parents and teachers. The child chooses the parents necessary to lead it into physical adulthood. It is therefore important that the parents fulfil this responsibility to the utmost of their beings. Now the sociological format in which this is to take place will obviously vary depending upon the cultural traditions of the society in which the parents live. Nevertheless, I view the idea prevalent today of breaking up the family unit as being motivated not by a change of consciousness but by a desire to avoid one's commitment to what one has created.

Q: Many people argue that it is better to break a family unit up and to divorce rather than to carry on if the two people in the marriage are unhappy and are making their children unhappy by their behaviour. They say that it is better to part than to bring up children in disharmony. What do you say to that?
ZT: It is impossible to generalise and to draw up rules for all the situations which occur within the many marriages which take place but, in principle, I would say that it is nearly always better for the parents to stay together. Even if the marriage itself is dead, emotionally or physically, it is not dead for the most important aspect of the marriage which is the children. The parents can, and should, raise their children together, giving of their vibrations in harmony to fulfil their divine responsibility towards what they have conceived and brought into manifestation. They may feel unhappy,

but what is happiness but a state of mind. They should sacrifice their happiness for their children.

Q: Women have a great ability to nurture and love which men do not seem to possess. I see a danger of women being drained by men because they latch onto the nurturing and love of women and use that energy for themselves. Is there not a way of teaching men to bring out the feminine side of themselves?

ZT: I would not agree with you that only Woman can nurture and love. Man can do it just as much as Woman. Obviously the energy of motherhood is a unique quality, but both Man and Woman can love and nurture a child. Indeed, both the parents are essential for the balanced evolution of the child, for each of them provides their own special quality of human nature which contributes to the wholeness of the child. Obviously Woman possesses the gift of motherhood and the energy that goes with it and that is very special to her, and Man, not possessing that energy, can sometimes find this difficult to understand. But, apart from this, there should be an equal giving and sharing of their creative energies within the family unit. Man and Woman should give to each other that which they have incarnated to ground and manifest. Each will learn from the other. If that balance is not maintained then, as you so rightly say, one will tend to lean more upon the other, but it is not necessarily always the male upon the female. It can be just as much the other way around depending upon the individuals and the relationship concerned.

Q: So many people come to the centre who have been through the experience of a broken marriage, sometimes more than once. Therefore I would like you to state very clearly what are the responsibilities of such people when a marriage ends and how can we reduce the ever increasing divorce rate?

ZT: The talk was, in a sense, trying to pre-empt the situation that you are now talking about. What was said was that if Woman used her divine intuitive power in the first place, if she chose her husband more carefully, if she used her discrimination and wisdom, then these marriage break-ups would not take place, or at least not to the degree that they are at present. Woman today rarely uses her discrimination and she usually marries for the wrong reasons, either surrendering to pressure from the male or else marrying for personality rather than for spiritual reasons. She thus enters into an undestined union. With such a marriage inevitably there comes conflict and tension which usually results in divorce and subsequent unhappiness both for the husband and wife and for the creations of their marriage. I therefore ask those women who are not yet married to be responsible, to exercise your divine intuition. It is not the end of the world to say "No", to wait until your destined partner comes along. As long as people marry wrongly you will continue to have the problems of divorce. That is something which Humanity has to contend with.

In the final analysis, therefore, the problem can be reduced to how great a sacrifice the people involved are prepared to make. For example, are they prepared to sacrifice for their children or not? If they are not, then they will divorce and go their own ways, but if they place their children before themselves, if they recognise that their children still have all their adult lives ahead of them, if they truly love their children and wish to see them grow to the highest perfection that they can manifest, then they must sacrifice their own happiness, their own desires, for the good of their children. That is the nature of what life on this Earth is about: sacrificial service in love. There are many who cannot do this, and I have great compassion for them. It requires great love to sacrifice one's personality desires, for that is what one is doing, sacrificing not one's soul but one's personality desires for a child whose life is seemingly unimportant compared to that of an adult. But that child *is* the future. If the child is unbalanced it will in turn create an unbalanced future and who is going to return to that unbalanced future but you, in your next life. So by your actions now you are preparing the conditions of your next life. You cannot escape your karma. That is the Law.

Q: In a broken marriage, therefore, both the partners have to be prepared to make the sacrifice and stay together for their children. It is no good just one being prepared to do it?
ZT: Yes, of course. That is what marriage means: the two becoming the one in creativity.

Q: So if one partner did not understand that responsibility it would not work?
ZT: It would be difficult, if not impossible, for it to work.

Q: At this time of the Earth's evolution are there many soul-mates marrying to produce the children of the New Age?

ZT: Indeed, yes. Perhaps the greatest number of soul-mates that has ever incarnated on the Earth at one time is present now to be the fathers and mothers of the leaders of the New Age. Perhaps only once before, in Atlantis, at a certain critical time in its evolution, was such a large number of evolved souls committed to the physical plane of Earth as there are now.

Q: If you have a situation where the wife is quite willing to stay and support the children, and wants her husband to do the same, but he falls in love with someone else and goes off, what can she do about that?

ZT: This is a very common situation. The first point that I want to make is that the woman who is responsible for attracting the man away, for taking him from his family, must also share the karma for the breakdown of that marriage, for she is betraying the feminine aspect of Creation.

Q: No! Surely it is the man who is karmically responsible for going, not the other woman?

ZT: The man becomes attracted to the other woman, but it is how that woman responds that decides the future of the relationship. Any attraction that is repelled and denied soon withers and dies.

Q: But surely the man is still karmically responsible? If he's married it behoves him not to go off chasing other women.

ZT: Yes, I would not deny that.

Q: So he is the one responsible, not her. She was just walking along minding her own business until he came along!

ZT: You are not understanding what I am saying. Obviously, both the husband and the wife have equal responsibilities, each according to their soul evolution, towards the preservation of the marriage. That must be understood. What I am talking about now is the responsibility of the feminine aspect of Creation, which every woman can, and should, understand and manifest. The woman that is attracting that man away from the marriage is aware of what she is doing. She is destroying that marriage. She is helping to destroy a family. She does not have to do it unless she chooses to do so. She

is betraying the feminine aspect of Creation. That is why Woman
has fallen from her pedestal and that is why the World is in the state
that it is today.

Woman must accept her divine responsibility. She is the wisdom
aspect of Creation. She is the force of God in motion. She 'knows'
so much more than Man. She has a direct link to the Godhead
through her intuitive channel. She has a greater sense of right and
wrong than Man. She is the virgin aspect of the Goddess in
manifestation. Every time she denies that responsibility, for
whatever reason, be it the love of a man or the love of the personality, she is betraying not only herself but the whole female
species. So, in a sense, in the eternal triangle she is destroying two
people by saying "Yes" to the man.

Q: I would like to know if you have already taken a man from his
wife what you can do to remedy the situation?
ZT: There is little that you can do, for the act is done.

Q: Surely you can learn from it and not do it again. We do a lot
of these things out of ignorance because we are not aware that it is
wrong and because in society it has become accepted.
ZT: No, I would not agree with you. There is no such thing as an
ignorant woman, and I mean that seriously! A woman always
knows in her heart right and wrong very clearly in such a situation.
The reason that all this sexual seduction and manipulation goes on
is because many women do not want to know the truth.

Q: I would like to ask about the meeting of soul-mates. Is this just
applicable to a select few or to many people at this time?
ZT: I think we should be very clear about what we mean by soul-
mates and what we mean by affinities. Affinities are the two
aspects of one spirit that was created by our God. They are the two
sides of the coin which when complete make the whole coin. Due to
the evolutionary pattern of our planet, which teaches through
opposites, the spirit is split into two at birth, but after thousands of
years of evolution it will eventually become one again. Usually one
affinity incarnates on Earth whilst the other watches from the other
side of life. A soul-mate is the term which is associated with a group
of souls who were all created at the same time and who have experienced many incarnations together, often being brother and sister,

husband and wife. They are very closely linked karmically. There are many soul-mates around at this time because of the nature of the Earth's evolutionary cycle, and it is almost inevitable that people of an evolved consciousness will marry a soul-mate. Whether or not affinities incarnate together and marry depends entirely on the work they have come to do and how best they can ground and manifest their energy on the plane of Earth.

Q: I am divorced because my little daughter couldn't cope with the tension between my wife and myself. Now I ask what I should do. Should I stay divorced or go back and recreate a family situation?
ZT: Obviously, if the parents cannot live together because of extreme physical or mental conflict and so cannot provide an environment in which the child can prosper and grow to adulthood in harmony and love, then, inevitably, there has to be a separation. However, a separation merely means that one's responsibility for ensuring that one's child is nurtured correctly increases tenfold. So if the parents have separated, the child must have an equal opportunity of experiencing both the energies of the father and the mother in order to help it grow into a balanced adult. It therefore requires greater energy, greater sacrifice and greater understanding to help that little child to grow to maturity.

Q: Does that mean that both the parents should live close to the child and should be available on a daily basis?
ZT: Absolutely.

Q: Some people feel that it is necessary to leave their families in order to become spiritual teachers and help save the World, but I would have thought that the way to help save the World is by being responsible for one's own creations first. What do you think?
ZT: What I am to say now may sound harsh and judgemental, but I say it in love. Basically, the natural response of anybody who has failed in one aspect of their lives is to want to succeed in another. So if one has failed in one's marriage one wishes to put one's energies into succeeding somewhere else, and since we are talking about creation, which is children, if one has failed in that aspect of creation one wishes to help Creation itself. It is the same energy, the same desire, merely being diverted into another form. But, in truth, it is difficult to save the World if one cannot save one's marriage.

# CHOOSING ONE'S MARRIAGE PARTNER

The three most significant rites of passage which you will celebrate as human beings are birth, death and marriage. Over birth and death it would appear that you exercise little choice, although the truth of the matter is that on the higher levels of life, before you incarnate, you choose very deliberately and with great consciousness both your moment of birth and your moment of death. Nevertheless, because at birth and death you are transferring your spiritual consciousness from one plane of life to another, the fact that you have made a choice is not always readily apparent. But with the act of marriage, because you are living on the physical plane of life in your bodies of matter and because the density of the World's vibrations dulls your senses, that inspiration which is present on the higher levels of life appears to be denied to you. Many of you therefore experience great uncertainty as you seek out the partner that you have chosen to marry in this life.

It is important that you realise that evolved souls choose their marriage partners with as much care as they choose their moment of birth and their moment of death. There will always be a destined partner to complete a destined marriage, a partnership agreed on the higher levels of life by the souls involved before they even came down into physical matter on Earth. As in all things it is the point of soul consciousness that decides both the level of the marriage and the nature of its destiny. For young souls it does not matter so much if a destined marriage does not come to pass because they will learn lessons no matter whom they marry. Moreover, the lower the point of consciousness the more the souls that are available from which to select a partner for marriage, but as you progress up the evolutionary ladder so the choice becomes more restricted. If you do not choose your destined partner and marry someone else then your destiny is restricted, and in the case of an evolved soul is severely restricted. It is therefore important that you both find and marry your destined partner.

In the World in which you live today when perhaps twenty five per cent of all marriages end in divorce and when another twenty five per cent are marriages only in name, with husbands and wives simply living together in a joyless union, it is all the more remarkable that there are some people who still regard marriage as a lifetime's commitment. Such people insist on finding their right partner even though they know a legal release can easily be obtained from a marriage if they think they have made a mistake. It is indeed a rare soul, a soul of aged evolution, that regards marriage as a spiritual act and invokes the blessing of its Creator on that union, that dedicates the creativity of the union to its God. Marriage is a sacred sacrament and its significance is never lost on an evolved soul. That is why old souls always seek to find their destined partner in marriage. They recognise both the sanctity of the union and the purpose for which they agreed to marry on Earth.

The temptation is always present for an evolved soul to marry a less evolved soul. The magnetic quality of an evolved soul will often attract a less evolved soul to it like a moth to the flame. An evolved soul sometimes succumbs to this temptation because of the apparent personality attractions and so has to face the lesson of being married to a less evolved soul. This often proves to be a painful lesson for not only does such a marriage limit its destiny path but it also places severe restrictions on the creations of its marriage. Moreover, as the older soul grows in spiritual maturity and reaches the physical age when it wants to become a teacher, it finds that it is continually being restricted by its less evolved partner. The result of this is that unless karma is to be created it must restrict its evolutionary pace to that of its partner. An old soul will make this mistake only once or twice in its evolutionary cycle and will then learn the lesson and will never need to repeat it. It is important, unless your destiny requires it, not to marry a less evolved soul. You should always seek out your true partner in marriage, the partner you have chosen for this incarnation. You should seek your true partner not just to fulfil your destiny, not just to fulfil the spiritual nature of your being but, above all, because you know that that is the commitment which you made before you came down into physical life.

How then are you to recognise that chosen person? The greatest mistake that you can make is to spend hours thinking about it, for thought does not come into the process of selecting and marrying your destined partner. Thought only creates personality alternatives. It is the heart that selects. There can be no alternatives for the heart, because the heart, which is the seat of the spirit, has already made its choice. Therefore no selection process takes place within the heart, only the process of recognising what has already been ordained. Therefore to think, to dream, to create images of the person you will marry, of the nature of the marriage and of what it will create, is a waste of time and energy and will only lead to confusion in the mind. Old souls choose their partners with their hearts. You use the expression of falling in love. That form of love is not the love of the personality emotions, the love of the thought-forms, the romantic love of the story books. No! True love is the love of the heart. It is the love of your Creator permeating through you. It is a recognition of the two becoming the one and of the strength that that energy produces, a strength that cannot be ignored. That recognition is as striking as the moment of birth and the moment of death. If you are seeking your marriage partner and have not felt this love then either you have not yet met the one you are to marry or, if you have, the moment for marriage has not yet arrived.

It is important that you recognise not only that there is such a thing as a destined partner but also that there is such a thing as a destined time for marriage. Many people meet their destined partners and will then wait for many years before they marry. The reasons for this are manifold but are usually either karmic or because of the differing rates at which the individuals concerned have evolved in their present lives. You all possess the divine gift of free-choice and can vary the rate at which you open and develop your centres of power and energy, the rate at which you bring forth your soul consciousness. Because of this free-choice many souls will deviate from their destiny paths and will take time to return to them, thus delaying the onward progression of their souls. Therefore until both partners are ready for marriage on a spiritual level there is no point in them marrying. Indeed, if either of them is not yet ready for marriage, then the destined time of marriage will be postponed until the individuals concerned are ready for that act of union. Such a decision is of course taken on the higher levels of life. So you must not only have met your destined partner, but both of you must be ready for that act of union, for the commitment to marriage on a spiritual level.

Old souls do not marry for romance. They marry to be of service to Humanity and to the Cosmos. They marry to serve the principle of marriage which is one of service, of service not to themselves but to Humanity and to the World as a whole. They come together at the appointed time to unite their energies as an act of service to their Creator. Therefore, individually, they should prepare for this event. They should develop their strength of character, they should eliminate their personality weaknesses and prepare themselves for their spiritual union. Marriage is not a ceremony which they should walk into with their eyes closed, fatalistically, just because they feel they should marry. Rather it is like a knight keeping his vigil before he earns his spurs. It requires fasting, prayer, meditation and one-pointedness to prepare for that blessed union. Until both the partners are ready there is no point in marrying, for the entrance into marriage is just as important as is the leaving of it.

The nature of the energy that is grounded as you enter into marriage and make your vows, as you establish your life together, will decide the nature of the marriage. It will create the pattern of the married life to come. If you enter with wrong motivation, with wrong thought-forms, if you enter in a world of illusion, then that will be the path which the marriage will take. It is therefore important that you enter into marriage with clarity. Look with the eyes of the soul, not with the eyes of infatuation, of romance, of the personality thought-forms. Look with the eyes of the soul for it is the one soul recognising the other that ignites the fire of the destined union. There is no choice for an old soul, just a moment of awakening within the heart, a recognition that the moment for marriage has come. If there is any doubt then that moment has not come. For an old soul there is never any doubt, only the certain knowing that you are embarking upon the destiny which you have chosen.

If you feel ready for marriage but cannot find your partner, it can be the case that the time has come when you were destined to marry but your partner is not yet ready for marriage. You therefore have to exercise patience and wait for them to evolve a little further along their path so that they may reach the point of consciousness when they can enter correctly into marriage and can make their presence known to you. You would not wish it otherwise. Your partner must be ready for that union. To marry someone who is not your equal in soul evolution, someone who has not yet fully awakened their spiritual consciousness and so cannot share with you on all levels, would be to destroy the marriage.

Marriage, therefore, is an important rite of passage. It is just as important as birth and death. The timing of your entry into marriage is known to your Creator, as is the destiny and point of consciousness of both you and your intended partner. There is no such thing as error in the plan of your life — your destiny. There is a Divine Force that knows all things, that is aware of every step that you take, of every hair on your head. There is no need for fear, no need for doubt. If you do have doubts then meditate on them, listen to the innermost murmurings of your heart. Talk to your Creator and seek Its peace, seek Its counsel, and what you desire to know will be released to you. Have faith, trust in the Divine Force that has guided you in your life so far and will guide you in the future. Your marriage partner awaits you just as eagerly as you await your partner.

## QUESTIONS AND ANSWERS

Q: I knew, on a soul level, that I was marrying the right person and so was happy to proceed with my marriage even though on a personality level I still had doubts. On the day before the wedding, at the rehearsal, I received a fantastic blessing of grace that descended upon me and let me know that I was doing the right thing. But I really was working on faith. Surely the female, with her intuitive powers, should be more knowing and more confident of her selection?

ZT: Have you ever considered that perhaps your husband knew! Do not forget that the male aspect of spirit is not always in a male body and the female aspect of spirit is not always in a female body. The male aspect will always pursue the female aspect and it is the female aspect that makes the choice, using her divine power, her intuitive channel. Nevertheless, sometimes the female aspect of spirit, with its powers of selection, can be in a male body. So outwardly it is not always the male that seeks the female and the all knowing female that accepts or rejects. It can work the other way around especially when a very strong female aspect of spirit is in a male body.

Q: Why does it so frequently happen that people who are sure that they have met the right person, enter into a relationship and then before very long that relationship breaks down?
ZT: The reasons behind this are infinite and it depends, of course, on the nature of the relationship. In the World in which you live today so many people have relationships before they actually get married that truly it can be said that they have been married several times and I mean this not in the true sense of the word but in the way that they live together and have a sexual relationship! If someone enters into such a relationship with selfish motivation, seeking only support from their partner, always taking rather than giving, then obviously the relationship is meaningful for them only so long as their partner gives, as they are getting what they want from the relationship. However when they have taken as much as they want, or they find someone else who is prepared to give more, they end the relationship and move on. This can be true on many levels of life. I would say that if you enter into such a relationship, never intending marriage, then your motivation is usually wrong and that you have a selfish, not a selfless, motivation. You are entering the relationship not to consummate a holy act of creation, but to satisfy the needs of your lower self. This inevitably leads to conflict and that is why so many people are continually changing partners.

Q: Very often there is a conscious reason for a relationship but underneath that conscious reason there is a very strong unconscious drive pushing one into a relationship. It seems impossible to expect someone to recognise that they are doing wrong when so many of our drives are unconscious. What do you feel about that?
ZT: When you talk of drives and urges you are using terminology which is difficult to quantify. However my understanding of physical life is that no matter what the urge, conscious or unconscious, before you actually allow that urge to become physical reality there is a moment of choice when you can either say "Yes" or "No" to it, when you can either accept or reject it. There is a moment when you can exercise the divine gift of free choice. You have to make the choice and that choice, of course, should be based

80

on your soul wisdom, but if, for example, you are so besotted with someone that you do not want to listen to your soul then you will not stop to meditate in your heart to see if what you are doing is correct. But that moment of choice is there and it is there more for the woman than for the man. It is the man who pursues the woman seeking her wisdom. It is then up to the woman to make the choice and to either accept or reject him.

Q:   If you are making a wrong choice does not universal feed-back very quickly show you that you are wrong before you actually enter into the marriage?
ZT:   If you have made a wrong choice and I use the word 'wrong' not in the sense of right and wrong but in the sense of not your destined partner, then, depending on your motivation for making that choice, the Universe would reflect back to you. But if, for whatever reasons, you had consciously decided that you were not prepared to proceed with your destined marriage and had decided to marry someone else, then you would be permitted to do that. The reason for this is that the lessons you would learn from such a marriage would be beneficial to your evolutionary cycle.

Q:   Is it a hard lesson for an old soul to be married to someone whom they should not be married to?
ZT:   Yes, but that should not happen to old souls who always choose their marriage partners with great care before they come down to Earth. They know who they are to marry and the possibility of an old soul marrying wrongly is remote. With old souls the force of the soul impulse is so strong that they will not go against what they know to be correct. Old souls may not want to know, but they know! They cannot avoid their soul responsibility.

Q:   I have recently ended a long standing relationship with a much younger person because I felt that that was the right thing to do. He now wishes to resume the relationship. Should I agree to this, for his sake if not for mine?
ZT:   You have been as a mother to him. You have aided his evolutionary cycle a great deal. But just as there are times after a child has left its mother's apron strings when it wishes to return to the security of those apron strings, so it is with your man now. He does not like being alone in the world. He does not like the challenges

and tests that he is having to face, and so he seeks to return. But that is not the nature of life. A child has to grow up and become an adult, and it has to do that by itself, learning its own lessons. The decision that you have made in your heart is correct. The time has come to part.

If you were to marry now, and you can choose to do that if you so wish, the marriage would not last very long. Do you know why? Because he would not evolve. He would not develop himself. He is still a young boy with much to learn and much to bring forth. He has to establish both his personality and his soul influence more positively, to identify with his work both physical and spiritual. All this he has to do by himself, standing on his own two feet, learning his own lessons in life. If you remove those lessons from him he will be a baby for the rest of his life. You can marry him if you wish, but you will not be happy in the years to come. You have other things to do. You have your own destiny to lead. He needs to be free in order to become a man. It might seem hard but that is what happens when you push little birds out of the nest. They learn to fly and fend for themselves very quickly.

Q:  I would take great care not to stand in his way.
ZT:  I know you would not consciously stand in his way but you would stop him finding his way.

Q:  I divorced my husband two years ago. We had no children. Would the fact that I've been married in any way affect my marrying again, for example, because I've got karma to pay for my first marriage?
ZT:  Obviously the karma, if any, which you owe for your first marriage will have to be transmuted at some time, but that should in no way restrict the nature of a second marriage. Many people make the mistake of marrying at too young an age, with wrong motivations. Many marriages break up simply because at the time they were entered into neither of the people concerned really knew what they were doing. But as you grow older and more mature, and perhaps see a more spiritual purpose in marriage, there is nothing to stop you attracting your true partner to you. You have just made a little diversion from your destiny path, a diversion which has taught you many lessons. You can return to your path with ease.

82

# DIVORCE

You live at a time in which perhaps a quarter of all marriages will end in divorce and that figure does not include the many unions which are not called marriages by society today, where people live together for many years, just as if they were married, and then separate. Let me begin by saying that the act of divorce is really only a legal process. It is not an act which is recognised by we of the Spiritual Hierarchy on the higher planes of life. In reality there is no such thing as divorce. As the Christian marriage ceremony states very clearly, 'Those whom God has joined together, let no man put asunder'. The meaning of that is very clear: that a marriage which has the blessing of the Creator invoked upon it cannot be dissolved, not only in this life but also in the hereafter.

When a man and a woman enter into marriage they link not only on the physical plane of life but also on the higher planes as well and the karma which they create between themselves in that marriage will link them for many, many lives to come. The process which you call divorce is but a physical instrument devised by the legal profession to separate those who have been legally joined together in marriage. It may have validity on the physical plane of Earth but it is not recognised on the higher planes of life. So as I begin to talk about divorce I would ask you to remember that fact above all else. You can be divorced on the physical plane but never on the higher planes because you are linked for eternity to that person you have joined in marriage.

Divorce, therefore, is a human concept. It signifies the ending of a marriage. However let us be aware that there are many people today who although they think they are married have, in truth, never really married. Such people enter into marriage as if it was a game, a playground for the ego, and for them divorce is of no more significance than the marriage ceremony. There are also many in the World today, especially amongst the young, who do not believe in marriage in any form, be it church, civil or a simple union under some form of blessing. Many people today just live together and then separate. That separation is also a form of divorce even if it is not recognised as such by the legal profession. However the divorce which causes so much pain and suffering in the World today is the divorce that comes from a marriage which was consecrated in a church and which should therefore not be dissolved, a marriage that is ending only because of the personality weaknesses of the individuals involved.

One cannot and, indeed, should not generalise about marriage or divorce. All that I can do is to present to you the aspects of Universal Law which apply to all things on the plane of Earth, including marriage and divorce. Everything on the physical plane is ruled by the Laws of the Universe and one of those Laws is the Law of Equalisation or the Law of Balance. In any divorce therefore there must be equality in all things. The balance between husband and wife must, and will, be preserved no matter what a legal settlement may decide on the physical plane of Earth, no matter who may appear to win or lose in the divorce court. The scales of justice wielded by the Lords of Karma ensure that no-one gains and no-one loses. Although either husband or wife might appear to gain an advantage now, that imbalance will be redressed in subsequent lives. Truly, if the karma of a marriage is not fully discharged then you will return to it again and again. You will marry that person again and will have to face the lesson of that marriage again. The physical form may be different. The personalities may not be the same. But the eternal spirit within the body will be and it is the soul, which is the memory of spirit, that retains the lessons of marriage both past, present and future. You are condemned to come back and repeat everything that you do not complete in total harmony to the highest of your point of consciousness.

It would seem to me that as you hold a ceremony of marriage in a church so a ceremony of divorce should be held there too. It would seem to me that if the husband and wife came together in a church, with due solemnity, preferably to the very place where they had married and made their vows, they would think more seriously about the steps which they were about to take. Through a divorce ceremony they might grow into an understanding that this step was not necessary and that the clashes of the personality could be reconciled and placed in perspective. They might realise that they can, and should, make greater sacrifices to their marriage partner so that they could continue to learn and evolve together and give to the Earth of their union. For those who have entered marriage selfishly, to satisfy their own desires, this is a difficult and painful lesson to learn. Because so many people today marry with wrong motivation, marry too soon, not waiting for their destined partner, marry the choice of their ego, of their lower personality, marry for some low personal motive, the union of marriage has become a prison, a prison from which they long to escape. For them divorce is the means of escape from that prison.

When a husband and wife have decided to divorce then it is essential that this act is done with love. It should be done with just as much love as was used to form the marriage. In the act of divorce there should be a mutual understanding and sharing, a recognition that although their marriage has failed in this life the seeds are being sown for another marriage in another life, perhaps under more favourable circumstances. They should recognise that they are not saying 'good-bye' for the last time, that they will probably meet again in this life and certainly will in their lives to come. Divorce is simply a parting of the ways, a parting which will last for a short time until they come together again. There should be no hatred, no bitterness, no laying of blame or seeking to justify their stated position; just the recognition that perhaps the marriage was too great a test for them, that the jump in consciousness required to make their marriage work was too great, that the sacrifice demanded could not be given. In the sadness of the inner knowledge that the marriage has failed, in spite of their vows to their partner and to their Creator, comes an understanding of what will be required in their lives to come.

Inevitably, in a marriage today, there will usually be children to consider. It is here, perhaps, that the greatest lesson of a marriage is presented. Although the purpose of marriage is not solely to have children, for most parents the act of creativity on the higher levels of life will result in the creation of a child on the physical plane. Universal Law is very definite about the responsibility of creation. It clearly states that you are completely responsible for what you create until the end of time and if a divorce will prevent you from fully discharging that responsibility for creation, then that divorce should not take place. The parents should recognise that even if their marriage has failed due to their personality weaknesses, and they want to divorce, they should nevertheless sacrifice their own lives, their own desires, for the sake of their children. This means that they should stay together, certainly until the child has reached the age of twelve when its spirit is fully inside its physical body, happily until the child has reached the age of twenty one when it will have finished its second cycle and grown to physical maturity. A child needs the physical, emotional and spiritual guidance of its parents until the age of twenty one. Those parents who deny their children that guidance are incurring great karma not only for themselves but for the World as a whole.

An imbalanced creation creates an imbalanced World. An imbalanced child becomes an imbalanced adult and will in turn perpetuate that pattern of imbalance and will create disharmony and discord in the World. Some parents today, through their immorality and selfishness, are creating a generation of children that will destroy human society because they have become imbalanced in so many aspects of life. The result of this imbalance is that as these children grow to become adults they will create an even more imbalanced world. The pattern which you are now witnessing on the Earth will become accelerated during the next twenty years.

Now I recognise that it requires great consciousness to overcome the weaknesses of the personality and to sacrifice your being for the good of the whole, but many are called upon to do this. Some people are asked to sacrifice their lives, to give up their physical being in order to save another. Parents are rarely asked to do this, only to sacrifice twenty years of their living in order to be responsible for the children that they have created. If they cannot do that then they are not worthy of the Human Race and of the heritage that is freely given to them, a heritage earned by the sacrifice of past generations.

Look at the example of your Creator, that being whom you call God. Your Creator is totally responsible for every aspect of Its creation: you and all the other beings on Earth. At no time does your Creator divorce Itself from that responsibility. At no time are you separated from Its love and protection, Its guidance and wisdom. You are one, and always will be one, with your Creator and so should you be with your children. For those parents that

86

divorce and ignore their responsibilities to their children the karma will be with them for many lives to come. They will witness the results of what they have sown even unto the third generation. Parents must be responsible for what they have created. That is the Law of the Universe and if that responsibility involves sacrifice, then so be it. That is the way Humanity evolves and becomes divine.

So for parents with children divorce should not take place. Inevitably, it will, because Humanity is not yet of the consciousness to make the sacrifice involved. After a divorce has taken place the parents must at all times ensure that their physical presence, their spiritual energy, is available to their children whenever it is needed. It is essential, therefore, that the family energy and feeling is preserved even though separation has taken place. The male and the female energy must be present equally to hold the child in balance. A child needs the energy of the two that have created it in order to grow and become a balanced adult.

Even amongst people who have no children the decision to divorce should be considered very carefully, for many creations come from a marriage apart from the physical creativity of a child. A husband and wife create on many levels besides the physical. Every time they perform the sexual act not only do they create an etheric child on the higher levels of life which then becomes their responsibility, but they also create on the emotional and mental levels as well. So during their married life a husband and wife will create many thought-forms for which they are responsible. It is easier to handle the karma of all that they have created if they stay together in love. They can transmute everything that they have created as they grow old in wisdom. When they are in their sixth cycle of life, their fifties, and have achieved spiritual maturity, they can then look back together on the life that they have led and can see the creations of their marriage. They can agree where they have erred and, together, can transmute those errors and so go forward to become the teachers of the young.

There are some people today who believe that they have to sacrifice their marriages in order to become spiritual teachers, to fulfil a divine mission. I would say that if they cannot hold their marriages in balance then they have no destiny to be spiritual teachers. If they cannot be in balance on the physical, the external level of life, then they are certainly not in balance on the spiritual, the inner plane of life. Sacrificial service cannot be manifested on the higher planes if it cannot first be manifested on the physical plane of life.

For many people divorce signifies the ending of a marriage which, in truth, was never a spiritual union. Today many marry, many divorce, without thought for the effects of their actions on the World. It means nothing. They were never married in spirit anyway, although of course their union has linked them karmically for many lives to come. What concerns us of the Spiritual Hierarchy is that so many of the people who enter into a spiritual marriage today, who invoke a divine blessing, who ask that their Creator bless them and guide them in the years to come, should then renounce their vows and seek to end their marriage by divorce.

One of the great failings in modern society is that a husband or wife is usually not allowed to make any mistakes, especially where adultery is concerned. There seems to me to be little forgiveness in marriage today. Each partner is held to be perfect and when one slips from that perfection that is considered to be grounds for ending the marriage. Remember that it is by forgiving that you are forgiven. People will make mistakes in marriage. People will slip from their pedestals. That must be understood. If there is love in a person's heart, if they recognise the true quality of their husband or wife, then they will not punish them for their slip but will support them in their time of need. To make mistakes is human. It is a necessary part of human evolution. It is not grounds for divorce.

There are many who divorce today because they feel that marriage is preventing them from becoming what they want to be. They feel that marriage is restricting them, that the personality traits of their partners are stifling their potential, that they cannot be what their Creator intended them to be, that they cannot serve their God in some noble cause because their husband or wife will not permit it. This, to my mind, begs the question, for they have not recognised that their partner is the other half of human creativity, the other half of their being. Marriage is an act of union between two divine sparks of creativity. God is present in both halves of the marriage, and by denying one half you are denying your God, and to embark upon some great quest when you have already denied your God is pointless. If you cannot hold a

88

marriage in balance then you cannot be of true service in the Divine Plan. That surely is obvious.

So many people today are seduced by the material possessions of life. Perhaps this aspect more than any other today tests a marriage and leads to divorce. When certain material standards are not achieved, when either the husband or the wife thinks that they need more material possessions, more money or status, then the marriage becomes threatened. What is threatened, of course, is not the marriage but the ideas that the husband or wife have of that marriage. The spirit that was present at the altar when they were married is still there, but how many people seek its wisdom. If people today listened to that still, quiet voice within there would be very few divorces. If people truly loved each other, loved not the personality but the spirit, there would be no need for separation, no need for denying what they have already created on the higher levels of life.

So I urge you all, especially if you are considering divorce, to think clearly of what you are doing. You can separate the bond of marriage for just a short time on the physical plane of life, but that is all that you will achieve and what will you have created by that act: the karma you owe to your marriage partner, the karma you must discharge to your Creator, the necessity to come back and repeat that marriage again, the karma you owe to your children if there are any in that marriage, the karma you owe to your country, to the World, indeed to the Cosmos, for the ripples you have created on the pond of eternity. Weigh the balance carefully before you make that step.


## QUESTIONS AND ANSWERS


Q:   If only one person wants to get divorced and the other person does not, if one person wants to keep the marriage going what is the position then?

ZT:   Divorce should be a mutual agreement, with both husband and wife agreeing to the separation. If that agreement is not present and one of them wishes the marriage to go on then the other person should make the sacrifice and should remain in the marriage to help that person. That is the spiritual ideal: that the sacrifice should be made to help the other partner who still has need of the marriage. On the legal side, as you well know, the fact that one person wishes the marriage to go on very often cannot prevent a divorce if sufficient 'evidence' can be manufactured to produce grounds for divorce before the judge. The divorce will still go ahead, without regard for the other person's feelings in the matter.

Q: Let us suppose, as is so often the case, that it is the wife who is looking after the children who does not want the divorce, and that it is the husband who has found someone else and gone off. Where does she stand regarding karmic responsibility for the divorce?
ZT: It is impossible to generalise about all divorce situations. The Law of Karma does not proportion responsibility in percentages, nevertheless, the person that wishes to preserve the marriage would probably attract less karma than the person who wishes to end it.

Q: But why should she attract any karma since it may not be her fault that he has left?
ZT: I am not talking about fault. That is the human way of looking at life. A divorce is no-one's fault. Usually both aspects of the marriage are to blame for that situation arising. The husband and wife must both accept responsibility for all that they have created in the marriage, including the divorce. They must together face and transmute the karma that they have created.

Q: I would like to ask a question about karma. Would it be true to say that karma is what happens to you when you wrong some-one?
ZT: Karma is the eastern name for the Law which you in the West call Cause and Effect and which I call Equalisation. What you have sown, what you have done in thought, word and deed has an effect and that effect will in turn be felt by you. It is as simple as that. What you have done not only in this life but also in your many previous lives has had an effect on the pool of life, and when you step into that pool you will be affected by the ripples that you have created both now and in the past.

The essence of the Law of Karma is that everything in Creation is held in perfect balance. There is no such thing as inequality. Karma ensures that equalisation takes place, ensures that the balance is held between all human beings and all cosmic beings of the

Universe. Do not see karma only as a plus or minus column in a divine accountant's book in which is recorded what you owe to someone because of the wrong that you have done them! It does not work in that way. It is rather a teaching process in which you learn from what you have done. It is you that has created those ripples on the pond of life and they will in turn affect you. The purpose of karma is not punishment. It is rather a process of balance and education.

Q: I feel that I have incurred a great deal of karma because I divorced my husband. But surely life is a learning experience and one is expected to make mistakes. You make karma sound like a threat, like an axe hanging over my head waiting to come down if I do wrong. I don't believe a God of Love would use such a weapon. He would teach his children in a gentle way. How do you feel about that?

ZT: I would agree with you. I hope I have not presented karma to you as an axe hanging over your head! Karma is not a punishment. Karma, for the most part, is a course of action agreed by yourselves after death. After you have passed over to the higher planes of life you go over your total life with a very wise being. In consultation with that wise being you agree as to where you have erred, the lessons you have to learn and the steps to be taken to redress the balance in the future. Karma is not something which is imposed upon you against your will. It is something which you choose to work out both for yourself and for the energy pattern which you have created in the pool of life. It should not be seen as a punishment.

Let me give you an example. Supposing that you murdered someone in a fit of jealous rage. Now that does not mean that the karma for that murder would be that that person would be allowed to murder you in another life. That is not karma. What it would mean would be that after your death you would look back on what you had done and would see why you had murdered that person. You would assess the motivation behind your act, the effect that it had on his and your family, on the World as a whole. You would then determine the lessons which you had to learn from it. You might also decide that you owed that person a degree of service because of what you had done. You might decide to repay that person by returning in another life to help him with some evolutionary lesson.

91

You might come back as his child with a destiny to die at a young age from a painful disease. The man who you had murdered would therefore experience the pain of losing his child at a young age  and would be placed in a position of growth and evolution. He would learn many lessons from that experience. That incarnation would be your sacrifice to him to help him along his evolutionary cycle. You must see karma not as a punishment but as an evolutionary tool designed to balance all the deeds of Humanity and to ensure its further evolution.

Q:   I still feel the whole concept of karma is very dangerous. It can be used as a threat to make one act correctly. It can stop me from doing things I want to do out of fear of the karma involved.
ZT:   The Law of Karma is just one of many Cosmic Laws that govern your physical and spiritual behaviour on the plane of Earth. These Cosmic Laws govern every aspect of your being. They are all powerful, all pervasive, and even if you are not aware of them you are still governed by them. Ignorance of the law is no excuse for breaking it. Many people break a law and do not know that they are doing it. The karma for this is obviously less than for someone who knowingly breaks a law. Obviously the corrective action necessary for a child would not be the same as that for an adult who has broken a law. In just the same way a person who breaks the Cosmic Law without being aware of it is corrected far less sharply than someone who is aware of the Law and knows that they are breaking it. There are degrees with which the Law is applied, as you can well imagine.

Many people enter marriage and then discover that they have made a mistake. That is a fact of life, something which we all know takes place. It has been going on ever since Humanity came down upon the plane of Earth and the bond of marriage was created. What is important is the way in which the husband and wife handle their marriage and handle their divorce. It is recognised that two people can marry with every intention of fulfilling their vows but later realise that the time was not right for them to fulfil their obligations. They would therefore seek release from their marriage. They are free to do this provided they remember that the karmic responsibility for their marriage will have to be faced in another life, at a later time. So there are some who will marry twice in a lifetime for this very reason.

Q: When a woman divorces and remarries, her children are then brought up by their stepfather. Should the original father still stay close to the children or is it better for him to go away and allow the new family unit to grow together?

ZT: Again I cannot generalise because every human being is unique, every situation is different. Nevertheless, if a child is under the age of twelve it should be able to experience the physical vibrations of both its creative parents whenever it wants them. This will not be possible if one of the parents does not live near the child. Beyond the age of twelve, in the second cycle, the child still needs the support of both its parents but not to the degree that was present in the first cycle. It is therefore desirable that the parents should still be available for contact when, and if, the child needs it. If a parent lives a long way away then that is not possible. So it would seem to me that you can only discharge your parental duties to your child if you live fairly close to it.

Q: What about the stepfather? Cannot he take the place of the original father?

ZT: The stepfather can substitute to a degree, but inevitably this will create confusion in the child's mind, especially if it has experienced and loved its father's vibration for any length of time. Psychological problems will present themselves later on in life.

I will end by making this analogy. Let us suppose that you have a garden and in that garden you plant some very special, very rare, priceless seeds. You take great care to prepare the soil and when the first shoots come up you nurture them with great love. You protect them and care for them as they grow to maturity. In return the flowers give you great joy as they prepare to bud and bloom. Indeed your love is so strong for them that you will not let anyone else cultivate and look after them. Eventually the flower blooms and because of your love it releases its colour, perfume and essence to the World. Naturally you obtain great satisfaction and joy from what you have done.

Now that seed is a child and it seems very strange to me that you would want that seed to be tended by anyone else but yourself, that you would want it to grow up away from your vibration, to be denied that which is its birthright: your divine energy, your love, your light. Do you really want your child to be raised by a foster parent, a parent who either consciously or unconsciously may thwart your child's ambitions in life. For in spite of the good intentions of the husband or wife who remarries, the other half of that new marriage will not fully respect the creations of the first marriage. He or she will rarely have the same feeling and love for the child unless they are exceptionally evolved souls. You are therefore handing over a part of yourself, a part more precious than yourself, to be nurtured by a complete stranger.

# PROBLEMS AND TESTS

As you pass through life on Earth you all have to face what I will call problems and tests. Indeed, for some people life appears to be nothing more than a continual series of problems and tests which they have to face almost every day of their lives. So let us consider the real nature of problems and tests and see what is involved in facing them. I will begin by defining what I consider as being problems and tests.

Tests are something that originate on a soul level. They are obstacles that have been placed in your destiny path for you to face, to come to terms with and resolve. Tests therefore are usually associated with the major decisions in your life. Now that does not mean that there is no such thing as a small test, there is, especially since minor personality irritations are very often made into small tests because of the way in which they are handled. But, basically, most people will incarnate simply to face and resolve one major test in their lifetime and as such they will be given many opportunities of facing and learning from that test throughout their whole life.

If your soul is seeking to change an established pattern of behaviour then it will probably take the greater part of a lifetime to bring about a change in that pattern, to bring you to that moment in time when you will respond correctly to the test. For example, if in past lives you have frequently stolen things and have persistently misappropriated other people's property and possessions without thought for their needs, if you have failed to recognise that physical matter, although placed in human guardianship, belongs not to Humanity but to a Divine Being, then that pattern is not going to be changed in the twinkling of an eye, in one test. What will be necessary will be a gradual process of teaching and learning over several lives so that when you are finally put to the test again you will respond correctly because of that learning, because you have attained the necessary point of consciousness.

You therefore face tests only infrequently and they usually demand your attention for many days, even months, before you reach a decision. Remember, however, that when that decision is reached, because you have been given the divine gift of free choice, that you are making a conscious decision, a decision that is neither right nor wrong but simply reflects your point of consciousness at that time. As you walk down the path of life after that decision so you will attract aspects of the Universe unto yourself according to the note that you sounded at that moment of decision.

Let us now consider what are problems. Problems are the creation of your physical brain, your thoughts. They are not of a soul origin. They are of an earthly origin and, as such, are nearly always concerned with earthly things. Problems very rarely involve major decisions such as those you find in a test of a soul nature. Usually they come to you as a result of your own actions, of your abuse of Natural Law. For example, a man who has many possessions usually worries about his possessions. This worry, this mental conflict, creates problems which he then has to face and resolve. However the problems are what he has created. They are of his own making. The result of this, of course, is that very often such problems demand his energy and attention to the exclusion of the more important aspects of his life, for whilst his mind is concerned with his physical problems he has little time for anything else. Now do not think, just because I have used this example, that wealthy people always have more problems to face than those who are poor, for a wise person can be both rich and poor. It is how a person faces the test of wealth and poverty that creates the problems. The example that I have used could be replaced by many other conditions of life.

A curious link sometimes exists between problems and tests. Very often on a soul level you know that a test is coming. You sense in your innermost being that a moment of test is approaching. For example, perhaps you are going to move house, to leave the area where you have always lived and change your job or career. Very often in a situation such as this your intuitive channel senses the change some time before its moment of physical reality. This feeling is registered in your brain and subsequently your personality

96

begins to play with it, anticipating the change that is to come and thereby makes a problem out of it. So very often you try to face your test before its right moment in physical time. Because of this, taking the example of moving house, you could begin to look for a new house before the right time and as such you will probably look for houses in the wrong area, choose one for the wrong reasons and so create problems which will have to be faced and resolved at a later stage. So in this instance tests and problems can be linked together, but for the most part I make a clear division between the two.

A problem, in earthly terms, can best be compared to a mathematical problem. There is a solution. The answer always lies within the realm of the human physical brain. Any problem can be resolved into an acceptable and comprehensible answer provided enough energy is directed towards the solution. No matter what the problem if you sit down and apply yourself to it, if you consider the choices open to you, the cause or causes of the problem, what steps can be taken to solve the problem, your physical brain can and will solve it. If you cannot do it by yourself then you will probably enlist the aid of friends or relations to help you. If enough energy and attention is devoted to the problem it will be solved. It is as simple as that. So what, therefore, is the problem with having a problem? A problem remains a problem only so long as it remains unsolved. It remains a problem only so long as time, energy and attention are not given to its solution, indeed, only so long as the individual does not want to solve it. Very often some people like to have problems. For them problems are the salt of life. Problems give them something to worry about, something to talk to their friends about! If they did not have problems with which to concern themselves there would be a big void in their lives and there you have the crux of the matter, for without problems the intuitive force of their being would enter that void and would fill it with the wisdom of the Cosmos.

It is obvious that physical problems must be solved on a physical level. You are all aware of that fact. If you have a problem with your car, your house or your business then it must be solved by giving time, energy and attention to it. Recognise, however, that the way in which you give that time, energy and attention is important. If you do it half-heartedly, without thought, without one pointedness, without energy, without seeing clearly what is involved, then a problem that could have been solved in a minute may take hours, even days to solve. The longer you have a problem, and ignore it, the more complex it becomes since a problem grows. What could initially have been solved in a moment may later take months to resolve. The longer you leave your problems unsolved the greater the conflict, the greater the demand of your time, the more debilitating they become, the more they divert your mind from what it should be doing. So the first thing you must realise is that problems must be resolved as, and when, they occur. The conflict that they create within your mind must be resolved as soon as it arises. If that is not possible, for whatever reason, then time, energy and attention must be reserved so that you can resolve them at the first opportunity, so that at the end of the day, before you go to sleep, your problems have been resolved. If they are not, then you wake up the following morning with those problems still present, still demanding your energy and attention and obstructing the learning process of that day.

It is important that you separate your problems from your tests. If you face a test then you know that it comes from within and that your soul is aware of it. Your soul links you to the tests of life. If the Universe is testing you, then your soul knows that fact and if you will but listen to that inner voice you will soon be aware of that fact on an outer form level. A test, therefore, is something that *you* have chosen to face, something that *you* have chosen to master. As such, a test is rarely something that can be rushed into and solved in a split second of time. Whereas the understanding of a problem might occur in that way, the resolution of a test usually takes place over a longer period of time. Indeed, very often it can take months, even years, before you learn the universal lesson and accept it into your point of consciousness. Moreover, very often the realisation of the lesson comes through a series of smaller tests which point to the bigger one. Often a test can simply confirm what you already know to be true. Something that you learnt in past lives will be tested again and again until your soul is sure that that aspect of Universal Wisdom has become a part of your consciousness. Many of the minor tests that you face are confidence tests, to prove to yourself that what you already know to be Truth is indeed Truth and that you will follow your soul consciousness.

If you are faced with a test and if you fail to recognise it, or ignore it, then rest assured that it will be presented to you at another time. You cannot bypass a test. Tests are presented to you at every opportunity, for that is the reason why you incarnate on the Earth, the reason why you are here. Tests will be presented to you again and again and again, but they will come in their own time and in their own way. The Universe will automatically present you with the tests which you have to face and resolve. You must ensure, however, that you do not let your brain, your intellect, confuse the nature of the test, that you do not let your earthly conditioning colour the soul aspect of the tests. Do not let what is a test of a spiritual nature become a test of your personality. Remember that your soul looks at a test with the eyes of the soul. It does not recognise the personality, the influences of this life-time, this earthly conditioning. It seeks only to see the wisdom of eternity in a test. Many people, faced with soul-tests of a high nature, very subtly turn them into personality tests so that what should have been solved at the soul level, deep within, is lowered onto the personality level with all its emotions, fears and worries, likes and dislikes, and in the morass of the personality the test usually becomes insoluble.

So let us recognise our problems and tests for what they are. Let us fear neither. Let us welcome them as a necessary part of our life: tests of our spiritual life and problems of our personality life. Let us recognise the way in which we are going to solve them. The soul can assess and solve a personality problem but the personality cannot, and never will solve a soul test. As you face the problems and tests in your life be aware of the true nature of what you are really facing. Give energy to it. Meditate on it. If you have to solve a problem by tomorrow morning and if that problem was of such an important nature that it would result in, shall we say, your death if you did not make a correct decision, then you would apply all your energy and attention to it. But, alas, you usually do not apply such energy and attention because you view your problems only as irritations on the face of your personality living.

I, of course, do not live in your world of matter with all its attendant problems. You wake up each morning to face your physical, earthly responsibilities, but can you not see that if you wake up each morning with the burdens of yesterday still upon your back that the way you live the day, and respond to it, will be greatly affected by those burdens. So wake up free, with no burdens of the past, and you will have the energy and the awareness to live life as it should be lived. But if you wake up burdened down then life itself becomes a burden. The person who walks through life with the least possessions walks freely and quickly, and when I say possessions I do not mean possessions in the sense of money and property but in the sense of physical memory, personality possessions. Release these and you release your burdens. Be open to the moment. Listen to the voice of the Universe speaking to you, respond to its pattern and design and your problems will disappear.

Above all remember that you are given no problem, no test, which you cannot face, which you cannot solve. Your physical brain can solve any problem which it creates. Your soul can face any test which stands before it. If, after much searching, you cannot truly see the answer then invoke the aid of your Creator, listen and receive. Remember, however, that the answer which comes may not be the answer which you seek or desire, for the response of the Universe may not necessarily reflect what you want to know, only the truth which you must face.

# EDUCATION FOR THE NEW AGE

You live at a time when the very fabric of human society appears to be disintegrating. Your world today is more competitive, more greedy, more self-centred, more violent than at any other time in living memory and yet the opportunities that exist for education at this time have never been greater. More children are processed through schools and colleges and have opportunities for higher education than at any other time in the history of the Western Civilisation. Nevertheless, in spite of all these opportunities, you have the situation today where some 'educated' children, whilst still in their 'teens, commit suicide, give birth to illegitimate babies or else have abortions, regularly use drugs and alcohol, steal, vandalise property and are, of course, often totally unprepared for the World in which they must live and find work. Whilst all of this cannot be laid solely at the door of education, education is a great deal to blame, and when I say education I mean not just the educational system that exists now but the systems which gave birth to that system. You, the older generation, are the product of a formal system of education which has evolved gradually throughout the centuries.

It would be true to say that society gets the educational system that it deserves, just as it can be said that society gets the government, the church or the legal system that it deserves. Humanity creates, and only Humanity can change, that system. When the numbers of those who are suffering under the system reach a certain proportion then the demand for change becomes irresistible. But those who govern the country and control the educational system, having been through that system themselves and being a product of it, will always endorse the system because it supports their way of life and their ideas of society and of the roles that people play in it. It is only those who have failed in such a system, who have not benefitted from it, who have indeed been handicapped by it, that will recognise the need for change. That the present educational system is not meeting the needs of many young people can easily be discerned by looking at the World today, for although it can be said that educational standards are high, especially here in the Western World, you still have young people leaving school totally unprepared for the World in which they have to live and quite unable to earn their living. Many young people are veritable misfits in society. Now partly this is because industrial society is changing dramatically, partly it is because here in the Western World the rate of technological innovation is increasing rapidly, but mainly it is because you are moving into a new Age, an Age that is manifesting a new sense of being and purpose, an Age when Humanity is revealing a new aspect of its being on the plane of Earth.

The educational system that exists today is the creation of politicians and scholars during the past three hundred years. It is essentially a patriarchal system. That is to say that it has been created, for the most part, by men and so reflects the evolutionary characteristics of the Piscean Age which has witnessed the dominance of the male over the female. This dominance led to the growth of the belief that it was only necessary to educate men, and that women could be ignored since they were only destined to fulfil the role of being wives and mothers. Successive generations have tended to support that belief and therefore the present educational system reflects that imbalance. Education today is concerned solely with the development and training of intellect to the complete exclusion of intuition. Now it cannot be denied that Humanity has considerably developed its intellect and that this has enabled it to discover nuclear power, to reach the Moon, to create complex computers and so on. But Humanity has not developed its intuition at the same time which would enable it to use what it has created correctly and with the right motivation. Humanity has also not learnt how to change or even modify the pattern of its thought. It has become moulded in purpose and intent and this is reflected in its educational system.

Now the development of intellect is an essential part of any educational system. You have to learn to use and develop your physical brain, to develop that computer which your Creator has given you as a means of expressing yourself on the physical plane of life. You must learn the human skills necessary for communication: reading, writing and arithmetic. You must learn the technical skills of the civilisation in which you live. You must learn to drive a car, to work an electrical machine and so on. You must also learn about your physical bodies, about the country in which you live, about the very planet on which you walk, about the atmosphere which you breathe. That is the kind of technical knowledge which should be given to you in school in order that you can function efficiently in your environment and can come to terms with it.

What your forebears have discovered and have painstakingly written down in books is the human heritage which is handed down to you, but hand in hand with all that knowledge must also come the intuitive force, the ability to look at that knowledge anew, to receive further inspiration, to develop and expand what has been established as truth by the society in which you live. Unfortunately, today, in most of the major fields of scholarly activity what has been established as truth is regarded as 'God' and those who dare to challenge that 'God' are declared heretics and are ignored, mocked or even excommunicated by the establishment. It must be recognised that many of the great advances that have been made, for example, in the field of science have been made by those who have totally opposed the current trend of scientific thought and understanding. This is also true of most human activities including even simple domestic living. Many of the great advances made in human evolution have come from outside the recognised educational systems.

Now it is not my intention simply to point out some of the faults of the present educational system and then to say that the system has failed. You can see that it has failed. It has failed because it no longer reflects the hopes and aspirations of the children of the New Age. It has failed because it is conditioning children to support a way of life that is dying. It has failed because it is producing young people who cannot adapt to the environment in which they find themselves after leaving school. The purpose of education is, surely, to prepare young people for that moment in time at the end of their second cycle, when they complete their twentieth year, so that they can leave their schooling as mature, educated beings, ready and willing to be of service to the World. If they cannot be of service then they will experience frustration and will inevitably turn against the system that has fathered them.

The educational systems of the past, being patriarchal and, therefore, imbalanced, since they have concentrated solely on intellect to the exclusion of intuition, have created imbalanced children. These children have, in turn, grown to become imbalanced parents who have unwittingly perpetuated those systems. However, as Humanity now approaches the dawning of the Age of Aquarius it is evident that the educational systems must change, not only to reflect the nature of the New Age but also to prepare the many children who will pass through the systems in the next few years for the changes that are to come. Already there are rumblings coming from within the systems themselves. Many teachers feel that the education they are giving children is not correct and that if it was, there would be more balanced and fulfilled children entering into the World at the age of twenty one.

What, therefore, can one do at this time to prepare the ground for education in the Aquarian Age? Firstly, remember that education must reflect the nature of the Cosmos and be balanced in every respect. It must reflect the balance of the male and the female. It must reflect the balance of intellect and intuition, of knowledge and awareness. The curriculum of any school must surely reflect that balance. You must learn knowledge, you must develop the intellect to be a tool to help you walk your path in life but, equally so, you must develop that intuitive channel which links you with the wisdom of the Cosmos. Intuition is the source of inspiration, not intellect. Intellect can never create. Intellect can analyse. Intellect can be logical. Intellect can reason and can draw conclusions but it cannot innovate. Intellect is like a computer. A computer can create only from the data that has been put into its memory. It is the same with the human brain. The educational system that is to come must place emphasis on intuition, both on the need to bring it forth in children and to teach them to respect it.

Education in the Aquarian Age will establish the correct relationship between teacher and pupil. There are two paths of teaching: the path of experience and the path of awareness. Teachers can teach their pupils of human experience, of what they have learned: reading, writing, arithmetic, the nature of their universe, all the knowledge that has been gleaned and written down in books. All that can be passed on to their pupils as human experience, with the proviso that they do not regard it as 'God', as the infinite and ultimate truth, but only as the sum total of what has been discovered so far. But what can teachers teach their pupils of awareness? Nothing! The teacher's job is to awaken within their pupils the divine gift of their own awareness. Teachers should not teach their pupils of their own awareness and then invite them to follow in their path. Teachers should encourage their pupils, through right relationship and right observation of the World in which they live, to bring forth their own understanding of life, to discover for themselves the purpose of life and the destiny which they have chosen.

There is prevalent today, because of the nature of your educational systems, a tendency to catalogue children and to channel their activities along narrow paths, to attain a desired object at the end. But how wonderful it would be if every single child when they left school had walked along different paths, had fulfilled different roles, had developed the talents they had discovered within themselves in their school. Today, however, children leave their schools as successes or failures, classified by examination, often self-centred and unable to sacrifice to themselves let alone to the World, unprepared to be a part of society or to respect social values which are held sacred even by the Animal Kingdom.

Teachers, therefore, must establish complete equality in the classroom between the male and the female, recognising that both have to give to society, that both have to create in society. They should recognise that if any aspect of their teaching, either to the male or the female, is in imbalance then that will produce an imbalanced child. The educational system of the future, therefore, will demand complete sexual equality and from this children will obtain an understanding of the true purpose of life and of the wholeness of the World in which they live.

Is it also not strange that even today your educational systems can still divide science and religion for, in truth, there is no such division. They are one. Science is religion. God is in all things. God controls every atom of the Cosmos. Scientists are not investigating science. They are, truly, investigating God, but as yet they have not understood that basic fact, so divided are they amongst themselves, so narrow is the aspect along which they look. This is also true of medicine, of industry, of agriculture, in fact of every aspect of human existence, for God is in all things, is in all beings, is in every human activity.

Education in the New Age will therefore teach of the Earth as a whole, as a balanced sphere. It will reflect an understanding of the World around it, of the planets and their influences. Astrology will therefore be an essential part of any school curriculum. The knowledge of ancient religions, the wisdom of past civilisations, the lives of great people who have transformed the nature of human activity, all these will be discussed openly in New Age schools. Such information should not be accepted automatically as truth just because the teacher is saying it but should be considered, meditated on, debated and the child left free to accept or reject. Why should any child accept as truth what its parents or teachers tell it if the child itself has not experienced that truth. If you impose your truth you are, in fact, suppressing a child's birthright, to discover the truth of this World for itself and to choose the life that it wants to live. The greatest gift that you can give any child is the gift of discrimination, to weigh all things in the balance, to accept nothing that it has not learnt as truth for itself.

The educational systems of the Aquarian Age will be designed to allow children to fully investigate the facets of life to which they are drawn, to establish the truth of life for themselves through their own experiences and decisions. To learn, children must be allowed to follow a path of their own choosing. Now I am not advocating that children should have complete freedom to choose what, when and how they wish to study. They are young. Like many adults they have probably not learnt the discipline of work and so they need a structure within which to learn and be taught of life. It is essential that in this structure there are teachers who are born to teach, that is souls who have come on Earth with the destiny to teach.

Today many teachers teach for the wrong reasons. Many are wrongly motivated and lack the necessary humility to teach the young. They are intent only on impressing their opinions, their view of life upon their pupils. Many who should be teaching are seduced into other walks of life, are seduced not only by money and status but by the attractions of pursuing intellect for intellect's sake and of living in a world of scientific make-believe rather than human reality. I ask that those of you who feel it within yourselves to be teachers should come forward and be of service. The sacrifice is not great. For once you have recognised that the generation which you teach, if correctly taught and motivated, will then in turn pass that on to the next generation, so you will recognise that the most priceless gift that you can give to this World is to educate children correctly.

Your world is dying because your children are dying. Save your children and you will save your World. For the most part older people are beyond change. They are fixed in the patterns of their thought and the society in which they live. They cannot release what they believe is truth, what they believe is their security: the world which they have created. It is only the young who can do this. You therefore have the opportunity of giving them the priceless gift which was denied to many of you: a balanced education, one that will bring forth the talents which they have gathered over many, many years. They demand an education that will prepare them properly for the physical life they have chosen to lead, one that will develop their intellect and their intuition to the highest but, above all, one that will recognise their individuality, one that will respect the level of their soul-evolution and the destiny that they have come to fulfil. No one is the same. Everyone is unique. Every child on this Earth demands respect for itself as an individual spark of light and the recognition that it has its own path to walk, its own destiny to fulfil. Recognise that fact. Educate the child into a knowledge of itself and this World will be saved.

## QUESTIONS AND ANSWERS

Q: That all sounds very wonderful but there is no way that the schools around here do any of the things that the speaker was talking about. We have children and we want to do the best thing for them so what should we do? Start our own school?

ZT: It is obvious that you can only use an educational system that is already in existence, but it seems to me that you are forgetting the meaning of the word 'teacher'. A teacher is not only a person who stands up in a school classroom. Parents are teachers. Relatives are teachers. Above all, the World in which you live is the greatest teacher of all. Obviously it will take time to change the educational systems of your schools. It will take time to create a new system and to find teachers who will teach it. But classroom teaching represents only a small percentage of the teaching available from life. I would say that a child learns thirty per cent at school and seventy per cent elsewhere. You can control that elsewhere.

Q: I find that in most schools there is a tremendous amount of competitiveness, not just on the playing fields but in the class-rooms as well. Is competition a necessary part of this new educational system? I am concerned because uncompetitive children find it very difficult to achieve in our schools and, indeed, in life outside school.

ZT: Obviously you must prepare your child for the World in which it is going to live and earn its living. If you yourselves have lived in and are a product of a competitive society, and you intend your child to follow in your footsteps, then it too must learn the nature and the practice of competition. Some children thrive on such tests. Competition in itself is not necessarily a bad thing. Consider that natural selection through competition takes place in many species of the Animal Kingdon. You can see this not only in the struggle for survival but also in only the fittest being selected for mating and reproduction. Where the human race errs is in the beliefs that are attached to competition and, in particular, to the winner/loser syndrome.

There is an old saying, which has great wisdom in it, which states that what is important is not who wins the game, but the game itself. Sometimes in human competition you lose sight of the fact that what is important is not who wins but the game. You are part of the game of life. To stress the competitiveness of the game is to obscure the purpose of the game for, in truth, there is no winner, no loser. For example, if five people go for one position and one person wins, the other four have not lost. Perhaps the right person has that job and the other four were not meant to get it. Nevertheless, competition for competition's sake is a lesson to be learnt. Those who live by the sword will die by the sword. Those who live by competition will die by it. That is a fact of living. So recognise the need for competition in its place. See it as, at times, a source of natural selection. Never place your child, never ask it to take part in a competition unless, firstly, that child wants to do so and chooses of its own free will and, secondly, it realises that what is important is not the result but the competition, the learning process of the game.

Q: As a teacher I am forced to teach both children who benefit academically from my teaching and those who do not, for the system demands that everyone be taught the same subjects. The result is that we have achievers and, unfortunately, non-achievers. How can I get out of this system?

ZT: If as a teacher you are true to yourself you should not teach something which you believe to be wrong. You should not support a system which you believe to be wrong. In a sense many teachers have already made that choice by not entering the teaching profession, not on a conscious but on a sub-conscious level. The choice for those who are already within the teaching profession is whether to try to change the system as much as is possible or to reject the system and create their own.

The trouble with Humanity is that it is very conservative. It does not like to change, but you are living at a time of great change, a time when the whole of human civilisation is about to be plunged into the fire of the Aquarian Energy, a time when all the dross will be burnt off and out of the ashes will arise the new phoenix of Aquarius. It is at such a time that a new educational system can be built. There are many who would welcome such a step and who, if a school were to be established with new ideals, with new purpose, new disciplines, would indeed support it. The situation which faces parents today is that they have no choice and until those who are true to their profession establish that choice parents are forced to use the systems that presently exist.

Q: As a teacher, I find it difficult to give individualised attention because of the numbers and variety in my classes. There are just too many human aspects to encompass.

ZT: All that you can do as a teacher is to be true to your own understanding of what teaching is, to create the right atmosphere in your class-room, to give of your best. What you begin many will continue. It takes only one match to start a forest fire.

Q1: Yes, I agree with that. One man in France advocating a new form of childbirth has caused a revolution in attitudes to childbirth all over the World. The same can be true for education. It only needs one person to stand up and fight for what they believe to create a new system of education.

Q2: One of the problems facing teachers today is that they have a

109

great deal of technical knowledge to impart to a child and this takes a considerable time, especially if a child is a slow learner. If we were to spend half the time developing the intuitive channel we would not be able to teach the knowledge we have — or should school be extended?

ZT: Let us realise firstly that everything you teach, all the facts that you are presenting to your pupils, at the very best, is second-hand knowledge and, at the worst, is centuries old. Let me make an analogy. Until the advent of Copernicus children had been taught and had religiously copied down in their text-books that the Earth was the centre of the Universe. Along comes a man of vision, who expresses a new concept, but they are taught to fear him, indeed are told that he must be destroyed for he threatens what is established as knowledge. So what is the real value of that knowledge?

The purpose of education is to make children aware of the whole spectrum of life. Perhaps the greatest weakness in the educational systems of today is that they specialise too much, that the child does not have a balanced understanding of the wholeness of life and of the part that he or she plays in it. How else can your scientists justify conducting such terrible experiments on animals? How can they be so far removed from the reality of what they are doing that they put their experiments before the sacredness of life?

Education should be extended until young people have reached the end of their second cycle, the age of twenty one, but that does not mean that we are extending the period of education merely to teach more things or to teach at a slower pace. It means that we teach the child initially of the wholeness of life and then allow the child of its own inclination and being to choose what it wishes to learn, to study what it is drawn to. Therefore in essence the child creates its own syllabus. You would say to me that this would demand many more teachers. Then so be it.

Q: This idea of having school terms and then very long holidays. Is that a good system?

ZT: No. There should be balance in all things. Sometimes I am not sure who needs the holiday more in your present system, the pupils or the teachers! That surely speaks for the system under which you suffer. As I have said many times before, and heard, in return, many exclamations of dismay, old souls do not need holidays. If you are a balanced and evolved being you should live your life in such harmony that you need no such thing as a holiday!

Q: We can attempt to teach young people these ideas but is it possible, for example, to teach existing scientists, psychologists and politicians to respect the four Kingdoms of Matter, to stop them from experimenting on live animals and starting wars out of national egoism? Can we teach the older generation?

ZT: One lives in hope, but the history of your civilisation has proved otherwise. We of the Spiritual Hierarchy always live in hope, but the nature of the path upon which Humanity is set today must inevitably lead to its own destruction unless it changes its ways. We pray for this change. We seek to bring it about, but if individuals will not stand forth and be counted then you will not change those who lead society. You have to change society from within. You cannot, for the most part, expect your leaders to change, for they are not true leaders: they merely reflect the opinions and views of the society which they lead. If you will but change yourselves then you will have the leaders you deserve, the leaders you need, the leaders that are there waiting to be of service. These new leaders will only bring about change when they are supported by the people who elected them.

For example, let us suppose that you had a government today which on hearing that there was starvation in a certain country in Africa wanted to give half of this country's grain supply to that country. This would mean that this country was then short of grain but could live on other sorts of food. Would this country support such an action, or would it rather say "You can only have the grain of which we have no need. Our country, our people, our needs must come first." A selfish people elect a selfish government. A holy people elect a holistic government. You can change all this by changing yourself. That is all we ask, that you change yourself.

Q: There is a society which encourages parents to teach their children at home and for groups of parents to teach groups of children. Do you think this is wise?

ZT: I feel that this is an excellent system for young children. Up to the age of ten years old such a system of education would be most beneficial and could be easily arranged. You do not need formalised education for young children. The child thrives more in the home environment because it is more secure, provided of course that the home environment in which it is living is whole, healthy and balanced. The problem today is that parents have to send their children to school because the home is unholy!

Q: But after ten you feel children should go to a school?
ZT: Yes, because then a child has to learn more than the parents can give, has to learn to mix in society, to cope with friends and enemies, with energies it has not yet met, to learn to stand alone, to be away from the home.

Q: But could this not be done in a small school formed and run by a group of parents?
ZT: Yes, all things are possible. What you have to recognise is that everyone is different. Every school is different and reflects the needs of the people that go to that school. You would not teach a Chinaman the same as an Englishman. The needs of an African are different from those of an Eskimo. There is no blueprint for the perfect school for all beings. Just as communities, groups and friends come together on a certain note, so do schools. The best teachers are the ones that recognise the individuality of their pupils and seek to recognise and to strengthen that individuality, to let them be what their Creator meant them to be.

Q: What part does television play in education?
ZT: Television can be a very useful tool. It can present to your child what is true of life but, equally so, it can present to your child what is totally untrue of life. To allow your child to watch television unsupervised is to destroy its educational value. If you cannot point out to your child what is true or untrue you should not allow it to watch television. If your child cannot understand that what it sees is but an entertainment, is but a drama on a stage and has little to do with the reality of life, it should not watch. Young children should most certainly not watch television alone. To leave your child in front of a television to watch what it chooses is creating the very world which we are seeking to change.

If I could leave you with one final thought it would be that the greatest service that you can do to Humanity, the greatest service that you can do to your World, to your Planet, to your Creator, is to educate yourself.

# THE END OF THE WORLD?

I must begin by emphasising that there is a question mark after the title of this talk. I have not deliberately chosen this title in order to be provocative but merely to reflect the viewpoint of many people in your World today. Even amongst spiritually minded people there are those who question the reason for the events now taking place on this planet, who ask whether the Earth can survive, whether it should survive, who ask whether the Earth-changes to come are something to be avoided or to be welcomed. All that I want to do in this talk is to present a point of view from another plane of life and to ask you to hold it in your minds in the years to come.

I will begin by making the simple statement that the Earth, like you, is imbued with spirit. It will, therefore, never die. Whilst its physical form might change as it experiences periods of transformation and transmutation, the spirit that is responsible for its creation will never die. In the same way that you in your physical bodies die and are born again onto a higher plane of life so the Earth, on another level, undergoes a similar experience. It is a cosmic fact that all forms of life, no matter what the level of evolution, are born, die and are born again in the endless cycle of evolution. The Earth has done this many times, obviously not as frequently as you reincarnate in your physical bodies, and it will doubtless do this again.

Those of you on the plane of Earth who fear death, who do not understand the real nature of this act of transformation, will also fear the ending of the World because the result is apparently the same: the ending of physical life as you know it. But those of you who are aware of life beyond death, who recognise that death on the plane of Earth is but the opening of a door to a higher level of consciousness, a return to the place of your true being, must also see that the same is true for the Earth as a whole. Humanity must

113

recognise that the Lord of the planet, that being known to you as the Goddess, since she is female in energy, who created this form that you call the Earth, must also die, must eventually be transformed onto a higher plane of consciousness. This will one day come to pass. Now this death of the Earth should not be confused with the Earth-changes which you will soon have to face. The present cycle of the Earth's evolution will continue for a long, long time yet. The changes of which we talk now are the Earth-changes that are associated with the introduction of the Aquarian Age. It is essential that you who live at this time of transition should understand the nature of and the purpose for these Earth-changes.

The planet Earth on which you live has felt the presence of Humanity for only a very short cycle of time. The Earth had been in existence for hundreds of thousands of years before Humanity walked upon its surface and began to evolve itself. Humanity is but a pinprick on the time scale of the evolutionary cycle of the Earth. The Earth was evolving before Humanity came into being. It will continue to evolve when Humanity has gone, for the Lord of this Earth, the Goddess, the Earth Mother whose form it is, is a great and evolved spiritual being. Even though Humanity has incarnated on the plane of Earth for only a relatively short period of time it has achieved great technological and evolutionary advances as befits its soul origins. In but a few short cycles Humanity has reached that moment in time when it apparently possesses the knowledge to destroy not only itself but even the planet on which it lives.

It is only natural, therefore, that people should ask the question "Will the planet survive?". There is a fear in the minds of many people today that now that Humanity has the means to destroy itself it will indeed do so, for if there is one thing that is certain it is that in the past when Humanity has had weapons of war it has *always* used them. Never has the spirit of sacrifice been present in the act of war. Humanity wages war for one purpose only and that is victory, if necessary, at any cost. Various countries today possess the ultimate weapons of war, both for offence and defence. At the push of a button the major powers can exterminate their enemies, or threaten to do so if they are attacked. Moreover, with the proliferation of nuclear technology all over the globe many smaller countries now, or soon will, possess that ultimate power. With such an arsenal of nuclear weapons, an arsenal which is capable of destroying this planet many times over, it is easy to see why countries are afraid of each other and especially of the people who control the use of those weapons. Where there is fear, where there is hatred, then there is the possibility, indeed the probability, of nuclear war. But I can assure you that the great Beings who watch over this planet and are responsible for Humanity's evolution will not permit that to happen. The great Beings who truly control the destiny of this Earth can, and will, prevent the total destruction of this planet, but note that I say total destruction. This Earth will continue on its evolutionary cycle and will be protected by the Higher Forces of life. They have the power to prevent any, or all, nuclear explosions if that is their will. The existence of your planet is therefore assured in that respect.

There is, however, another factor that we have to consider, and that is the cycle of Human Evolution. If you look at the rate of human reproduction during the past one thousand years it is not difficult to see, merely by considering Earth resources and projecting figures forward into the future, that the way in which Humanity lives today cannot be carried forward into the next century. Humanity is growing at too fast a rate for its spiritual understanding. It is reproducing itself in too many numbers and by so doing is polluting the very land which provides the necessary food for its existence. It is using agricultural methods which will soon be unable to meet the demands of an ever increasing world population. Furthermore, Humanity is now tampering with that sacred being, Mother Nature, in order to achieve a short-term gain without considering the long-term implications. There is therefore approaching a time of famine, of drought, of pestilence, as Nature reacts to what Humanity has done to her. This reaction should not be seen as a form of punishment by the Divine but rather as the flowering of the seeds which Humanity itself has sown. These two factors, the increasing numbers of Humanity and the pollution of the planet itself, more than anything else will demand a change of a cataclysmic nature to redress the balance.

This change will take place both on an inner and an outer level. It is something which you should welcome if you do not fear death and can see the purpose of rebirth. Remember that the symbol of the Aquarian Age is the phoenix. The phoenix is the mythical bird which consciously sacrifices itself on the cosmic fire, releasing its old form in order to come forth purified in the new. Does not the

115

phoenix symbolise the desire within your own spiritual being for the purification of the Earth to take place so that the old human form can be cast off and the new Aquarian form may come forth? As you look around the World today you cannot help but notice the increasing tempo of human conflict all over the globe as both nations and individuals oppose each other for political, ideological and religious reasons. But Humanity is suffering not only on an outer level through famine, earthquake, disease and war but also on an inner level through its lack of spirituality, its self-centredness, its greed, its concern only for the self at the expense of its fellow human beings and the other Kingdoms of the Earth. All these events bear witness to the approach of Armageddon and the ending of the Age. Humanity needs to be purified. Humanity needs to experience the cosmic fire of purification in order to come forth reborn in the Aquarian Age.

I know that there are people, some spiritually motivated, who believe that this event will not come about and that it will be prevented either by the intervention of some great Master or by Humanity reversing the path upon which it is now set. I would ask you to remember the impact of the last great impulse of the Christ energy, of the Master Jesus who came on the Earth two thousand years ago. Consider how long it took for that energy to become an effective force on the plane of Earth even after that Master's great sacrifice. Even if the Christ energy was to return at this time it could not move Humanity from the course on which it is set. That is why the prophets and the seers of old could make their prophecies with such certainty. To ground cosmic knowledge on the Earth, to manifest it through the cycle of human evolution, takes time, human time. The spiritual consciousness needed to save this World cannot be grounded in the time that is now left before the Earth-changes.

Those of you who recognise this fact, not knowing when this great moment of transformation will come about but trusting only that it will be a divine act, inspired by Divine Will, might ask what is the purpose of your being. As I have said in the past, the analogy of a lifeboat should come to mind. You sail on the great ship of Mother Earth. At present you are sailing in calm waters, for you are living in the rosy days of the Western Civilisation, the civilisation of the White Race, the Race which is to lead the World in the New Age. This civilisation has attracted unto itself souls of great evolution, souls whose consciousness has manifested the technology and the human understanding which gives you the high standard of living that you now enjoy. You have the best of this Earth. That is a fact. However, you should also remember that the consciousness which gives you your high standard of living came down to the White Race because it is the Race primarily responsible for the birthing of the New Age. Deep down, on a soul level, that consciousness is prepared for the great changes to come.

See yourselves, therefore, as lifeboats of consciousness, as lifeboats designed not for this moment in time but for the storms to come. If I may use an analogy, you are the Noahs of the last great cataclysm. You are receiving your divine inspiration now to build your arks, not arks of physical matter but arks of spiritual consciousness, consciousness to understand the Earth-changes that will come, consciousness to understand the death and destruction that must inevitably follow and, above all, consciousness to rebuild human civilisation and to ensure its continuing growth in the future. That is what is important: that human civilisation rises up again set on a new path, set on the path of the Aquarian Age. This Age will see the physical manifestation of the divine principles which you now hold only as ideals, as spiritual concepts in your innermost soul beings. Everything of the highest that you wish was upon the Earth will be grounded upon her. All things will be possible in the New Age.

How, and when, are these Earth-changes to come about? They can come about in several ways depending on whether they are initiated by human destruction or by divine intervention. As to the timing of this event there are many opinions but, in truth, there is only one being who possesses that knowledge and that is your God, the Creator of us all. Furthermore, that knowledge will not be released to anyone until the actual moment in time draws near. I believe that the major Earth-changes to come will be initiated by what I will call the Fiery Messenger. There is even now a star of great power proceeding towards our Solar Body. The star, at this moment, is invisible to the human, or even telescopic eye, but it is set on a path which will bring it into conjunction with our Planetary System. As it passes by it will affect the motions of all the planets of our System and, therefore, will bring about changes on the surface of the planets themselves. The effect of this passage will be to set in motion the Earth-changes that are prophesied. Various

117

lands will sink, others will rise, to fulfil the karmic pattern of evolution of this Earth as was the case with Atlantis.

Humanity has the power to influence the nature of this transformation through its behaviour now, through its use of nuclear technology, through its use, or abuse, of the three Kingdoms of Matter on this Earth. It can either add to, or moderate, the path and the influence of this great star. How you as individuals behave now, how you lead your lives and manifest your consciousness will affect this great transformation of the Earth. So I say to you now, as I said to you five years ago, that these Earth-changes are coming. They cannot be avoided. They are part of the destiny of the Earth.

Is it not strange how Humanity finds it difficult to plan beyond the year 2000? It is almost as if the ending of the century is the ending of a cycle. Now I am not saying that that is the year when these changes will come to pass, but certainly the final ending of the Piscean cycle will indeed take place around that time. This therefore gives you two decades in which to prepare yourselves, to prepare your lifeboats, to establish your true values, to shine your light and to prepare for the ending of your world. I hasten to say *your* world, not *the* World, for it is your world that must change, not the World. The Goddess of this World manifests only perfection. What is wrong is the world that Humanity has created upon her divine being. The divinity of planet Earth will not be extinguished by any human action. The Goddess was in existence long, long before Humanity came into being. She will be here when Humanity has gone. Although Humanity has the power to destroy itself, it will destroy itself not by nuclear explosions, not by destroying the planet which it abuses out of ignorance and greed, but by destroying its own soul.

When Humanity finally dies, when it finally leaves this planet to proceed on the next cycle of its evolution on some other planet, in some other form, in an entirely different Age, Mother Earth will still be here. The Goddess will still give birth. The planet will then return to its former beauty and will take its rightful place in the planetary body of this Solar System. You will then, perhaps from another planet, see the true beauty of the Goddess and appreciate the priceless gift that was placed in your hands. You will then realise what was given to you in an act of great cosmic evolution and what you were, perhaps, responsible for abusing. May you look back at that time and say that you were not guilty of that great crime.

118

Q: I know that things have gone really wrong on the Earth and that I have contributed in part to what is going on. I also feel that I never really knew that I was doing wrong and that it was just a process of growing up. Still I feel guilty for what I have done. Is there any way of removing this burden of guilt?

ZT: Obviously as you have lived your many lives on the Earth you have contributed to the pollution of the planet, and I talk now not so much of physical pollution but of the far greater pollution of Humanity's thought-forms. Mother Earth is very clever at getting rid of physical pollution. Is it not amazing how even today she copes with most of the demands that are made of her by the Western Civilisation? But what she finds more difficult to cope with is the pollution of Humanity's thought forms, for they are most powerful and require great energy to transmute and dissipate.

You may find it a hard fact to understand but ignorance is no defence for wrong doing. What you have done in ignorance you are still responsible for and as you grow to spiritual adulthood and recognise what you have done so you must transmute that evil and wipe the slate clean. That is the nature of this School of Earth of which you are a part. You are expected to make mistakes, there will be wrong doings, but you will learn the nature of those mistakes and those wrong doings, come to an understanding of them and transmute what you have done. You will then be able to go forward more easily and to build on that knowledge and strength. Mother Earth accepts and understands your wrong doings, recognising them as part of your evolving process. Therefore there is no need to feel guilt for what you have done.

Of course, there are many today who, lacking the spiritual consciousness, cannot accept that they have done wrong, cannot recognise that Mother Earth is a divinity in her own right, that everything on the Earth possesses consciousness and understanding and has as much right to freedom and respect as have you at this moment in time. So what we are now witnessing on the Earth is not a punishment but merely the flowering of the seeds that Humanity has sown. It is something which Humanity has drawn unto itself by its thoughts, words and deeds. If you are not a part of those thoughts, words and deeds then you will not suffer. It is as simple

119

as that. The purity of your soul emanation will ensure that you will survive the destruction that is to come unless, as a soul of great consciousness, you have agreed to die with the mass of Humanity and to hold the balance in that moment of destruction.

Q: What baffles me is the fact that from the very creation of the Earth it must have been known that we would come to this point in time. I hear people talking about the Divine Plan and Divine Destiny and saying that everything is planned. I do not understand why the destruction and these mistakes were planned.

ZT: The destruction and the mistakes were not planned in the sense that you are meaning. Humanity has free choice. It has chosen to live in a certain way and so has attracted these events unto it. The only thing that is planned is the cyclic pattern of evolution and death is a necessary part of that evolutionary pattern. You would not want to live forever on the plane of Earth. That would indeed be hell! Surely you can see purpose in your own death. Surely you can understand that death releases you to the plane of your true being, to the plane of your true consciousness. Death, therefore, is simply an act of transformation. You must view the Earth changes in just the same way. How else could Mother Earth bring about the necessary transformation? How else could she correct the imbalances on the planet, imbalances which would indeed destroy her if Humanity had its way. A teacher allows his pupils at school to make their own experiments and to learn from what they are doing, but when the experiments become too dangerous then the teacher has to intervene, not only for the safety of the pupils but for the safety of the class-room as well. You are not aware of the power which Humanity now has under its control. You are not aware of the vast energies which the military people of your World have under their control. If you were, then you would see why intervention is necessary.

Q: Can not an aware group, by meeting together and sending out light and love, have an influence on world affairs?

ZT: The influence of any group sending out light and love into the World is obviously of great value, but the situation in which you find yourselves today is that even if the Christ Impulse was to come down on the Earth It would not be able to avert the path on which Humanity is now set.

Q: Is there any point, then, in trying to stop people raping the Earth and polluting the environment if it is all going to be destroyed anyway?

ZT: It is important, right up until that final moment of transformation comes about, that people keep on learning and growing in consciousness. You are in a school. Every single person that can be lead into an understanding of the true nature of life will be, so to speak, a soul saved, a soul taught the lesson. Indeed many will learn that lesson at that very moment of change, for in the twinkling of an eye they will suddenly understand.

Imagine that you had been living at the time of the Flood, almost seven thousand years ago. You would have been aware of the nature of life in the cities of the Middle East. You would have been aware of the wise souls who spoke out against the evils of the day. You would have been aware of the prophets saying that unless Humanity transformed itself then what, in those days, was called the Wrath of God would descend upon them. Then there would have come this great planetary movement setting in motion an enormous wave which would cause the Flood. As it came down upon the land, in that moment of supreme transformation, many souls would experience a great shift of consciousness. It is rather like a soldier in war who has killed many other soldiers and then as he himself is killed, at the very moment of his passing over, he suddenly sees very clearly the import of his life, of what he has done and the justice of what has been done to him.

Q: How can a centre such as this help best? In what way can we be of most service?

ZT: By helping to create a lifeboat of consciousness and by building that lifeboat not just for yourselves but for all those who will seek its shelter in time of storm. You must ensure that the lifeboat is well built, is capable of withstanding the storm and of being of service when it is required. Remember that in times of great physical disaster the Animal Kingdom knows what is to come. It hears in the quiet before a thunderstorm, before a volcano erupts, before a tidal wave comes. The other Kingdoms know that that destruction is near and can flee if they so wish. You have a similar right.

Q: Does the destruction of which you speak mean only physical destruction?

ZT: The destruction that will take place will be on both the physical and the higher levels of life. It will not be just the physical. It will initiate the release of energies to transmute thought-forms on the higher levels of life.

Q: The star that was spoken of, has it passed through this Solar System before?

ZT: Yes.

Q: Is it Haley's comet?

ZT: No. It is far bigger than that.

Q: Will you tell us more about the destruction of the thought-forms? On what level will this take place?

ZT: The thought-forms of Humanity have been accumulating over thousands of years. They grow in intensity as Humanity multiplies and produces more powerful thought-forms. Whilst the Goddess could, if she so wished, destroy those thought-forms, she does not do that because the thought-forms of Humanity are part of its evolutionary cycle. They are something for which Humanity alone is responsible. They are an essential part of the school of life and are something which Humanity itself has to transmute. They are the burden which Humanity has to carry. Therefore to destroy such a burden would negate the purpose of the evolutionary cycle.

However we are approaching a time when a Force greater than the Goddess will intervene and the consciousness of the Force will decide the nature of what is to happen. The evil of Humanity can only be transmuted by Humanity itself. However, evil can be temporarily suppressed or locked away by the Higher Forces, to be transmuted at a later stage in the evolutionary cycle when Humanity has the consciousness to do it. This was the case with Atlantis. The evil of Atlantis has never gone. It is still there. You will have to face it when it comes to the surface again and transmute it.

Q: Many people believe that beings from other planets will come in their spaceships to save selected members of Humanity at the time of the next cataclysm. What do you say to this?

ZT:   Obviously the beings who live on the other planets of this Solar Body are aware of what is taking place on the Earth. They have already intervened on many occasions and have prevented great destruction on the Earth. They do this not to remove Humanity's lessons but simply to ensure that Humanity is able to go on learning. It is therefore possible that at the appointed time they will come down in their spaceships and will lift the chosen ones to safety. But let us consider this.

If you are not of this planet, if indeed you have come from another planet and are here as a servant to help the evolution of the Earth and Humanity upon it, then you will already be in touch on the higher planes of life with the planet from which you came. Therefore nothing would be more natural than for your people to come and remove you before the moment of disaster, and then to put you down on Earth again when the transformation was over. It would be, so to speak, a country taking care of its own. Since there are beings here from the different planets then there could be incidents of such people being helped.

However the question which must be answered when one considers the theory of intervention on a large scale is why have the space people not intervened up to now? Why, with their wisdom, with their understanding of cosmic energy, have they not already imposed a solution from above to prevent Humanity's self-destruction? They could, for example, have neutralised all atomic weapons and made nuclear war impossible. Why has this not been done? Because Humanity has to evolve itself. There is no point in removing the lesson from the classroom. Humanity has to learn through its own mistakes, through its own sacrifices, through its own evolutionary consciousness and, above all, through the great teacher, death. That lesson is paramount and they would never intervene and remove that lesson. But that is not to say that they would not help Humanity on the higher levels of life as it faces its moment of test.

123

# THE TRUE NATURE OF THE ANIMAL KINGDOM

I am going to talk to you about the true nature of the Animal Kingdom and how it will manifest in the Aquarian Age. My purpose, however, is not only to make you look at the future but also to make you look at yourselves now, to get you to examine your relationship with the Animal Kingdom and so help to bring about the basic shift in consciousness which must take place. For when the destined Earth changes have taken place, when the conflict between the Animal and the Human Kingdoms has been resolved, there must be lifeboats of consciousness which can present to the children of the Aquarian Age a vision of life very different to the one that we have seen during the last millenium of Human evolution. For the Aquarian Age which is now dawning heralds a millenium of peace and harmony and if Humanity is to live in association with the Animal Kingdom it must see clearly the correct relationship that should be present.

Before we look into the future we must first examine the past. We must go back beyond history, beyond even Humanity's first footsteps on the planet Earth. We must go back to the very beginning of time when this Earth was first created. We must realise that the creator of this Earth, that being whom we call the Goddess, being female in energy, not female in shape or form but female in energy, created this Earth as part of her divine responsibility to her Creator, the Lord of the Sun. This Earth then is her body, her plane of life, and everything that she has created upon it are manifestations of her soul and personality character. Everything which manifests in the Animal, the Vegetable and the Mineral Kingdoms portrays an aspect of her being.

These three Kingdoms therefore, the trinity of physical life, existed for thousands upon thousands of years before Humanity was placed upon the Earth to walk its evolutionary path. At that time all the Kingdoms coexisted in peace and harmony upon the plane of Earth. The animals were directed by the beings whom you perhaps know now as the Titans, great beings, some half animal and half human, others half angelic and half bird. They were a mixture of the plane of Earth and the higher planes of life. They responded to the authority of the Goddess as they guided the Animal Kingdom along its evolutionary path.

It may seem a strange concept to you that a being can evolve within the body of another being, but consider that there are beings of consciousness evolving even now within your own physical body as you evolve within the body of the Goddess who in turn evolves within the body of that Being whom you call God, Whose physical form is the Planetary System of which you are aware. Let us therefore simply accept that these great Beings manifest aspects of themselves to fulfil the plan of evolution and that the Animal Kingdom is linked directly to the Goddess through this divine authority in a growing evolutionary cycle.

Then, for reasons unknown to us, that great Being, the God of our planetary system, placed the soul of Humanity upon the Earth. Humanity was not of the Earth, was not born of the Earth, was not the creation of the Goddess. It was the sacrifice of the Goddess to have Humanity on her being, to allow Humanity to evolve itself according to its own evolutionary cycle and pattern which was very different to the one which she had created. But the Goddess being female in energy, a being of creativity and love, accepted that challenge, that request made to her by the Creator of us all. At first Humanity lived in peace on the plane of Earth heeding the guidance of the great Titans, the great angelic beings, learning of the Mineral, the Vegetable and the Animal Kingdoms, recognising the unity of the three and the necessity for harmony and balance in order to fulfil the evolutionary cycle. But then Humanity fell from grace.

Possessing the gift of free choice, which the great Titans did not, and thus having the ability to choose both the direction and the timing of its evolutionary cycle according to its own point of consciousness, Humanity could affect the nature of the path upon which it walked. Inevitably Humanity clashed with the Titans. The result of that clash was the gradual withdrawal of the Titans from the plane of Earth and the Animal Kingdom, recognising that a new god had come upon the face of the Earth, turned to Humanity for the guidance and leadership which had formerly come directly from the Goddess. This the Goddess allowed for she knew of the great potential that lay within the hearts of Humanity. She knew that they were gods in the making, capable of rising to even greater consciousness than her if they would but grasp the challenge presented to them and ground the qualities, at present latent, which were given to them by the Creator of our Planetary System.

So Humanity became the masters of the Animal Kingdom. Humanity now had the authority previously held by the Titans, and those great beings disappeared, often to reside in the Mineral Kingdom. This is made manifest today by the many legends which tell of great beings lying under the shape of the earth, in the fold of a hill or inside a mountain awaiting their moment of recall, to come forth to play their part again. They are the hidden aspects of the Goddess which she does not release at this time in order to impose her authority. She has given Humanity freedom of choice, freedom of movement, to do with her subjects, with her aspects of personality, with the very heart of herself, whatsoever they wish in this cycle of evolution.

Consider that the Animal Kingdom has evolved over literally hundreds of thousands of years in order to reach the various points of its evolutionary cycle. Humanity has been but a short breath on the surface of the Earth, but witness the rate at which Humanity has evolved. This shows the potential that lies within the Human Race, that lies within each one of you, a potential far greater than that of the Animal Kingdom and of the Goddess which created it. That surely demonstrates to Humanity the potential that it has to manifest not only on the Earth but in the Cosmos as a whole.

As the Titans withdrew so Humanity took control of the Animal Kingdom. But Humanity had fallen from grace. Humanity was now using its powers not to follow the evolutionary cycle planned by its Creator, to create in Its image, but rather to create in its own image. Humanity became self-centred rather than God-centred. Humanity sought to acquire possessions for itself rather than to recognise the universality of all that was around it. Humanity no longer recognised the essential truth that everything belonged not to it, but to its Creator and to the Creator's servant, the Goddess. The animals followed the authority and the example of Humanity. They, too, fell from grace and as Humanity began to hunt and to kill, began to compete and to strive, to hold material things only for itself not heeding the needs and the sacrifices of lesser beings, so to an extent did the Animal Kingdom.

If I could show you only one thing in this talk it would be that you recognise that you see yourselves, you see your own weaknesses, your own failings through your relationship with the Animal Kingdom. As you abuse and exploit the animals so you are doing just the same to your fellow human beings, for the animals are but a mirror of Humanity's character. They are a mirror of Humanity's evolutionary path on the plane of Earth. Is it not true that you exterminate your fellow human beings just as readily as you exterminate your fellow creatures? That is the true nature of Humanity's consciousness at this moment in time. Nature is but a mirror for Humanity. That is its prime purpose: to reflect to Humanity what it really is doing. If you cannot learn from your fellow human beings, if you cannot learn about the true vibration of your being from them, then look at the Animal Kingdom. Look at the way Humanity treats that Kingdom and you will see how you treat yourselves. Of course, I am not saying that all of Humanity's relationships with the Animal Kingdom are evil. They are not. Many people do relate correctly to it.

So the Animal Kingdom was given over to the authority of Humanity. That was the priceless gift of the Goddess, to give of her own beauty, her own wisdom, her own essence, to place that in the hands of a young evolving god, Humanity, a race of beings that was struggling to attain the consciousness necessary to receive greater powers and greater wisdom. You yourselves know only too well of the path that the Animal Kingdom has taken and of Humanity's relationship to it. You may witness the downfall of Humanity and the degradation of the Animal Kingdom until the present day when we have perhaps the greatest degradation of all, which is animals being used by Humanity purely for its own selfish ends without any regard whatsoever for the destiny, the purpose or the consciousness of the Animal Kingdom, without even considering the part it might play in the evolutionary cycle of the Earth.

The Goddess created the Animal Kingdom for a very specific purpose. It was to combine in the trinity of the Vegetable and the Mineral Kingdoms to husband this plane of Earth. The Animal Kingdom is the divine link between the Mineral and the Vegetable Kingdoms, and if you remove that link you will destroy the evolutionary pattern of this Earth, for you need the three Kingdoms together in balance and harmony in order to preserve the atmosphere, the fertility and the environment of the Earth for the Human race. What the Human Race is doing now, if it did but know it, is to destroy that link, and with every species that is exterminated, with every species that is corrupted, over-bred, abused, deformed by Humanity, that link is weakening. You are approaching a time when it may break for good and that will herald not only the downfall of Humanity but of the other three Kingdoms as well. I say this not to frighten you, not to fill you with gloom, but to make you aware of Humanity's responsibility in this respect so that if it does happen you will not see it as an act of a wrathful God, or even as an act of chance, but rather as the direct result of Humanity's actions over the centuries towards the Animal Kingdom.

The link right now is very thin. The balance between the Kingdoms is near to breaking. When the Bible speaks prophetically of the plagues to come, that is indeed one of the events which will take place if the link breaks. At present Humanity controls the Insect Kingdom with its poisons and its pesticides, but that system will fail. Soon Humanity will be unable to hold back the advances of this aspect of the Animal Kingdom. The insects will begin to multiply more and more and to bring a scourge across the face of the Earth, for the force which would keep them in check has been destroyed by the Human Race. The natural balance has gone. The Insect Kingdom will cover the Earth and will bring about much Human destruction. There are scientists today who recognise this fact and are working desperately on new methods to control this potential and lethal invasion.

Humanity therefore has broken its bond with the Goddess. It has abused the sacred trust given to it by the Goddess. It has treated the Animal Kingdom as slaves. It has ignored its purpose, its destiny. Humanity regards the Animal Kingdom as unfeeling matter, to be freely used to further its own selfish interests and aims. Because Humanity has just gone through an Age of intellect, an Age where intuition has been suppressed, where the wisdom of the female has not been allowed to manifest to balance the intellect of the male, so there is current on the plane of Earth today the intellectual approach to the Animal Kingdom. It is an approach where the ends justify the means, where the animals can be sacrificed for the so-called good of Humanity, where they can be used for scientific experiments, where they can be used for food, where they can be

129

used for pleasure, where they can be used as personal possessions to satisfy Humanity's ego. Those days are soon to end. The Goddess is soon to reclaim that which is hers by birthright and creativity.

What can be said of the Animal Kingdom in the Aquarian Age? The human population balance on the Earth will have been drastically reshaped. The continual demand to use the Animal Kingdom for food will no longer be present and, moreover, the consciousness that will exist upon the Earth at that time would not seek it anyway. There will come a recognition of the Animal Kingdom as the husbanders of the Earth, with the role of making it fertile, of cross-pollinating, of carrying the wishes of the Goddess to every part of this planet, of manifesting the many aspects of the Goddess in all her beauty and wisdom. The animals will be recognised as responsible co-creators on this plane of Earth. Humanity, under the impulse of the Aquarian energy, will begin to manifest the highest of itself, not the lowest. It will seek to follow the will of its Creator and to establish once more that sacred link formerly held by the Titans. This indeed will be the sign for the re-awakening of those great beings. They will once again manifest on the plane of Earth to aid Humanity in its evolutionary cycle, to guide and to help it to recognise the nature of life on this Earth.

You are not of the Earth. You are from another planet, from another plane of life. The conditions that exist on the Earth are foreign to you. You are not used to these bodies of clay. You are not used to the concept of feeding, of clothing, of looking after a physical shape. You therefore need help and guidance in this matter. You need to be taught of the nature of the Earth and of the responsibilities that you bear to the creatures who live on her. The great angelic beings will do this. You will learn to communicate with the animals as did the Titans: mind to mind. Speech is not necessary. The animals will listen to you and will obey you. They will seek your guidance, they will seek your help and your wisdom. You will give it, and in return they will aid you in your evolutionary cycle for they will teach you of the Goddess. Those of you who walk with awareness in a garden can see there manifesting in the cycles of the garden and the animals the wisdom of a great being. That being gave you the bodies in which you now live, feeds the bodies in which you now live and will eventually reclaim the bodies in which you now live. For when you die and leave your physical body to return to your true spiritual home the Goddess will take back that which is hers.

130

The animals, therefore, are your direct link to the Goddess and to her wisdom, and you incarnate onto this plane of life to learn from the Goddess, to partake of her wisdom. You have the choice: to listen or to ignore. You are gods in the making. You have the potential to become a God. That is the real nature of the experiment of placing Humanity on the plane of Earth. So far Humanity has betrayed the trust of the Goddess. It has destroyed. It has weakened. It has ignored the hand held out by the Goddess for evolutionary advancement. That hand will soon be withdrawn, and when it is offered again it will be to a different race of Humanity, to the chosen ones who will have survived the changes to come, who will have the consciousness to grasp and accept it, to heed its wisdom, to recognise the Animal Kingdom for what it is: the servant of the Goddess, not the servant of Humanity.

## QUESTIONS AND ANSWERS

Q: Today we have the factory farming of animals and animals being used for experiments in laboratories. How do we make a start towards changing this system, apart from just not using the products of these industries?

ZT: The important thing to realise is that what you are seeking to change is not the results of Humanity's consciousness but Humanity's consciousness itself. If you seek to attack or change only the results then you are wasting your time because, like the weeds in your garden, even if you remove them they will come back again. What you can do to change the consciousness of Humanity is to change yourself. This of course takes time. You change only by example, by reflecting the truth in light and love, by right education, by talking to those who will listen, by showing Humanity in love that the path on which it is set is incorrect. As people begin to sense that things are going wrong, that perhaps all is not well in the relationship, they will then listen to those who can point out with clarity why this is so.

Q: There are activists on the physical level, such as those who disrupt hunts and raid experimental laboratories, who believe very sincerely that by physically opposing what they believe to be an evil

and by demonstrating to make the public aware of what is going on that they are helping the Animal Kingdom. Is this actually the case?
ZT: The fact that hunts and experimental laboratories exist is known to most people, as are the so-called benefits that result from them. What we are talking about therefore is violence as a means of drawing attention to something which is already known. Is that violence for the animals or for the people committing it? What we have to recognise is that you may lance one boil but others will soon come. Now you can keep on lancing the boils but how much better to get at the cause of the boils and to prevent them coming. What we have to change is people's consciousness. We have to touch the hearts of people so that they see clearly that such activities, such places, are not necessary, are not desirable. The necessity to trap animals for skins and coats will only stop when the ladies of this world do not wish to wear them. While the market is there the cruelty will continue. You must change the consciousness. You must educate that consciousness, and education is an act of love, not violence.

Q: Do not the animals suffer?
ZT: Yes.

Q: Then is it not worth while stopping a little of the suffering and at the same time making people more aware about things?
ZT: You will obviously save some animals and alleviate some suffering on the day, but will it really benefit the suffering of the Animal Kingdom as a whole?

Q: In the pharmaceutical industry there are many tormented animals being used in evil experiments. Is it not right to stop that suffering?
ZT: Yes. But the demands for such testing is the direct result of the many people who use the pharmaceutical products. Until such time as that stops, the testing will continue. Humanity as a whole is suffering. I wonder which is suffering more: Humanity or the Animal Kingdom, bearing in mind what the first speaker said, that the Animal Kingdom is but a mirror of Humanity?

Q: Is the link between the Human and the Animal Kingdom definitely going to be broken? Is it too late for us to change that?

132

ZT:   Obviously while there is time all things are possible, but I feel that the path on which Humanity has set itself is so fixed that I cannot see Humanity changing.

Q:   What about pets? There is such a link between humans and their pets. Is this a good thing or not?
ZT:   The link which exists between humans and their pets is merely a reflection of the higher link that has just been mentioned. The greater will of the human inevitably controls the lesser will of the animal. That involves great responsibility. What therefore is of supreme importance is one's motivation for having a pet. That should be examined most carefully before you take on the responsibility of a pet. Next, you should ensure that the pet which you choose is the one that is in harmony with you. You should ensure that the pet has as natural a life as possible, and if you cannot let it have a natural life then you should not have a pet. Remember that your pet has consciousness, has will and has an evolutionary cycle to fulfil. You should give it the freedom to do so. If you are not prepared to do that then do not take a pet. The joy that you receive from your pet comes from a sharing of the oneness of life, from a mutual recognition of the beauty of the plane of Earth. Perhaps the best example of having a pet is where you approach an animal that lives in the wild and establish a relationship with it, based on mutual trust, so that both parties have the freedom to meet and share and then go their own way as they so desire. This was how it was in the very early days of Humanity on the plane of Earth.

Q:   What about having animals neutered? That stops an awful lot of suffering from unwanted babies, but it does interfere with their will.
ZT:   I do not believe that your God, even in this moment of extreme over-population of the world, neuters humans! There is a natural cycle and a natural rhythm to all things. The only reason for human beings neutering animals is because the environment in which the animals live is artificial to them and to the human. Having said that, if you introduce a pet into an artificial human environment, then you must take complete responsibility for doing that and protect the pet. Nevertheless, can the relationship be complete when the animal has been neutered? The answer is no. You are getting a half-animal, a half-pet. If this is what you desire then

133

so be it, but be aware of that fact. Of course, there can still be great evolution and joy in the union even when the pet has been neutered, but I would always advise that you seek the real thing, which is union with the spirit of a free animal on its own terms.

You live in an imperfect World which reflects the imperfectness of Humanity. The Animal Kingdom is cruel, as is Humanity, the Animal Kingdom over-breeds, as does Humanity. Inevitably the Animal Kingdom reflects Humanity's actions and is also out of balance and that is why Humanity has to modify the pet's behaviour pattern, so that it can live in a world that is divorced from reality. An artificial human world demands an artificial animal world. What you can do is to create a new relationship between Humanity and the Animal Kingdom. How can this be done? By giving of yourself, by giving of your time and energy in relationship. That means communication. That means giving of yourself as you would give to a child. It means teaching and love. It does not mean patting your dog on the head once a day when you feed it. Obviously the best relationship is the one established in the wild where you can meet the animal on its own terms.

Q: Is it right for us to eat dairy products?

ZT: We must begin by recognising the way in which we obtain these dairy products. It was intended that the Animal and Human Kingdoms should give to each other. The animal will give freely of its surplus to Humanity. In return Humanity can give of its surplus to the Animal Kingdom. Unfortunately today, as in all things, Humanity's greed has led to the creation of a vast dairy industry which produces great surpluses. The human body in the Western World has been adapted to what you call a lactic diet but that does not mean that Humanity would die without that diet. The times when Humanity needs dairy products are relatively few. It should not be a daily thing. It should be reserved for rare occasions, for times of ill health, for times of stress. Indeed you can do yourself much harm by eating too many dairy products. Moreover, the system which produces dairy products today is cruel, since it exploits the animals and gives them no say in their own evolution because they are totally controlled by Humanity. As a result of this many dairy products are lacking in the essential vitamins and nutrients, both on a physical and a spiritual level, which would be of true benefit to Humanity. You must make your own decision as

134

to when to use such a diet. All that we ask is that you recognise the sacrifice that has gone into it.

When you are very young and when you are very old milk is a beneficial form of food. In the case of the human baby this should be mother's milk, but because many mothers today do not feed their children long enough, so the need will arise to use other forms of milk because this is the food that the baby can most easily assimilate. Likewise when one is old and eats very little, as the body begins to decay, so certain essential nutriments and vitamins are needed to prevent that decay and are to be found in dairy products. For the normal healthy adult these vitamins can be absorbed from other sources of food and there is no need, from a nutritional point of view, to use dairy products.

Q: Do you think that it is possible that the day will arrive when people will stop killing animals to eat them, not just a minority of people but a majority of people? Also, do you think that day will arrive before a major cataclysm?
ZT: In my opinion I do not believe that such a change is possible, if only because people do not want to change.

Q: Is it not true to say that all of us are at different points of evolution and that what is right for one is not for another? If we look at life today it seems totally unreasonable to imagine that everybody living will suddenly realise that it is wrong to exploit animals for food. But is it wrong for *all* people? It might be wrong for us, but can you say that it is wrong for everyone?
ZT: What we are concerned with here are two things. Firstly, the human aspect and, secondly, the animal aspect. Let us take the animal aspect first.

Can there be any justification for the support of a system which is becoming increasingly cruel, oppressive and, indeed unhealthy, for that is what is happening now in the farming industry. As the financial aspect intrudes more and more into farming so the drive to become economic, to make more money, to produce more meat for less cost, becomes the important factor in meat production. Animals become a gain on a computer. People forget they are dealing with living animals. There can be no justification for the continuation of this system at any level.

Let us now consider the human aspect. Humanity is by nature

135

very conservative. Most of you come from parents, grandparents and even great grandparents who have probably eaten meat. It has become an established practice. Now that does not mean that you cannot change but it does mean that the traditions of generations have been impressed upon you. It means that you are accustomed to animal sacrifice and that you accept it as your natural right. Those of you who have changed, or are indeed considering the change, are breaking with those traditions because your consciousness demands it. Inevitably you will have to battle with those traditions to accomplish that change, facing opposition from your family and friends around you, for by your very actions you are causing them to examine their own.

It is difficult to change Humanity's consciousness other than at times of great crisis. Only the fire of purification can bring about sudden change. Nevertheless, people are beginning to realise what is really involved in the production of meat: the sacrifice, the pain, the destruction of an aspect of Nature. Until Humanity sees that it is itself that it is destroying when it kills animals there will be no change.

Q:   If people enjoy eating meat and do not want to change, how can they be persuaded that eating meat is not good for them?
ZT:   If you eat meat, just consider what it is that you are really eating. If you are seeking to purify yourselves, to make your bodies finer instruments, to feel more with your senses and to go beyond your physical body, then you should eat only the purest and the best food, that which has grown naturally and reflects the purity of the Goddess. If you eat food, either animal or vegetable, that has been grown in distortion, if you eat meat which has come from a diseased animal, an animal which is in imperfection because it reflects Humanity, if you eat meat which is imbued with the animal's fears and aggressions, then you are partaking of those fears and those aggressions. What you eat controls what you are. It influences your temperament, it influences the very nature of your body as an instrument of service, as an instrument of the Godhead. Finally, the next time you kill an animal, perhaps, just before you kill it, consider what aspect of the Goddess that animal represents.

136

# HOLDING THE LIGHT

What do you understand by the word 'Light'? In the duality of the physical plane of life Light is the opposite of Darkness. Where there is Light there can be no Darkness. Indeed, the absence of Light is Darkness. Springing up all over the World at this time are what are called Light Centres. People today talk of increasing the Light, of grounding the Light. The term 'Light' rises above race, above language, above religion. It is a symbology that is understood throughout the World.

Light opposes Darkness and the struggle that is manifesting on your planet today is but a reflection of a greater struggle on the higher planes of life between the forces of Light and the forces of Darkness, for nothing manifests on the physical plane of life unless it has already manifested on a higher plane of being. You, souls of aged evolution, are fighting a battle on the Earth against Darkness. If you look at your World today and think that Darkness is triumphing, that the forces and powers of Darkness are really controlling this planet, then recognise that that is because the Light is not shining strongly enough. You are not holding the Light.

The Red Indians of North America practised a noteworthy custom. In the last stages of that Race it did perhaps become a degenerate custom, but in the origins of this symbolic act lay a great cosmic understanding. At a time of battle a warrior, usually the chief of the tribe, would stake himself to the ground. He would knock a wooden stake into the ground, tie a piece of hide to it and then attach the hide to his leg and there he would stand and fight, either to win or to die. It was a supreme act of bravery, of sacrifice. Its meaning to the rest of the tribe was clear: here I stand. In order to do this the warrior had to possess a certain understanding of life, a certain state of mind. The warrior had to have confidence in his physical abilities at that moment in time. He also had to have an understanding of life and death, an acceptance of his destiny and, above all, of the fact that the will of his Creator would be done.

How many of you would be prepared to stake yourselves in such a way for your Race, let alone for your Creator? I ask this question because in the World today so few are prepared to hold the Light. There are many aged souls now in incarnation on the Earth. They chose with great deliberation to come down on Earth in order to be present at this time of planetary transformation, to witness the changing of the Ages, to take part in the great battle between Darkness and Light at the end of the Piscean Age and to welcome the Aquarian Principle. However many of these souls are not fulfilling their potential. They are not demonstrating the spiritual qualities which they can, and should, manifest.

There are often people in the World who are prepared to stake themselves to that piece of ground but who are not ready for that act in body, mind or spirit, and so they fail. In that very act there is Darkness, for to fail in that test was a sign of defeat for all who fought with the warrior and the effects of that defeat were felt by the whole tribe. If you hold the Light, if you stake yourselves and fail, remember that you drag down those around you. So before you actually make that symbolic act, be sure of yourselves. Be certain of the wisdom that lies within you. Be certain that the many aspects of your being are in perfect harmony. To arrive at that moment when you can make that act of sacrifice to your Creator means that you have looked at the innermost part of your being and are shining the Light that you came to manifest on this plane of Earth.

Darkness flourishes today because there is too little Light. There is too little Light because the Light is not being shown. You live in a dense physical World, of that fact you are well aware. That physical World can and never will be perfection. Even a great soul such as the Master Jesus on descending into the plane of Earth was corrupted, to a degree, by that plane. So there can and never will be perfection on Earth, but that does not mean that you should not strive to the utmost of your ability to shine the Light that you possess in order to bring out the Light in others. This requires sacrifice. This requires giving. This requires that you support all those who stand in the Light with you. Above all, it requires that you recognise the source and the purpose of Light. You are but mirrors of Light. You are not the source. It is only the perfection of your being that reflects the Light.

138

Light destroys Darkness. There can be no Darkness where there is Light. There is this philosophy in the Western World today that Darkness will be defeated in some great battle, that Humanity will be saved from Darkness by a Saviour, perhaps by the Christed Being, Who will come down and release Humanity from the bonds of Darkness. That is not so. The Christ Principle came down on Earth two thousand years ago and released the impulse for the Piscean Age, but there is still Darkness. It will be just the same in the Age to come. It is Humanity alone that can save this World. It is only by evolved souls holding their Light and standing for what they know to be true in their hearts that Humanity will bring about the redemption of this Earth. That is the destiny that lies before you. That is the task that you have come to carry out. That is the duty which you must begin to fulfil. It is so easy to be seduced by the temptations and the pleasures of the World in which you live today and to succumb to the limitations of the physical plane of life. If you regard yourselves solely as physical beings then you are limiting yourselves, for you are beings of Spirit. You are Light living for a short time in a body of physical matter.

The great human institutions of the World are for the most part corrupt. In Government, Church, Medicine, Law and Industry, in almost every human organisation and endeavour, there is to be found corruption and Darkness. How are you to remove that Darkness but by shining your Light, for where there is Light there can be no Darkness. You will only bring about this transformation by demonstrating your spiritual consciousness. Whether or not you are trained in any particular profession, in any particular career, does not matter. It is the Light of your soul-being that will illuminate the Light of others and lead them to self-discovery. You cannot change the World, you can only change yourself and by shining your Light you will lead others to recognise and to shine their Light.

The vast mass of Humanity lives, and will die, in Darkness. That is a fact of life. As Jesus said, "The poor are always with you", the poor in spirit, the poor in soul experience. It is the souls of aged evolution who bring about transformation and initiate change on the plane of Earth. They are the chosen ones, the beings of soul-experience, the beings who agreed before they came down into physical manifestation to play this part at this most critical time in the Earth's evolution. They have come to show their Light. They have come to disperse Darkness, to bring about this great evolutionary step forward. But where is that Light today? How many of you are strong in yourselves? How many of you would die for that Light? The Light is not a philosophy, an intellectual concept. It is the innermost, the most sacred part of your being, the part which you know as Truth, the part which you know to be divine. That is the reality of the Light which you must shine.

You are faced with the World of Matter and the World of Spirit. You must balance that duality. You must lead a life of Spirit in a World of Matter. The Matter will try to corrupt the Spirit. You must not allow that. Even the most corrupt human system on the plane of Earth can be changed by the Light of Spirit. You do not have to change the system yourself. You merely have to shine your Light and the Darkness will disappear. That, after all, is what Jesus did. He was on the Earth for but a short time. He spoke to relatively few people. He personally touched the consciousness of only a handful of disciples, and yet his Light went forth all over the World. That Light transformed Western thinking. That Light was responsible for the cycle of evolution that has gone on for the last two thousand years.

Light: that which is of the Divine, that which does not permit Darkness. I wish that all of you who possess a bright Light would take account of yourselves, would realise that if there is Darkness then you are to blame. If you shine your Light and are true to yourselves, if you resist the temptations of the material World and rise above the restrictions of physical life, if you would only be what you came to be, then you would transform this planet. You would transmute the Darkness which is present on the Earth today. As you read your newspapers and see the reports of death and destruction, of collective and individual violence, of selfishness and greed, so you must surely realise that the path upon which Humanity is set must lead to self-destruction. Even now you live under the threat of a nuclear holocaust. How is this to be avoided? There are some who believe that by actively campaigning against nuclear weapons, that by abolishing nuclear weapons they will bring about peace. They will not. The only path to peace is the path of Light, for where there is Light there can be no Darkness. Over and over again I will say this to you because you are beings of Light, you are the Light of the World. You have the potential to change this World. It lies in your hands.

Individuals can unite into a centre of Light. Many pin-pricks of Light can come together to become one unified source of Light: a thousand light-bulbs instead of one. Where there is unity of purpose and will the power is much stronger, but you must also recognise that more is to be lost when a centre of Light fails than when an individual fails. This is because many people, like moths to a flame, will have seen that Light and will be looking at it, will be assessing it critically, to see if that Light can withstand the powers of Darkness. There are many centres of Light springing up all over the planet but, equally so, many are failing because of the personalities of the people involved, because their consciousnesses have not evolved to the point when they are ready to shine the Light, to stand and stake themselves on the plane of Earth.

Recognise that you are a point of Light, that one day that point of Light will become part of a centre of Light, that one day that centre of Light will become a planet of Light and that that planet of Light will one day return to the Source of Light. You must fulfil your part in that evolving cycle. To fail now will affect your destiny for life-times to come. You are here not as a test, for you have passed this test many times before. You are here simply to do what you have done many times before at similar moments of crisis in past lives: to stand and hold the Light, to hold the Light not for yourselves but for the planet, to hold the Light not for your families but for the families of Humanity. You live to serve the Light. Therefore stand and hold that Light. Accept that responsibility. Listen to the voice of your Creator, listen to your hearts and follow your soul murmurings. Reflect the Light.


## QUESTIONS AND ANSWERS


Q: The speaker seemed to imply that Darkness was an evil thing, which does not quite fit in with my understanding of Darkness. Is Darkness evil?

ZT: When we use the terminology Light and Darkness we are using terms that reflect the duality of the life that you lead. There is always a choice before you, an opportunity to exercise the divine gift which you have been given, a gift which is given to few planetary bodies. Both Light and Darkness are of God. Evil is a

141

creation of religion. When we talk of Darkness we are talking of energies that wish to assert their influence on the plane of Earth. These forces have a spiritual hierarchy controlling them just as do the forces of Light. The purpose of the forces of Darkness, put simply, is to test the forces of Light. The choice which faces Humanity today is the choice between Light and Darkness. The forces of Darkness are not evil in the sense that religion talks of evil which is as a sin against its beliefs. Evil is really the opposite of live, which is why evil is the same as live but spelt backwards. It is the same energy used in an opposite way. Darkness is that which darkens the face of the Earth, that which darkens and oppresses the soul of Humanity. Light is that which uplifts the soul of Humanity, that which brings forth the divine aspect of its being.

What we are talking about here is Humanity's cyclic pattern of evolution which has been going on for thousands of years. This struggle between Darkness and Light has been going on for many cycles, on many levels of life. If Darkness appears to triumph that does not mean the end of Light. It simply means that for a time Humanity will have to live in conditions unfavourable to Light and the people who incarnate in that time will have a greater challenge on their hands. You live at a time when you could be led into thinking that you have seen the worst of Darkness. That is not so. There are forces in existence now that are capable of unleashing Darkness beyond your comprehension. So how you shine your Light now is important not only for yourselves and your children, but for your children's children and their children. Darkness is not evil. It is the Satanic, the Saturnic side of the Creator testing Humanity, presenting it with the choice of Light or Darkness. It is through that choice you evolve not only yourselves and this planet but all the spiritual beings associated with it.

Q:   What part does faith play in the act of staking oneself out, to use the first speaker's analogy?
ZT:   There are two kinds of faith: blind faith and certain faith. Let me use the example of an athlete to illustrate the difference. An athlete trains his body for a race. He knows that he can attain a certain performance which, although varying from day to day according to his motivation and will, he can reproduce under most conditions. The athlete enters the race in the certain faith that he can reproduce his training performance. However if he was to enter a

race without any preparation or training, just because he felt inspired to do so, he would be entering that race in blind faith. Now there are times in life when blind faith is the only faith available and therefore has to be used, but almost always that is because the person involved has placed himself or herself in that situation. Our Creator, in my understanding, never demands blind faith.

Faith is a necessary part of Humanity's make-up. Inevitably, in life, you will meet challenges that you have not faced before. You will face new tests, new problems, new conflicts, but always there is within you the understanding of your capabilities, the knowledge of your destiny, the wisdom of your soul. These will help you to face and answer any challenge. You will always have the potential within you to face any challenge in certain faith.

Q: Is there any formula, is there any technique, that we can follow to help us to shine the Light?

ZT: Whilst I recognise that your libraries abound with 'Do it yourself' books and that this has become quite an accepted way of learning, nevertheless, you should also recognise that it is not possible for many people to learn in this way. There are many would-be do it yourself carpenters who even with a book in front of them will never become carpenters! People are all individuals and as such will all excel at different aspects of living. You are all unique aspects of Spirit, possessing different talents, qualities and abilities. These you should manifest naturally to the highest of your motivation. If you do this in harmony with your being then you will automatically be shining your Light. It is not something that has to be practised, followed step by step from a manual. It is an act of being. It is an act of God. If you are a God-centred being then you will naturally shine your Light. Of course there will be times when you will fail, that is recognised by the Higher Forces, but there will always be many more times when you will succeed.

Above all, I would ask you to consider the example of the light-house. Your spirit is like a light-house and when your light is bright it can be seen for many miles and can help many people. If you are an aged soul then remember that many will see your light and will use it to illuminate their pathway. You are not aware of how much one bright light can help the World. Never underestimate the influence that one correct act has on the plane of physical life. One correctly motivated thought, word or deed can transform a hundred-fold. It requires therefore that you always act with responsibility, not for yourself but for those around you.

Q: What about the point that what is Light to one is Darkness to another? For example, a farmer will lovingly raise and nurture his sheep and then think that there is nothing wrong in sending them to market for slaughter because he feels that what he is doing is correct. Someone else, however, might think that what the farmer was doing was exploiting the Animal Kingdom. Can one person's Light be another person's Darkness?

ZT: You are forgetting what is the source of Light and Darkness. Let us not be drawn into the individual reflections of Humanity. Let us remember that the source of all life is the Being who not only gave us life but created all things. We simply reflect Its Light according to the nature of our being. That Being does not judge. That Being does not compare. It accepts us for what we are. Consider the example of the Master Jesus and his Light. By your definition everyone around him was Darkness, but that was not the case. Jesus shone his Light and the Light touched many people. He was the spark which ignited their consciousness and placed them on the path towards Light. Do not worry about the deeds of others. Do not try to change them or convert them. Just show them your Light.

Q: The purpose of a spiritual teacher obviously is to teach others but if your teachings are opposed to the way of life around you then are you not being judgemental and divisive by teaching?

ZT: No. The teachings of the New Age that are now manifesting on the plane of Earth are not intellectual concepts with which you can play mental games. Either they are, or are not, realities to you. If they are not realities then continue in your present lifestyle and forget about them. If they are realities then live them. That is the way you are going to change this World. It is no good talking about a New Age lifestyle but not living it. Only right thought, right speech and right action will transform this planet. You must be prepared to show your Light and to shine it in the face of Darkness.

Q: We have had many teachings given to us by the teachers who speak through this instrument. I consider them to be true in the light of my own experience but when I repeat these teachings either in conversation or discussion some people think that I am being judgemental. I often wonder whether it would be better if I was to say nothing, or is that being a coward, rather than staking myself out and standing for what I believe to be true?

ZT:  I will begin by saying that belief does not enter into it. The Indian warrior would not stake himself out just because of a belief. This supreme act was not an everyday occurrence. The warrior did not stake himself out just to encourage other warriors because they were losing a battle. He did it because he was motivated to do so by a deep inner feeling. He was prepared to commit himself to, what I will call, the Force of Destiny, the Force of God. He was prepared to demonstrate that understanding and commitment before all people. The fact that he did this did not mean either that he and his tribe would win the battle or that he would survive. That was not the point of staking himself to the ground. It was an act of spiritual initiation.

Many of you are approaching a similar point of spiritual initiation. You have acquired a new awareness of your Creator and of Its will for you and this planet. Because of knowledge released from the higher planes of life you are beginning to understand and to come to terms with a lifestyle which is very different from that which society practises today. But until you live and practise that way of life you cannot say that it is Truth. You must live it to know it, and until you know it you are not in a position to stake yourself for it. People will come and observe you. People will come and listen to you. You cannot be responsible for what they say or feel. All that you can do is to show your Light.

Finally I ask you all to be courageous. It is difficult to oppose the World. It is difficult to overcome the conditioning of a lifetime, the conditioning of generations. Only an old soul can, and will, do it. It takes a Copernicus or a Galileo to have the inner strength to say, "No matter what society or science says, I know this to be wrong and so I will oppose it. I will shine my Light on this Darkness." That is what is required of all of you.

# THE TRUE NATURE OF THE MINERAL KINGDOM

You live at a time when Humanity regards itself as being at the very pinnacle of the human evolutionary cycle. Western Civilisation, in particular, regards itself as being superior to all other forms of life, largely because it has made such great technological advances, because it has indeed reached the Moon. In the pursuit of these achievements the White Race has, for the most part, regarded the other Races and, more particularly, the three other Kingdoms of Matter, as being completely subservient to its aims, to its understanding of life, to its cycle of evolution. The idea of co-operation, of co-creation with these Kingdoms, has never been a part of its thought. The White Race has pursued its evolutionary cycle with a remarkable single-mindedness. In my talk, therefore, I would like to present to you a cosmic view of one of those subservient Kingdoms, the Mineral Kingdom, so that you may understand a little of its true nature and purpose and try to establish a correct relationship with it in the years to come.

I wonder if you ever recognise the divinity of the Mineral Kingdom, if you are aware of its purpose, indeed of its consciousness, or do you perhaps think that the Mineral Kingdom is without life-force, without spiritual energy, inanimate matter to be used by Humanity as it so wishes. If we were to go back to the very creation of the planet, before human evolution on its surface was ever considered, we would see that the Earth was born out of a union of the Sun God and the Goddess of the Earth plane, and that from that act of cosmic fertilisation the Goddess created her physical body, the Earth. Creation on a cosmic level is similar in design to that of human creation. Life is breathed into the molecules of matter by vibrations of spiritual energy. As the vibratory level varies according to frequency so the form which the matter takes varies also. The divine Goddess therefore breathed of her energy into the molecules of physical matter and created the form of the Earth: the rocks, the earth, the sand, the precious stones which Humanity seeks today. Every aspect of the Mineral Kingdom was created by her to fulfil the nature of her evolutionary cycle.

The Goddess created the planet Earth to ground the energy of her being on the physical plane of the Solar Body of which she was a part. The Earth was to give of her energy on the physical plane to the other physical aspects of the Solar Body. The planet was intended as a transmitter of her love, of her creativity. The energy of her being therefore flowed through every aspect of the Mineral Kingdom. Her wisdom, her consciousness, manifested the many aspects of the Mineral Kingdom of which you are aware today and some which Humanity has yet to discover, for the higher aspects of her being are still hidden from Humanity. There are, even today, elements of the Mineral Kingdom that Humanity has not yet discovered and indeed will not do so until it has achieved the consciousness to handle those elements with responsibility.

The Mineral Kingdom therefore vibrates directly to the energy of the Goddess and displays her power. Every aspect vibrates according to a different aspect of her consciousness. The Kingdom is controlled by her servants in the Angelic Realm. In the days of old that control was exercised on Earth by those beings called the Titans, a race of giants who possessed the authority and the power to control and to oversee the passage of life on the Earth. The Titans were conscious that they walked on the divine and that everything which they touched and with which they came into contact was an aspect of the Goddess manifesting for the evolution of the planet Earth and for the two Kingdoms who lived upon her: the Vegetable and the Animal Kingdoms.

For many cycles of evolution the three Kingdoms lived together in perfect harmony. Then Humanity was placed upon the Earth from a source far beyond this planet and, as I have said elsewhere, gradually control was released by the Goddess and by her servants, the Titans, into the hands of Humanity, and as the Animal Kingdom looked to Humanity, to the new god that was walking the face of the Earth, so did the Vegetable and the Mineral Kingdoms. Humanity was given dominion over the three other Kingdoms of Matter to help it in its evolutionary cycle to become a god. So the Mineral Kingdom, whilst possessing the energy and intelligence of the Goddess, was allowed to be directed by the thought-forms of Humanity. Humanity could use the Mineral Kingdom according to its own ideas, its own thoughts, its own desires, to fulfil the nature of its being.

You may not recognise the fact, but Humanity does indeed control the elements of Nature in many subtle ways. You might think that the motions of the Earth, such as an earthquake, a volcano, a flood, a drought, are something which Humanity cannot control, that Humanity is merely a spectator of the transformation of any aspect of the Mineral Kingdom and then has to learn to live with it, but that is not so. The idea that Humanity is responsible for these motions is looked on with scepticism today, but looking back to the ceremonies of the ancient civilisations of the Red Indians, of the Aztecs, of the Egyptians, we can see that they better understood this relationship between Humanity and the Mineral Kingdom. They knew that co-operation was necessary and that a joining together, a union, was vital, since they shared a common evolutionary cycle. They therefore sought that co-operation in their spiritual worship. They realised that when that union is not achieved then there are droughts, floods, earthquakes, volcanic eruptions, the transforming of physical matter, with the result that parts of the Earth become inhospitable to the human race.

The first point, therefore, that I would make, not just for you but for all Humanity to understand, is that the Mineral Kingdom is under the control of Humanity. By its own thought-forms, by its own patterns of behaviour, Humanity influences the Mineral Kingdom. Humanity can, and must, co-operate with that Kingdom if it is to continue on its evolutionary path on the planet Earth, but for so long has the Mineral Kingdom been abused and vandalised by Humanity in order to serve its own ends, no matter what the cost to the Mineral Kingdom, that this co-operation has broken down. It is because of this that Humanity now approaches a time of planetary transformation when the minerals of the planet will move, will vibrate to a different note. If Humanity does not change to that note, does not recognise it, then it will perish.

You live on this Earth by virtue of the Mineral Kingdom. It gives you the means of physical expression. It provides you with your physical body. It also feeds that body. Without its energy you would be dead. The atoms of your body vibrate to the Mineral Kingdom. They are at one with each other in both purpose and

149

destiny. The food which you take in is full of the elements of the Mineral Kingdom and it is these which give you the energy to fulfil your physical and your spiritual evolutionary cycle. It is a very crude analogy to consider the Mineral Kingdom as a provider of energy, but that is what it is. The Mineral Kingdom radiates the energy of the Goddess over a wide spectrum for the use of Humanity on the planet Earth. Every single aspect of the Kingdom gives of her vibrations to fulfil the whole.

It is inevitable, indeed natural, that Humanity should be attracted to certain aspects of the Mineral Kingdom and, in particular, to what you call the precious stones. Humanity has established some stones as precious, precious today not because of their innate qualities but because of their monetary value. In ancient days a stone was regarded as precious because the priests recognised the energy that flowed through it. A stone was seen as a provider of energy from the Goddess for the use of Humanity, as a source of power to be invoked and used. In ancient days stones were used as a means of protection, as a means of transportation around the planet, as a means of attracting animals to one, as receivers of cosmic energy, as instruments of healing and so on. Stones are in fact channels for cosmic energy. They give and receive energy in the infinite cosmic pattern.

When you are attracted to a stone you are attracted to the energy with which that stone pulsates. The energy of a stone will help you to walk your destiny path. It will help you to attune to all the other elements of the Mineral Kingdom. The stone serves the individual by merging its energy with the energy of the human being and following a common path. In that way the human being is uplifted and so is the Mineral Kingdom. Evolution takes place together. Some people use stones to help with their spiritual work, to be of service in many fields, for stones channel energies which can raise the level of human activity. Stones can help the individual to advance along the path of his or her chosen field or profession. That is why even today you carry on the ancient practice of wearing rings containing stones. They are an aid to human evolution. Here I must say that stones should be used only with consciousness, with respect. The buying and selling of stones as a means of investment is a degradation of their very act of being. Recognise also that stones absorb energy. They absorb the thought-forms of everything and everybody with which they come into contact.

You would perhaps think that a diamond is of more value than a piece of granite. However I would say to you that a piece of granite can contain more wisdom, more power, more energy, will uplift you more than a diamond, but who would pay the price of a diamond for a piece of granite today? Beware, therefore, of the human values placed on stones. Instead, seek their cosmic value. Feel intuitively for the stones which you need and then let them come to you. Do not seek the stones of your desires. Allow the activity of your own being to attract the stones unto you that you need for your human evolution. Remember that the Divine works through people and that to you will come the stones which are necessary for your evolutionary path. If you follow the desires of your lower self, your ego, then you will attract that level of stone to you and, far from helping you, that stone will mislead you, perhaps even destroy you. You are aware that some stones have the reputation of being jinxed, of possessing negative energies. This is a true fact and those that attract such stones unto them have a troubled path ahead. If you place a curse upon a stone and give it to another human being then that energy is transmitted to that being and that being will be affected by that thought-form.

Remember that stones were here long before Humanity incarnated on the Earth. They have been impregnated with the vibrations of millions of points of consciousness from, and beyond, this planet. They will tell you, if you will but listen to them, a story of evolution far removed from the one which you accept to be correct today. They have seen many, many cycles of evolution. They have witnessed the coming and going of many forms of life. They have witnessed the rise and fall of many human civilisations. As you touch a standing stone, realise that you are tuning into the Akashic Record of the Human Race. Within the walls of your house now is the record of all who have lived in it. If you have the sensitivity to receive from those stones you can learn of the nature of life within that house since it was built. You can learn of the energy that went into it, of everything that has taken place within its walls.

When you touch a piece of granite you are touching the oldest rock on the planet Earth. You are touching the most sacred of rocks. You are touching the very source of the Akashic Record of this Earth, for that rock can tell you of the true nature of the Goddess. That rock can tell you of the cycles that have taken place and of the cycles that are to come. Rocks, stones, do have consciousness. They

151

possess the consciousness of the Goddess. They also contain the consciousness of every single form that has been in contact with them. All that is stored within them and they give that energy out. Therefore a stone that is honoured by someone, that has been blessed, when given to another will transmit that energy, will transmit that love. A stone is a carrier of energy.

As I said earlier, be cautious as to how you choose your stones, both the stones that you wear and the stones that you give. It is better to be without a stone than to have an incorrect one, for an incorrect stone can, truly, limit your destiny. It is not a coincidence that usually it is the female of the species that desires to wear stones. Outwardly it would appear that they wear them for ornament, but that is not so. The desire of Woman to wear stones is born of her direct link to the Goddess, the Creator of physical life, the Womb of all that is and all that ever will be on the Earth. Woman creates just as the Goddess creates and she therefore realises, often on a subconscious level, the significance of the stone as a giver of energy, as a symbol of purity, as a symbol of Mother Earth. Woman, of course, creates at a lower level than the Goddess but she fulfils a similar role. The stones which you wear also affect that which you create: your children.

Tune into the stones which you have and see if they are in true harmony with your being. Look for the consciousness of those stones. Seek to contact the elemental spirits of the stones and listen to them. If you discover that a stone is not in accord with your innermost being, then part with it no matter what you believe its monetary value to be. You may possess the most expensive diamond in the world, but if it is not in tune with your being it will destroy you, and of what value is that?

Allow the magnetism of your being to draw the Mineral Kingdom to you just as it does with the Vegetable and Animal Kingdoms. The nature of your soul evolution, your point of consciousness, your vibratory note, will draw to you the stones that you need to walk your evolutionary path in life. Stones can be, and are, of great influence in developing spiritual consciousness, in developing psychic ability, in developing your healing powers. They can be used for physical transportation, for co-creation with the Vegetable Kingdom to improve the vegetables and crops that you grow. They can help to fertilise the soil and to create a Garden of Eden out of a desert.

The real power of a stone is beyond your comprehension. It is a study which Humanity has never made. In the Age to come there will grow from within Humanity an understanding and an appreciation of the true nature of the Mineral Kingdom, of its purpose and of its destiny. Humanity will realise that the Mineral Kingdom was here for millions of years before Humanity came on Earth following its own sacred and divine path. Humanity will recognise that it is out of respect for that divinity that it should try to co-operate with it. The Mineral Kingdom will give of its energy freely to you. You in return must use that energy responsibly, must co-create and so fulfil the true nature of your being: to be divine.

## QUESTIONS AND ANSWERS

Q: You said that stones could be used for transportation and for healing. Has Humanity used these techniques before?

ZT: In the past Humanity has used stones for many purposes. In an evolved civilisation such as Atlantis, for example, stones were used for healing, not only by placing the stones on the human body but also by light being reflected through the stones to shine upon the human form. The Atlanteans used stones as a source of energy and power to create what you now call electricity. They used stones for transportation, for moving themselves around the physical plane of Earth. They also used stones for planetary travel.

Q: What about this craze today for crystals? I feel very wary, not that I do not believe that they have the power but I just feel that we know so little about crystals and energy, and yet we seem to use them so indiscriminately.

ZT: I would agree with you that some people today use a crystal like they take an aspirin. Both can be equally poisonous! As with medicines, so with stones or crystals, one must understand what one is doing. To put a loaded gun in the hand of a young child would be stupid. Indeed it could be said that one man's crystal is another man's poison! A certain crystal may be of value to one person but not to another. The idea that one crystal or one shape can be universally applied to all human beings is wrong. Every human being needs a different crystal, a different vibration, a different

153

note, and to mass-market them and send them around to people will I am afraid not be of much value and indeed, in some cases, could cause harm.

Q: People can see that it is wrong to buy and sell humans and they are even beginning to feel that it might not be correct to buy and sell animals, but nobody seems to realise that it is wrong to buy and sell stones.

ZT: What we are really talking about here is not buying and selling but the materialistic concept of life to which Humanity today clings. Humanity believes that it is the source of all life, the controller of all physical matter. It therefore finds it incomprehensible that anything could come to it except through its own actions. Ownership of anything is an illusion created by Humanity to satisfy its ego, for in reality Humanity owns nothing, nothing whatsoever. Although you might pay money for something and think that you own it, it can be taken away from you in an instant by the Divine Force. You are allowed to possess the elements of matter simply to help you along your evolutionary cycle. You attract certain things to you, certain lessons which you have to learn and, equally so, through your desires you may attract to yourself things that you do not need, that are an extra burden you have to bear.

Officially you recognise today that human beings should not be bought and sold. Unofficially, even in the civilised Western World, you still do it, but more subtly. The price is not openly displayed but the thought-form is there. You all know what I am talking about when I say that. Humanity today lives by buying and selling. Money is still, apparently, a source of power in the Western World. Those that are rich have what they want. Those that are poor do not. But I, however, would like to put it another way. I would say that those who are rich in spirit have what they need and those that are poor do not, and rich in spirit is *not* the same as rich in wealth. Any being who is rich in the knowledge and diversity of spirit can attract to itself everything that it needs for its evolutionary cycle. The nature of the spirit is that it will only draw to itself what it needs. There is the Law of Attraction and Repulsion which exists on every level of the Cosmos. In just the same way, a precious stone which you need will come to you. Indeed I would say this: that in ninety-nine per cent of the cases a stone that is given to you is nearly always of greater value than one which you buy for yourself, for the stone that is given to you has come to you freely, as a gift of love, whereas the stone that you buy is probably the result of a desire that you have created, something which you think you need. So the buying and selling of stones is a human weakness just as is the buying and selling of anything.

Q:   Could you say something about wearing stones as jewelry?
ZT:   Think about the stones that you wear very carefully. Meditate on them. See if you really need them and should have them. Do not think in terms of value and money. Feel whether the stones which you have and which you wear are meant for you. Having said that, I will also say that there are times of the year, even times of the month, when you would wish to wear one stone and not another. I would also say to you that if you have not worn a stone for over a year, then you should part with it.

Q:   Is it wrong to dig for precious stones deep down in the Earth? In parts of Australia, for example, they are laying waste vast areas in search of opals.
ZT:   The way in which Humanity digs and mines for precious stones is most wrong. Mother Earth gives to Humanity the stones that it *needs*. In the upheavals of the strata of the Earth, as that which was formerly underground comes to the surface, so stones are revealed for the use of Humanity. It is right for Humanity to search for these stones and to use them, but to dig deep down into the bowels of the Earth, to disintegrate layer upon layer of stone, to rip up from the Earth what Humanity greeds, not what is needs, is creating karma with the Mineral Kingdom for generations to come.

Q:   We also do that with coal and oil. Is it wrong to use them too?
ZT:   Coal and oil are, of course, part of the divinity of the Mineral Kingdom. They too have a pattern of evolution. It just happens that at this particular time in human evolution they represent an available source of energy, but there is no need for Humanity to use those minerals. There are other more natural and beneficial forms of energy available. What has happened is that because Humanity's spiritual knowledge has not kept pace with its material knowledge it has travelled along a limited path and so alternative sources of energy have not been discovered. But Humanity needs coal and oil to progress and therefore the Goddess

155

has allowed these forms of energy to be used by Humanity to further its evolutionary cycle. But the time is coming when that source of energy will be denied, not only in the sense that there will be no more stocks available but because of the damage which is being done to the atmosphere by the use of such fuel. This fact will be recognised by Humanity and another source of energy will then be discovered and employed.

Q: This leads on to nuclear energy. Is it right for Humanity to play around with this energy and to use it as a source of power?
ZT: The present advance in nuclear technology is a complete aberration. Of course the energy which is present within the molecules of matter, the energy of the sun, can be tapped and used, but the way in which the atom has been split and the energy used has produced disastrous side effects, disastrous not only for Humanity but also for the other Kingdoms of Matter. The time is rapidly approaching when Humanity will bitterly regret the use it has made of nuclear energy and nuclear fuels. This development is, so to speak, leading into a dead-end, literally, and will rapidly be recognised as such.

Q: From what you are saying it seems that we, as human beings, are very much out of tune with the correct use of the Animal, the Vegetable and the Mineral Kingdoms. It is most disheartening for me to think that even when I am trying to do my best I am constantly exploiting these Kingdoms. Yet there is only so much that I as an individual can do. It leaves me with a feeling of semi-despair that I am so way-off. How can there be any validity in what I do?
ZT: Perhaps it would be relevant to make a little analogy. Let us consider the example of a small child. Within that being there can be a very evolved soul, a soul of great wisdom and power, yet as it walks around the garden what greater pleasure can it have than pulling off the heads of flowers! That action does not relate to the true nature of its being. One day, however, it will grow up and the true nature of its being will control its physical body and it will realise what it is doing. It is the same for Humankind. Now I am not saying that all of you are children, because you are not. Some of you have grown up a good bit to become precocious teenagers!

It was allowed for in the evolutionary plan of the Earth that Humanity would make these errors. It was recognised as a necessary path of human evolution. Therefore do not feel despair. If Mother Earth did not want you to take of these sacrifices she would not permit it. The essential thing at this time is that those of you who have the consciousness set an example and through your understanding seek a new relationship. Now this is not something that is going to be established overnight, but even a change of attitude, even a recognition that everything that is around you is divine, is of the God-head, has a consciousness, has a meaning and a purpose separate to yours, is a beginning. I talk to you now in the knowledge that what I say will not bring about sudden change. Perhaps in ten years a part of you will respond to what I have said and in the gradual unfoldment of your spiritual being there will come an understanding of the correct relationship. All that I can do is to hold a mirror to your soul that the soul may bring forth what is within it.

Even the most simple soul can co-operate with Nature by listening to her. Even the most simple soul can understand the correct use of the Mineral Kingdom. When you pick up stones and place them around your garden you do not know why you have done it, but you have done it. When you plant a certain flower here, a certain vegetable there, you do not know why you have done it, but you have done it. The force of the Goddess flows through you all. To become more aware is not a conscious intellectual training process. It is the opening of the intuitive channel that will reveal the love and the wisdom of the Goddess in all her beauty.

The Earth is here to share with you. You know in your heart of hearts when you abuse that trust. You know when you are doing wrong. All you need to be concerned about is yourself. Others may do whatever they wish. You are accountable only for yourself and if you, through your love, create a better understanding, if you, through your energy, can grow things that other people cannot then you will change the World. Begin with one small radish. Do not be too ambitious! One small radish grown without chemical fertiliser is worth a whole field of potatoes fertilised wrongly.

Q:   Can you say anything about extra-terrestrial rocks, rocks that are not of Mother Earth?
ZT:   Just as the people who walk this Earth are not all human beings, there are some from other planets, so it is with the rocks. Rocks that come to the Earth obviously carry with them the

thought-forms, the energy, the vibration of the planets from which they have come. The effect of such rocks is to modulate the effect of the energies present on the Earth and to create a certain distinct pattern, to provide an energy form which will help the Earth's evolutionary cycle. Is it not strange that when they brought back the pieces of moon-rock and the scientists examined them they could find nothing spectacular about them? How disappointing to have spent so much money on bringing back such uninteresting pieces of rock! Of course they were looking on the wrong level. They did not measure the energy. They did not even think of the consciousness. Outwardly all rocks may look alike, but then so do human beings. It is only when you look within to the subtle levels that you realise the uniqueness of everything that is. There will be many more rocks coming to Earth in the not too distant future.

Q: Many people today wear diamond rings. It seems every woman's ambition is to own a diamond ring. Is there a spiritual purpose behind this?
ZT: Most people today buy diamonds and wear diamond rings without even being aware of what they are doing. They do not think of where the diamond came from, of the energy it attracts and of how that energy will affect them. A stone is like a radio receiver and as such receives not only the energy of the Goddess, its Creator, but also the energy, the thought forms of Humanity, both good and evil. If you have a stone, curse it and give it to someone, you can affect that person's life.

Q: Is that true of all stones, of all the gems?
ZT: Yes, it is true of all the precious stones and crystals, especially those that are found deep in the earth. Humanity should only use the stones that are near the surface of the earth. You should recognise that the Earth's surface is not as fixed as you would believe. The Earth's crust is constantly moving. The land which is necessary for a particular Age is brought to the surface and with it are the stones necessary for Humanity's path during that particular evolutionary cycle, be it ten or twenty thousand years. Thus the land of Atlantis was prepared for the Atlanteans and when their Age came to an end the land was removed and new land came up to the surface for the next Age. So the land which you have to work with is the land that is appropriate to your particular point of

consciousness, the lessons that you have to learn in this cycle. Very often, by digging down deeply into the ground you are tapping into past civilisations, past karma and past power which perhaps Humanity is not yet quite ready to handle. One should always handle precious stones with great awareness. Their primary function is to receive cosmic energy and balance the Earth. They are like the jewels in a watch. So when you wear a stone on your hand be aware that you are receiving a specific cosmic energy and that you are affected by it. In the days of old only the priests and initiates would have earned the right to wear certain stones. These were treated with respect and reverence and only worn after a ceremony of invocation and blessing. I would ask you to treat your stones in a similar fashion.

# THE TEST OF MONEY

You live in a World in which money has become God, a World in which the pursuit of money has for the most part replaced the pursuit of life, a World where the Animal, Vegetable and Mineral Kingdoms are happily sacrificed for a short-term financial gain, a World where Humanity sacrifices even its health, its individual well-being, in order to achieve the accumulation of money. But what is the real nature of money? Why has money become so important in the World today and why does the Western World, in particular, think that if it can acquire more money its problems will be over? Why do you as individuals think that money is the answer to most of your problems. Why do you believe that if you had more money your life would be happier? Why do you continue to support these illusions when in your innermost beings you know that they are not true?

Let us consider the lives of the great Masters. Not only did they not incarnate into positions of power and money but they had no need of money during their physical lives whatsoever. That is the true mark of a Master, for when you have attained that degree of Mastery and can control and manifest physical energy you do not need money. Money, therefore, is merely a substitute for spiritual energy. That surely is the test to be applied to those who would call themselves spiritual teachers today. The mark of a true spiritual teacher is that they do not charge money for the gift of their being. So when you encounter those who must charge, those who offer their divine talents on a monetary basis, recognise that there is a weakness, an understanding of life that has yet to be mastered. The really great Masters, like Jesus and the Buddha, never charged for their services for they did not need to. They understood the laws of manifestation and could attract to themselves everything that they needed for their destinies. That is your birthright as well.

161

Money is spiritual energy and as such is an energy that you have to handle when you incarnate on the physical plane of life. Money is a test, a test to be faced and mastered. Recognise it as a necessary test placed there by your Creator. The test of money is quite simple. You are to be the master of it. Money is not to be the master of you. How do you begin to understand the real nature of money? Simply by recognising that the form is not the reality. Money is only the form of an energy. Look at the example of your own physical being. You are aware of your form but you are also aware that there is a spiritual energy behind that form. This energy was there before birth and lives on after death. It created the physical body in which you now dwell. Energy manifests form. Before all form there is energy. Because you live on the physical plane of Earth naturally you are concerned with physical form. One of your major lessons is to learn to handle form, to be the master of form in its many aspects, but to understand the form you must always go back to the energy.

The essence of money is energy. When you use money you are handling energy, if not your energy then someone else's energy, for someone has given of themselves, of their spiritual energy, at some time, to create that money, to create that energy. So if money is spiritual energy you can now recognise that how you handle that money is of great karmic importance for, ultimately, you are handling the energy of your Creator. To have too much money is just the same as having too little. Both will adversely affect your destiny. Is it not true to say that someone who has a great deal of energy but does not share it, a miser, is just as miser-able or miserable as someone who has too little energy, who has not realised that money is a spiritual energy and as such can be manifested by simply asking the Creator that one's needs be met? The essence of handling money correctly in your World today, as in all things, is balance.

There is this tendency, especially amongst some young people in the Western World today, to avoid facing the tests of physical life, to run away from them. Because they have seen some of the evils resulting from the misuse of money they say that they will have nothing to do with money and will live without it. That is only possible if they are Masters, if they can manifest everything that they need for their destinies but, alas, few of them can do that. Everyone has to face the test of money, has to learn to handle

162

money correctly on both the form and the energy level. You have to learn to handle money correctly in relationship with your fellow human beings, your local government, your country, the World, for money belongs to the whole World and if you have too much of it, as does the Western World today, then other parts of the World will be too short for Humanity can create and manifest only so much energy. Only so much energy is available for the evolutionary process.

The basis of all monetary exchange is balance, is giving and taking equally. There have, of course, been civilisations where money was not used, where barter was the order of the day. Other forms of energy exchange have also been practised, especially amongst people more community minded than yourselves. It is a fact that a Druid would lend money expecting repayment in his next life, such was his belief in reincarnation! The principle involved in either barter or money exchange is that of striving to balance the flow of energy. You must give as much as you receive. That is the Divine Law. If you manifest spiritual energy for yourself then you must give back of your own energy an amount equal to that which you have manifested. If the scales are not balanced, if the energy flows are not equal, then you create karma for yourselves.

Many people today create wealth at the expense of their fellow human beings or the three other Kingdoms of Matter. In many countries I can see your less evolved brothers and sisters being treated as slaves, I can see thousands of years of mineral and vegetable evolution being sacrificed for an apparent short term financial gain. Humanity must realise that to hold the Earth in balance it must give back to the Earth just as much energy as it takes. What Humanity takes from the Goddess it must return to her with its love, with its creative energy, with its worship. Nothing should be taken from the Earth without something being returned and that which is taken should be shared equally amongst all Humanity for spiritual energy is not yours to hold, only to use in pursuance of your evolutionary cycle.

In the society in which you live today you need money just to live. That reflects the nature of your civilisation. Many of you can recognise the limitations of such a system. Some of you are seeking to change it through right action and right demonstration according to the inspiration of your consciousness. Others are simply refusing to support it. Nevertheless, as the Nazarene said, you must

163

render unto Caesar that which is Caesar's. The government of your country, the governments of the World, require that part of your energy be given to them in the form of money in order to help the whole. That is the basis of taxation. Trade all over the World is achieved through the exchange of money. Today, even aid is usually given by a gift or a loan of money. That reflects the nature of Humanity's point of consciousness at this time. It is not the correct way. I have spoken at another time on the financial aspects of charity as it exists today and have pointed out that for the most part such money is often given with totally wrong motivation. Once more I say that unless money is given with correct motivation, unless the energy is positively directed, it will achieve no good purpose. Money created through negative energy is worthless. If people create their money, for example, through the sale of drugs or through the abuse of the other Kingdoms of Matter, whilst outwardly they might appear to have the wealth which society envies, in reality their lives are doomed for they are amassing wrong energy which ultimately will lead to their downfall.

As you earn money always be conscious of your motivation for doing so. Recognise yourselves as beings of spirit. Recognise that the form of which you are so familiar is but an expression of that spirit. Recognise that money is spiritual energy. It is not wrong to have money. It is not wrong to earn money. It is indeed very often the destiny of some people to acquire great sums of money. Usually the lessons of wealth are associated with younger souls as they reach a certain degree of spiritual understanding. Recognise that wealth is always associated with destiny, it never happens by chance. People always accumulate wealth for a reason and sometimes the test of money is not for themselves but for their children or their children's children.

When you look at the lives of people who suddenly obtain large sums of money either through lotteries or games of chance you see there encapsulated the problems of wealth. For it is not by chance that such people win money. It is an act of destiny presenting them with a lesson they have to learn. Sometimes such money destroys their lives. Although in the short term they might appear to be happy and to have no problems in life, unless their understanding is correct misery soon sets in. The lesson of wealth is a difficult lesson to learn and all of you that have comparatively little money may thank the Lord that in this incarnation that is not your destiny, for to be responsible for the handling of large sums of money is a very testing destiny. That is the meaning behind the story in the Bible of the tests given to the Master Jesus after his forty days in the wilderness, when the Devil promised Jesus temporal power if he would but bow down and worship him. Money is the greatest of all temptations: to use the energy of your Creator for physical form power.

Therefore use the money, the spiritual energy, given to you by your Creator wisely. Recognise that the money that comes to you is the money that you have manifested. If you think that you need more money then go quietly within yourself and in your meditations see if your needs are real. If they are, then in all honesty you can manifest that money simply by stating your needs and asking your Creator to meet them. The money will come to you, perhaps not in the way that you desire, perhaps not in the form that you expect, but your needs will be met. Remember that although God works through people your needs are met by God, not by people. It is by appealing to the Godhead that physical form is balanced.

Recognise money as a test. Every time you handle it bless and transmute it, for whatever evil is in that money can be transmuted by correctly motivated energy. Every note that you bless, every note that you mark with the balanced cross and send forth with your love, is a messenger of your Creator. That is one of your purposes in life: to transmute the energy of money. Money is not evil. It is the use that Humanity makes of it that is evil. When Humanity places money before its God, when Humanity places money before the three other Kingdoms of Matter, then you know that devastation will surely follow for your Creator will not long permit Humanity to worship Mammon.


## QUESTIONS AND ANSWERS


Q: One of the things I have always been confused about is the charging of money for spiritual gifts, for example like healing or channelling. Is it correct to charge and, if so, how do you decide when, and when not, to charge?

ZT: I think it was clearly stated that until you are a Master and have achieved that level of mastery when you can manifest all your needs on the physical plane of life that a major part of the lesson of life is learning to balance what you call spirituality and money. There will always be some who feel that they need to charge for their spiritual services if only because that viewpoint simply reflects their own point of consciousness. From their evolutionary standpoint it seems right that they should charge. That is a lesson of life that they are learning and they should not be criticised for that. However you should also recognise that it is very easy for a charismatic spiritual teacher who can touch the hearts of people to earn a great deal of money and for you to equate that money with success. So there is a lesson to be learnt in charging only a fair amount, in charging perhaps just enough to cover one's costs. All of you are at different evolutionary levels learning different lessons. Each one of you has to learn to handle money according to your own consciousness.

Q: I know of groups that charge quite a lot of money for their spiritual services and they appear to be growing and becoming very successful. So can you say that that is wrong?

ZT: It is not for me to say what is right or what is wrong. You must decide for yourselves basing your decision on your understanding of life, on the teachings that have been given to you, on the example of the great Masters. You know, for example, that Jesus or Buddha had no need to charge. They could manifest physical form as they desired. They could create at will. If they had wanted a car, for example, then they would have created a car, in an instant, in front of them. That was the nature of their power. If they had needed money then they would have created the money right in their hands. But most people on Earth are still on the path to becoming Masters, with many lessons to learn, one of them being how to handle money. Money is a great temptation because of the power that goes with it. That was why the Master Jesus had to face that temptation. If you are a great soul then because of your magnetic quality it is relatively easy to touch the hearts of simple people, to inspire them and to make money out of them. That is one of the great tests of Mastery. Everyone, at their own level, must do as they feel right. They can either give freely or make a charge. They can either make a fair charge or an excessive charge. They can either earn a great deal of money or a little money. It is up to the individual to decide according to his or her point of consciousness.

166

Q: Is it true that spiritual teachers lose some of their powers if they do charge?

ZT: Shall I just say that the powers which they have, or think that they have, can be diminished by their example and demonstration. You cannot lose what is rightfully yours, what you have earned over many lives. Many teachers, of course, profess to have certain mystical powers which they do not really possess and it is only the support of their followers that sustains their powers. When people recognise the illusion their power goes. The powers of a true Master, like the Master Jesus, are beyond your comprehension. The power to destroy a whole civilisation at the invocation of a single word cannot be placed in the hands of initiates. Such power is only granted after thousands of lives of testing and tempering in the fire of life on Earth.

May I give you the analogy of a baker. If your baker was a great Master he would make his bread every morning by manifesting all the ingredients, imbuing the bread with his love and power and then offering the bread, free of charge, to all those who wanted it. His customers would get the maximum benefit possible from this wonderful bread. Now if a divine baker is not present, is it not desirable to have a normal baker around who makes his bread to the best of his ability and then charges for his service? At least the people are getting bread. You would all like to use divine bakers but it is not always possible!

Q: Using your analogy, at one stage would not a divine baker have had to charge for his bread and his services?

ZT: Yes. Before you became a divine baker you would have had to have been a normal baker for many, many lives. You have to accumulate knowledge and wisdom through the understanding of physical life. The Masters such as Jesus have experienced many cycles of evolution to reach their points of understanding and consciousness so that they can handle matter spiritually and correctly with the purest of motivation.

Q: Supposing a person decides he wants to be a healer. So he gives up his regular work and says "Now I am a healer I must charge because I do not have another way of earning my living." Would it not be better for that person to carry on working and to be a healer in their spare time and so not have to charge for being a healer?

ZT: We all have to begin somewhere. Inevitably we will make mistakes as we walk the path to Mastership. It is a beginning just to wish to be of service, to be a healer, even if the person charges for it. The World today would be a better place if more people were trying to be of service to each other.

Q: With most people today the biggest problem is an economic one so far as living is concerned. It does not seem wrong to me for a person gifted with healing to charge in just the same way that a person who has the gift of carpentry or some other skill does. If I had to take a full time job in order to exercise my healing gift then I would only be able to do it part time as compared to being able to do it full time because I am charging.

ZT: If we consider the ideal, to which we are all striving, to be the masters of energy and form, then no matter how noble your motives are to be of service you must recognise that in essence you are limiting yourself, you are limiting your own potential and growth by charging for the healing power that comes through you, because that energy is given *freely* to you. You heal by virtue of a Divine Force which does not charge you for the use of that energy. You are, therefore, using a freely given energy and then charging for it. Your motivation may be of the highest, but that is what you are doing. Recognise that you should freely channel the energy that is so freely given to you and give of your being to the whole of Humanity regardless of any monetary considerations. Look at the example of Nature and see how the three Kingdoms of Matter give freely to Humanity. Look at the example of the great Masters who would never charge because they would see that as a limitation on the energy. Unfortunately what you price you limit, and that which comes from the Creator is beyond limit.

Q: Is it a question, then, of balancing your life between your consciousness and the service that you can render?
ZT: Yes, I would agree with that.

Q: Is it not a fact, though, that a great many people have to pay money for something before they really place any value on it, no matter whether it be a learning process or a material object?
ZT: I would not agree with that. I believe, as I was saying before, that if you have to pay so much money for something, then that is

168

the value that you place upon it. If you pay four hundred pounds for a ring then that is the value that you place on that ring. But if someone in an act of love gives you a ring, then that ring is beyond value. You would not exchange it for a hundred times its value. It is priceless, it is limitless, and the joy that that ring will give you far surpasses any monetary value because it represents a flow of cosmic energy. You limit cosmic energy by placing values on material things. Of course I recognise that you need prices and values for the purpose of trade or barter but this procedure cannot be applied to the acquiring of cosmic consciousness. You cannot obtain enlightenment by paying large sums of money. The link to your Creator, the source of all consciousness, lies within you and there are no restrictions placed on its use except those that you choose to impose.

Q: You talk of young and old souls. What do you mean by that?
ZT: There is an immense range of soul evolution present on the Earth which ranges from a simple mongoloid child incarnating on the Earth for the first time to a Master such as you follow, Sai Baba. Between those two extremes of consciousness lie millions and millions of unique points of soul evolution. To say young or old is really misleading, but it is the terminology which I use to differentiate between soul evolution and the nature of the lessons in consciousness which a mongoloid child or a Sai Baba have come to learn. They are both manifesting different aspects of consciousness and will serve the World in different ways. So I use the terms young and old not as a measurement, not as a comparison, but merely to express the difference between what is expected of evolved and unevolved souls. We of the Spiritual Hierarchy speak to evolved souls because we desire them to bring forth from within their being the great wisdom which they possess and to manifest it on the Earth for all to see.

I will leave you with this thought. You have two popular sayings in your World: 'The important things in life cannot be bought with money' and 'You cannot take it with you when you go'. Both are simple statements of fact. Why does Humanity choose to ignore them? Perhaps you should consider what you will take with you when you do go!

# CHILDREN: THE SEEDS OF CREATION

You live in a world in which Humanity rarely lives in the moment. For the most part Humanity lives in its dreams, its desires, its memories, projecting itself either back into the past or forward into the future — more often into the future because that is more illusory than the past. At this time of great disharmony and imbalance in the World, as Humanity proceeds on its apocalyptic path, it is quite understandable as to why Humanity should do this, for what better way is there of avoiding the reality of the present than by going forward or backward in time.

Humanity has not yet realised that by avoiding the present, by avoiding the responsibility of the moment it is sowing the seeds of its own destruction. It has not yet recognised that the future of this planet rests in the hands of today's children. It is only by right upbringing, right education, right environment, right guardianship of its children that Humanity will create a balanced and harmonious future. For Humanity to ignore the needs of its children, to place them second in importance and to live only for itself, to concentrate its energies on obtaining financial or material prosperity for itself, to seek to fulfil its physical desires, is to ignore the reality of life, for without balanced children there will be no future, there will be no world, there will be no evolutionary life-stream.

Children are the seeds of creation. They represent the birth of Creation Itself, the Divine Breath. They are the gift of our Creator, the promise of our Creator, to further life and the evolutionary cycle of this planet. Without children there is no life, there is no purpose. They are, therefore, the supreme beings of the species of Humanity. Children *are* more important than adults, for it is the children who dictate the evolutionary future of the Earth. It is therefore imperative, if the future of Humanity is to be assured, if the evolutionary cycle is to continue, that the children of today are

171

made aware of their responsibilities, of their divine heritage and of the path upon which this world is now set.

Hand in hand with children comes their education. I have spoken of this at another time and I do not wish to repeat what I have said, but it is obvious that the education of a child is the most important aspect of parenthood. Education is two-fold. It consists of the training of the intellect and the training of the intuition. You live in a world which is born of intellect, believes only in intellect and ignores intuition. Most children therefore reflect that point of understanding, but it is imperative that the children of the New Age are educated intuitively as well as intellectually. Obviously you must strive to discipline and to train children's intellects, to make them aware of the physical reality of life and of all that Humanity has created, but equally so you must balance that with the training of their intuitive forces to help them to ground the inspiration of the higher levels and to tap into their birthright, the energy stream of human consciousness. Children, therefore, must have a balanced education. They must also have a balanced upbringing if they themselves are to become balanced adults. To create imbalanced children is to perpetuate the imbalance in Humanity today and accelerate the course on which Humanity is now set.

That you sit here today is because of the sacrifice of your parents. You were children once just like your own children are today. Recognise that the consciousness which you possess today you also possessed as a child. You have evolved little in consciousness during the years that you have been on Earth. So within every child is the adult. A child is adult in consciousness if immature in physical manifestation. Once the soul is fully in the body, by the age of twelve, a child has the consciousness, the spiritual understanding of life that you, as an adult, possess today. Of course that consciousness has to be grounded, it has to be manifested through its intuitive channel, but it is there. The child is as wise as the parent. The child is as all-seeing as the parent. The child knows its destiny and, what is more, the child knows the destiny of the World beyond your understanding for your understanding is limited to your lifetime. You incarnated on the Earth with the talents that you needed for your lifetime, for your destiny. You know little, if anything, of the destiny of the Earth beyond your moment of death: but your children do. They therefore come equipped for a different World, for a different destiny. So to make your children conform to your way of life, to your point of consciousness, to make them follow your destiny, is to restrict them, is to deny the very reason why they are here: to change Humanity, to be the seeds of a new race of Humanity on Earth.

Children must be free. They must be free to grow as they wish, free to experience every single concept that comes into their lives. The more that they experience the greater will be their understanding of life. All the parents have to do is to be the guardians of that soul, to create its physical body, to nurture it as the child grows to adulthood, to teach it of the physical nature of planet Earth, to help it to reach an understanding of its environment, of the nature of physical life, and then to release it in freedom to fly wheresoever it wishes, to be what its Creator intended it to be: a unique aspect of the Universe. The greatest crime that anyone can commit is to limit the consciousness of a child, is to impose upon it the discipline of the parent, the discipline of society, the discipline of religion, the discipline of the Earth. Now that is not to say that a child does not need discipline. It does, as you are well aware, but the purpose of discipline is not to restrict, it is to expand. Discipline is responsibility. Self-discipline is self-responsibility. You are educating a child to be responsible first for its body, then for its mind and finally for its spirit, to accept that divine responsibility and then to go forth and exercise it for itself.

Remember that the child chose you to be its parents. It chose you perhaps even before you yourselves incarnated on Earth. This is almost always the case where evolved souls are concerned. They choose whom they are to marry before they even incarnate on the Earth and so offer to be a vehicle through which important souls can come in order to fulfil the Divine Plan on Earth. Even if this is not the case, even if the conception of a child was not destined, if it was an act of lust, an act of desire, an act of personal gratification, then that unborn child still chose those parents as its physical guardians. That is the nature of the responsibility of parenthood. You are the guardians of that divine spark of spirit until it can be responsible for itself.

A child chooses its parents both for the vibratory level of their souls and for the physical attributes which they have manifested on the plane of Earth. It takes from the bodies of both the parents, from their genealogy, as you would say, to create for itself from the multitude of genes available the physical body that it requires for its life on Earth. Only a small fraction of the spirit is grounded in that body at first, but as the child progresses through the first evolutionary cycle of ten years so the degree of spirit, the soul content, gradually increases until by the age of twelve the soul is completely in the body. Once the first cycle has been completed the child is then committed to the plane of Earth. It has decided on a higher level to fulfil its destiny. It has decided that the physical factors of which it has need are present and that its destiny can be fulfilled, with purpose, according to the Divine Plan. For a child that dies before the age of twelve it is very often the case of the spirit withdrawing because the conditions that it desires have not been met.

After the age of twelve, when the spirit is fully in the body, a child has the capability and is the equal in spiritual qualities, in spiritual understanding, of an adult. Indeed a child can be more spiritually mature than a person of sixty if its soul understanding, its soul consciousness, is the greater. Even if you cannot see it, that soul consciousness is there. It may not manifest, it may not be present on a day to day level simply because a challenge has not been put to it. A prime function of parenthood, therefore, is to challenge the child, is to help to bring out its consciousness, its soul knowledge and wisdom, is to encourage it to manifest these qualities in its physical reality.

The child that evolves the most is the one that is presented with the most challenges, who sees clearly the true nature of physical life at every level, who understands the evolutionary patterns of the four Kingdoms of Matter, who is aware of the reality of life and death, who knows of the Divine through what it has experienced itself, not through what has been drummed into it by its parents and teachers. It is rare for a parent to know the destiny of its child. It is rare for a parent to know a child's vocation and the path that it will take. It is rare for a parent to know a child's destined partner in marriage. All this the child must discover for itself, in freedom, and if the mind of the child is encumbered by the burdens of the parents it will find that a hard thing to do. The greatest gift that you can give a child is the gift of freedom, to be itself; to be itself physically, mentally and spiritually.

Nevertheless, a child chooses its parents because it knows their points of consciousness and recognises the spiritual content of their beings. It wishes to share with them, to learn from them, to be

174

subject to their soul discipline. It is essential, therefore, that it is always the parent's soul which disciplines the child, never the personality. It is the soul which must be the guardian of the child. Any time you discipline a child ensure in your meditation that it is the soul which guides you and not your personality reaction, otherwise you will be perpetuating the present cycle of Humanity, you will be merely walking further down the path upon which Humanity is now set, the path which will ultimately lead to its own destruction.

If you want your child to survive the challenges that are to come it must be free. It must know itself. It must have its intuitive channel open. It must have been trained to discover for itself. Education must be an act of self-motivation, of self-discovery; it cannot be imposed from above. The primary tool of education is encouragement, encouragement for the child to seek, to discover for itself, to find more in life than the parents have discovered. It is inevitable, because of the evolutionary process, that a child will discover more of life than its parents and the sooner that stage is reached the greater the joy for its parents. There is indeed no greater joy for parents than to stand alongside their own child and to recognise that that child has surpassed them, indeed, can now give to them, can help them to see their own destiny more clearly, can lead them to a greater understanding of life.

It is obviously essential that two-way communication between parent and child is ever present. The channel must always be open. That sacred union must never be broken, for where there is no communication, no contact, then there can be no physical exchange, no physical discipline and no physical encouragement. Contact and communication are the essence. There must be contact and communciation between the parent and the child on both physical, mental and spiritual levels. The stronger the contact, the stronger the communication, the quicker the child will evolve and grow to adulthood. A child that has not had this contact can reach the age of sixty and still not have come to maturity. That fact can only be blamed on the parents.

Parents are the key to a child's evolution. That is their sole responsibility above all else, above even their own spiritual destiny. For to betray the sacred duty of parenthood, to ignore the education and up-bringing of a child, is to deny the future, is to deny Creation, is to deny the very purpose of one's being. No matter what one's hopes, no matter what one's ideals, if one fails that child, one is failing not just oneself but the whole of Creation. No great spiritual or evolutionary leap forward will ever come about through the sacrifice of a child. Parents must fulfil their divine responsibility to their child and release it on the path of life with its highest potential manifested, and from that sacrifice will come a surge of consciousness which will then advance the parents along their own path of spiritual progression.

What is a child but a gift of God. It is the seed of God coming to Earth with God's latest purpose, with God's latest design for the Earth. A child represents the future. It represents the World to which you yourself as a child will subsequently return. Deny your child, therefore, and you are denying yourself, for you are denying the World into which you yourself will eventually incarnate. Fail your child and you are failing not just the World but your Creator as well, for you are abusing the gift of creation, the highest gift that your Creator can bestow upon you. Self-reproduction, the creation of a child, is a divine gift. It is a gift not given to all forms of life. It is a gift not given to every being in our planetary system. The Human Race has been uniquely honoured by this gift. It requires the exercise of spiritual consciousness to be truly responsible for that gift.

I therefore invite you to consider the child in its true light: a divine messenger, a messenger not only to you, the parents, but to the whole World. A child carries the message of your Creator to the World. A child represents your Creator sowing the seeds of Creation. The future of your World, the future of this planet, the future of this planetary system lies in its children. The greatest gift that you as a soul can give to the Earth is to lovingly lead your child forward into manhood or womanhood, bringing out the highest of its divine capabilities, so that it may become a Christed one and change this World. But if, as so many do today, you live your lives in selfishness, always placing yourself before your child, always concerned with your own life, your own future, your own thoughts, your own needs, before those of your child, then that child will not receive of the highest.

Parenthood is a divine responsibility. It should not be taken on by everyone. The World is in the state that it is today because so many have taken on the burden of parenthood who are not yet ready to discharge it. The greatest karma you can create on this Earth is to accept the burden of parenthood and fail in it, for you

176

set in motion a chain of karma which will survive for generations to come, which will require many lives to discharge and transmute. For in that your child is imbalanced it will become an imbalanced adult and will, in all probability, itself create imbalanced children, and so the process goes on for generation after generation. You are responsible for that even until the final Day of Judgement.

I ask you, therefore, to recognise the responsibility of parenthood. Recognise that you are vitally concerned with creation. It is not a plaything. Children are the very seeds of Creation and the most priceless thing that you can do is to nurture those seeds, to plant them in fertile ground, to let them come forth and reveal a New World, a New Cosmos, a new aspect of our Creator. It must be your children first, your own life second. There can be no greater sacrifice than that you lay down your life for your child. Your Creator very rarely asks you to sacrifice your physical life, only certain aspects of your material being.

## QUESTIONS AND ANSWERS

Q: Can you tell us about children who are born with tremendous physical or mental handicaps. What is the purpose of that?
ZT: The first thing of which you must be aware is that what you call a handicap is only a physical handicap. There is no handicap of the spirit. The spirit of a handicapped child can be just as evolved as a child that is whole. Physical restrictions are a lesson for the spirit to understand and to come to terms with. You would then ask me "Why should there be such handicaps? If our God is a God of Love, how can that God permit children to come into the World deformed?" The answer is simple. It is because it is the parents who are creating. It is the physical behaviour, the thought forms, the spiritual consciousness of the parents that affect the nature of a child's physical body. It would be true to say that in almost every pregnancy a child is perfect at conception. Any deformity which is present usually takes place after conception and is entirely the result of the parents' actions, of the way they behave in thought, word and deed, of the way they lead their lives, of the way they treat their physical bodies and of their own points of consciousness. Only on very rare occasions does the spirit choose to come down

177

into physical manifestation with a deformity and that is when it has a very specific lesson to learn, a lesson which it has not learnt over many lives.

Consider the effect on the spirit of being in a deformed body, of being unable to express oneself fully on the physical level, even though one has consciousness and understanding. It is a demanding lesson with which to have to come to terms, for right from birth you are different from other people. You cannot live as other people. You cannot experience life as other people. You are always the one that is separate in a crowd. You are the one that is abnormal. You are constantly being reminded of your physical body and its imperfection. But the lesson of deformity is not just one of physical restraint, it is a far deeper lesson than that. It is a lesson for the spirit. If parents have deformed children I have to say, in love, look to the parents, for that is usually the cause of the deformity. That deformity is the result of wrong creation.

Q: Could it be that, as well as the child learning, maybe the parents had a lesson to learn by having that deformed child?
ZT: In that the parents have created wrongly it is obviously a lesson that they have to learn, but the learning process may take place over many years and may not be fully comprehended until late in life. Wrong creation attracts its own karma and initiates lessons which have to be learnt on many levels.

Q: What about children who are born and then are not wanted by their parents? They are fostered out to various families or put up for adoption. How does that affect them?
ZT: Let us begin by understanding that to deny one's child is to deny one's God. To deny one's responsibility to one's child is to deny one's responsibility to life. For a child to come on the Earth and to be denied that which it chose, the vibration of its parents, is to create the highest karma. However, if a child is denied its birthright, to be with its own parents until the age of twenty one, then inevitably a foster-parent will have to fulfil that role.

The role of a foster-parent is extremely difficult. One's motivation for taking on that role must be of the highest and of the purest. It must be universal and not personal. It must be born of a desire to help all children, not just of having children because one has not got them oneself or because one cannot physically have them. One should not adopt children simply to replace a feeling of emptiness in one's life. One must not adopt children for personal gratification. If one does adopt children with that motivation then great harm is done. Foster parents must exhibit a compassion for all living things. It requires a high point of consciousness to give of oneself to the Universe, to parent a child that is not of one's own seed, not of one's own consciousness, not of one's own destiny, and to give that child the freedom to discover what it was, what it is and what it can be.

It therefore requires great consciousness, great understanding of the purpose of birth and childhood, of the purpose of life and destiny, in order to be a foster parent. It is a task that should not be undertaken lightly. In most cases the reason why people do not have children is that children are not a part of their destiny. They have other work to do. I would therefore always advise that when children are adopted they are adopted by parents who already have children, where the marriage has already been prepared, where the responsibility for children has already been accepted as a part of their destiny, as a part of their evolutionary cycle. To adopt a child, even with the highest motivation, when one's destiny does not include that adoption will inevitably restrict the spiritual growth of one's own being.

Q: You mean it is better to put unwanted children with a family that already has children rather than to put them with a couple who have not got children. Of course the people who have not got children are usually the very ones who want them.

ZT: I know that is often the case. However there is usually a sound spiritual, and therefore a sound physical, reason why a couple cannot have children. You have been told on another occasion that a marriage should not automatically result in children. There are many people producing children today who should not be having them. Reproduction is not the automatic function of every human being. What the World needs is responsible creation. It is irresponsible creation that is destroying this World, for the constant creation of unbalanced children is affecting the destiny of the World. As you witness all the violence amongst the young today, remember that it is attributable not to today's World but to the World over the last twenty years, the World that conceived and nurtured them. What will the children of today's World manifest when they grow to adulthood?

179

Q:   If someone has conceived a child and believes that they have neither the consciousness nor the time and energy to take care of it and they feel it is not right just to have that child and then let it be adopted by someone else, are they not right to have an abortion?

ZT:    Let us fully understand the nature of abortion. Abortion is the ending of physical life. It is the ending of physical life by one being against the wish of another. It is, therefore, though I use an emotive word, murder, and the karma for such an act will have to be paid. It is no good saying that on a physical level one did not wish to create a child. The act of creation takes place because on the higher levels of life one *did* wish to create. It is difficult for you on the physical level to understand, but your thoughts influence creation on the higher levels of life. Indeed, on the higher levels of life thought is creation. The greatest contraceptive in the World, therefore, is thought. If you do not wish to create on a thought level then you will not create on a physical level. So many people today perform the sexual act without thought, without a contraceptive, as you would say in your earthly terms. The result that comes forth, the creativity, is a response from their soul. They have created because they chose to create. They have been blessed with a child because another being, on another level of life, vibrated to their union and agreed to come down to them. That is the nature of creation.

Do you think that your Creator, you God, would destroy your planet because it was inconvenient or not wanted? Is the life that exists on this planet to be got rid of, to be aborted, because a higher being decides it has gone wrong and is no longer wanted? No. The act of creation is an act of love. It implies responsibility and respect for what one has created until the cycle is fully completed and the divine duty discharged. I ask all those who are considering abortion to be aware of what you are doing. You are denying your Creator. You are denying the gift of life. You are denying the future of the World. You are denying the very reason for your being on the plane of Earth. It is a momentous decision to make and anyone who makes it must be fully aware of what is involved. To have that child may be inconvenient. To have that child may place restrictions upon the parents. To have that child may appear to thwart their dreams and their desires, but the conception is the result of a decision taken on a higher level of life. The parents have drawn that spark of life into their being because their point of evolution demanded and chose it. You may deny your destiny at your peril.

180

Q: Some people believe that the spirit does not enter the body until the moment of birth and that when you destroy a foetus you are not really destroying life. What do you say of that?

ZT: That is not correct. The spirit, or a small part of the spirit, is present at the very moment of conception. The amount of spirit present in the foetus gradually increases until at the moment of birth one seventh of the spirit is in the body. If there was no spirit present then there would be no physical body. It is the force of spirit which forms the body, decides on the genetic characteristics it wishes to include and controls the life and destiny of the foetus within the womb. The spirit is the architect that designs and builds the body that it needs for its incarnation. Therefore every foetus is a divine spark of life and, as such, is worthy of respect.

Q: It was said earlier that when disciplining a child you should discipline from the soul, not from the personality. I can understand that, but it is very difficult to do that when you have two strong personalities involved and they clash with each other. How at that point does one listen to one's soul and not react from the personality? Is there any help that you can give us?

ZT: At the very moment of clash between parent and child it is inevitable that it will take place on a personality level. This should be recognised if not by the child then by the parent. But the cause of the clash is not the clash itself. The clash is always the symptom of a deeper problem, a problem which can only be solved through understanding and love. The personality clash is but a manifestation of a lesson which the child has come to learn on a soul level. Therefore it is important that one talks to the child soul to soul. Now this is not possible on a physical level because of the age of the child and its limited point of understanding. Therefore it must take place on a higher level, when you are at prayer or in meditation. It is possible to talk to your child even when your child is asleep. It is possible to talk to your child even when the child is awake and playing. Communication is not only by thought, word and deed. You can communicate with its soul at any time that you wish. The soul is always present, always listening. You can communicate with the soul of the child and make your wishes and understandings clear, and that soul will respond, but so few today attempt this form of communication.

Q: When one parent is particularly violent either towards the other parent or towards the child are you saying that the parents should still stay together and should carry on looking after the child, especially if violence is taking place against the child?

ZT: Physical violence is usually the result of mental imbalance. One has to be mentally imbalanced, mentally sick, to want to use violence upon a child. Obviously, if a person is sick, it is as if they were sick in bed and incapable of looking after the child. So arrangements will have to be made for the child to be looked after in some other way. This is understood and recognised because there is no such thing as perfection on the physical plane of life. There will always be these tests, these obstacles to overcome, the creations of wrong physical living. There is no need to subject anyone, let alone a child, to physical violence. If that does happen in a marriage then that marriage cannot continue. That is not to say it should automatically end in divorce, but that there should be a separation whilst healing and reconciliation take place.

Q: Does that mean that there is no karma involved because you are sick?

ZT: No. The fact that one is sick is of one's own choosing, because of the way in which one has lived one's life. You are responsible for everything that you say and do. Therefore what you do even whilst you are sick and unbalanced is your karma.

Q: There are societies where men have more than one wife and they have many children who are then raised in a community atmosphere. Some of these societies appear to work very well. In the West we have a monogamous situation and live in single families. The stress created by this seems to be causing many marriages to break up. Is there another way of living that would better support marriages in our monogamous situation and prevent so many divorces?

ZT: The reason why so many marriages break up in the Western World today is not, in essence anyway, because of the mode of living. It is because of the values and the understanding of the individuals concerned. The difficulties that occur in most marriages are almost inevitably associated with a lack of consciousness, a lack of understanding of what the individual has invoked by entering into marriage. Today so few people recognise that marriage, let alone having children, is an act of sacrifice. In marriage one is being asked to place one's partner before oneself and to place one's children before one's partner. Unfortunately most people today marry for selfish and self-centred reasons and have children for similar reasons too. That is the way of your world, but remember that a broken home produces a broken child, produces a broken adult, produces a broken planet.

Q:   That is a frightening thing to say when you have a divorce rate of one in four in this country and of one in three in America.
ZT:   You may therefore understand in the light of what has been said how we can indeed approach Armageddon within twenty years from now.

Q:   It seems to me that there can be a very good reason for an abortion, for example, when one is bringing a child into a certain environment which would be very detrimental to it.
ZT:   One of the commandments is "Thou shalt not kill". That has always stood, and will always stand. Life is not yours to take. Life is the gift of your Creator. You would be most unwise to reject what your Creator has given you to fulfil your evolutionary cycle.

Q:   Even so, if a child comes down into a very difficult environment, one in which it is almost impossible for a child to grow up, is it really better off either being in that environment or on the other side of life awaiting another opportunity to incarnate?
ZT:   What you are describing now is the plane of Earth. Would you abort every child that comes on Earth? It is almost impossible today for a child to have a natural upbringing on the plane of Earth. Shall we therefore abort all children, or will not the strength of spirit within those children win through? Spirit is always stronger than the physical body. Spirit will out. Spirit will triumph. Spirit will transform this Earth, but it has to be on this Earth to do it. Some great spirits come in deformed bodies. Some great spirits come in the most tragic of circumstances. That has to be recognised and accepted.

Q:   I have had an abortion. Is there anything that I can do on a spiritual level to transmute the karma for this and to consciously work it out?

ZT: What we are concerned about here is consciousness. If we take not just an abortion but any form of killing, everyone has a reason for carrying out such an act. They can always justify what they have done, whether it be killing in war, slaughtering an animal or aborting a baby. But killing means the termination of life, the termination of consciousness. The very act of taking a physical life creates a great opening for your consciousness. One is constantly examining what one has done, why one has done it. One questions should it have been done and so on and so on. You are thinking about it even to this day. It is through the correct understanding of what you have done that you can then begin to transmute your karma. It is not a question of blame or guilt. One cannot and should not feel guilty for the past or even guilty for the future. One must accept what one has done, understand why it was wrong to do it, and then begin to transmute it. It is very often the case with people who have had an abortion that the same child is still waiting to come down to them and will reappear.

Q: Where does personal responsibility come into this? Who is to blame when children of fourteen or fifteen are involved in the sexual act and create children? Surely these youngsters can hardly recognise whether it is their destiny to have children or not. They have just been seduced by society which says you are supposed to enjoy yourselves in this way.

ZT: The situation in which you find yourselves today is attributable to poor education by the parents and poor education by society. If the parents are strong then children will listen to the parents before society, will respect the parents before society. Nevertheless, society still has an influence and children are educated as much by society as by their parents, but it is the correct relationship of the parents with the child that decides the balance and the influence of society.

What so many parents do today is to ignore their children until they are in their teens and then suddenly expect them to do what they wish, to conform with their ideas of society and life, when there has been no communication, no contact, no love. The time for the parents to establish a correct relationship with their children is in the first cycle. If it is not done then it will never be established. A child comes into your arms as a baby. It looks at you. It loves you from that very first moment. It is receptive to everything that

184

you wish to give it. It looks to you not only as the provider of life, as the provider of all its physical comforts, but as the provider of wisdom, of knowledge and of love. Mummy, tell me. Daddy, tell me. Tell me. Tell me. You are the source of life. You are the source of love. You are the source of understanding. That source should be constantly available until the child is twenty one. If it is not, then inevitably the child will look elsewhere and the parents have only themselves to blame.

Q:   I have always been fascinated by the Arthurian Legends. It seems to me that they are like parables and can apply just as much to our lives today. I always feel that what destroyed Arthur was not so much Guinevere's entanglement with Lancelot as the wrong creation of his son, Mordred, with Morgana. After all, it was Mordred who eventually destroyed him. Would you agree with this?

ZT:   All mythology is the history of Humanity's evolution on the Earth in story or parable form. Although you might regard many of the stories as myths they are all based on archetypes of Humanity and are a valuable source of wisdom for it. I would agree with you in that it was the lack of sexual purity on the part of Arthur and Lancelot, Morgana and Guinevere, that was the seed of destruction for Camelot. Humanity, today, should take heed of this.

# THE SIGNIFICANCE OF HUMAN CONSCIOUSNESS

You live in a world in crisis. This situation exists not just because there is the possibility of global warfare involving the use of nuclear weapons but because your world is in political, financial and ecological crisis and, above all, because it is in spiritual crisis. Many people in the world today have rejected the discipline of religious dogma but have not yet replaced that discipline by self-discipline, by developing their own intuitive understanding of the purpose of life. They have become so caught up in the physical reality of life, in the struggle to exist, especially here in the Western World where life is lived at such a frenetic pace, that they do not have the time to go deeply within themselves to seek the purpose of their being and the purpose of their life on the physical plane of Earth. It is not my intention, indeed, it is not possible for me to tell you the purpose of your physical life. That is for you to discover through your own intuitive channel. What I would like to do, however, is to present to you my understanding of Humanity's consciousness for it is only by changing Humanity's consciousness that you can change the pattern of human behaviour and so save your troubled World.

Nearly all of you live in the shadow of the fear of death. This fear is brought about because you do not understand the purpose of death. If you think about it, if there was no such thing as death, if you did indeed live for ever and never died, if you were in fact like the sailors in the legend of the Flying Dutchman, condemned to live for ever on the plane of Earth, there would soon come a time when you would beg for death, when you would pray to be removed from physical life! If you did but recognise it, then, death really is a saviour. It is for you the means of transition back to a plane of reality from this plane of unreality. Life on the Earth is not reality, it only has the appearance of reality. You dwell for the most part on higher planes of life, on higher planes of

187

consciousness, on planes of reality, and you incarnate on Earth, manifesting aspects of your spirit, in order to join this school of life and partake of its lessons.

A wise man once placed money in its correct perspective by saying that you cannot take it with you when you die. After death money is of no significance whatsoever, and that is also true of all physical matter. When you die you cannot take it with you. You incarnate onto the physical plane of life with spiritual consciousness, and that alone, and when you leave that plane you take nothing with you but that spiritual consciousness. Now that is not to say that there are not some beings who after passing over onto the higher planes of life are still so caught up in the material aspects of life that they are unable to release them. Such people look down on the physical plane of Earth which they have recently left and watch with great concern what is happening to their so called 'possessions', to all the material things they acquired on Earth and have not yet released. They can spend much time watching and waiting when they should be moving on to other planes of living, to other lessons of life. Most people, though, gladly release everything physical at death in just the same way as they release the higher planes at the moment of their physical birth. If you would but recognise it, therefore, the only thing of lasting value to you is your consciousness.

You incarnate onto the physical plane of Earth to evolve your consciousness. That is the sole purpose of your physical incarnation, the reason for you being in this school of life which you call Earth. Now that does not mean that you can ignore the physical reality of Earth. You must be responsible for the physical body in which you dwell, your fellow human beings, the society in which you live, the material possessions which are placed in your guardianship. That is all part of the lesson of physical incarnation: to handle the Earth plane with consciousness. But that is not the total lesson. You must learn to handle your physical reality with responsibility, but you must also learn to ground and manifest your spiritual consciousness. You must learn that your consciousness is a tool for you to use on Earth, a means by which you can express the deep cosmic knowledge which you possess.

In life today, for the most part, you tend to ignore your spiritual consciousness, the wisdom that you have gleaned over many, many, lives on many, many planes of existence. Remember that not only have you lived thousands of lives upon this plane of Earth but you have lived thousands of lives upon many other planes of existence. Life is not just the physical reality of which you are aware. A true understanding of the totality of life is beyond your comprehension at this time because you are limited by the physical body in which you are temporarily dwelling, but released from that body, living on the higher planes of life, you can truly experience cosmic consciousness. You can see the Universal Whole for what it really is: millions upon millions of beings, on many planes of existence, all exhibiting consciousness in the service of the one God of Whom we are all a part, the God in Whom we live, move and have our being.

You incarnate on the plane of Earth to evolve both your consciousness and the group consciousness of Humanity. This is achieved through the practice of right thought, right speech and right behaviour. Recognise that sacrifice, on many levels, plays an important part in your life. Indeed the example of all the great Masters who have come on the plane of Earth is that one has to sacrifice, sometimes even one's life, in order to evolve human consciousness. Recognise that you incarnate to serve: to serve the plane of Earth, your fellow human beings and, above all, this planet, the Goddess, on whom you live for your short lifespan. She has offered you her body as a school of life. Recognise that your own physical body is a part of that Goddess and that you will return it to her at the moment of death. It is a sacred temple, a fitting reflection of the spirit that lives within it. It is truly divine and worthy of your respect, and if you respect your own body then you will surely respect the bodies of other people in everything that you do in thought, word and deed.

Today you celebrate an ancient festival: the festival of Beltane or May-day. There are many in the Western World today who do not celebrate this festival because it is not recognised as a Christian one. But the Christian religion is only one small aspect of the total consciousness of Humanity. Christianity has existed for only centuries whereas the festival of Beltane has been celebrated for milleniums, for it is an Earth festival, a festival which links Humanity to the Earth, to the Goddess. Why do we have, why do we need, such festivals? It is not just to mark the seasons of the year or to bear witness to the dogma of a particular religion, no matter whether it be Christianity, Mohammedism or Buddhism. It is to link Humanity with the Cosmos, to make Humanity aware of its own mortality, of the passage of time, of the brevity of physical reality compared with the eternity of Nature, and of the need to tap into that reality beyond the physical.

We of the Spiritual Hierarchy recognise that the plane of Earth is but one twelfth of the whole. There are eleven other planes of existence which Humanity can experience through its higher bodies. It is your birthright to know of these planes, to witness them and to dwell on them, to be at one with them. That is the birthright of your spiritual consciousness. You incarnate with this knowledge, this reservoir of learning, the experiences of past earthly and cosmic relationships. Why, therefore, when you encounter the conflict of Earth do you surrender to that conflict and become a part of it? Why do you not go within yourselves to seek the aid of the cosmic wisdom that you possess? The World is in crisis because you as individuals are in crisis. The world crisis is but a reflection of your own inner struggles, your own desires, your own weaknesses. If you wish to resolve World crisis you must first resolve personal crisis. This can be done only through consciousness, through an understanding of the true nature of your being and of the God of Whom you are a part. This means going within yourselves. This means listening to your inner wisdom and not to the dogma of others. In quiet moments, such as you are experiencing now, attune to the cosmic forces, to the reality of life, and just for a short time release the unreality, for that is what it is, of physical life.

Shakespeare recognised this when he wrote 'All the World's a stage and all the men and women merely players'. You are indeed actors playing out a cosmic drama. The drama appears real to you for you are in your physical bodies and are personally involved in it, but you must have perspective of that drama and recognise it for what it really is. The drama has a purpose. It is to teach, to evolve your consciousness. Everything that happens on the plane of Earth happens not by chance but because either you as individuals or the World as a whole have drawn it unto yourselves through your behaviour in this or in past lives.

So tap into that spiritual consciousness which you possess and use it. Use it to transform not only yourselves but the World as a whole and by doing that you will be fulfilling your divine potential, for you are one with your Creator. The force of Its love and Its energy flows through you at all times. You are never alone. Your

190

prayers never go unanswered. You are forever attuned to the planes of life beyond your understanding. Recognise the physical reality and serve it, but also recognise the greater picture. Do not be swamped by the little drama that is being played out at this time on the physical stage of life. Hold to your faith. Hold to your consciousness.

## QUESTIONS AND ANSWERS

Q:   Can you tell us about the twelve planes of existence that the first speaker just mentioned?

ZT:   The Creator of our Solar Body, that Being whom you call God, creates on the vibration of twelve. You have, therefore, twelve planets within our Solar System, some of which you still have to discover. Each of these planets supports what we call a plane of life, a plane of existence. If, for example, you were to look at Venus you would say that no life exists on Venus. This is because on Venus life does not exist on the same frequency band that it does on Earth. The vibratory rate of each planet is different and so manifests a different plane of life. It is just the same when you die and leave your physical body. You move onto a higher frequency, into a higher body. You can still move around on the physical plane of life but no one sees you. Remember that there are the angelic and the devic kingdoms operating around you right now, but you cannot see them because they too are operating on a different plane of life, a different frequency.

There are twelve planes or levels of life in our Solar Body and the purpose of your spiritual existence is to achieve Mastery, as the expression goes, on each of those planes of life. The total destiny of your being is to achieve Mastery on all twelve planes. Let us, for example, consider the case of someone like the Master Jesus. He had achieved Mastery on only seven planes of existence. There were five planes on which he still had to learn and evolve. You, at your level of consciousness, are aware only of the seven lower planes which are a part of your physical understanding. The remaining five planes are beyond your comprehension, indeed, are beyond my comprehension even though I dwell on a higher plane than you. So for the time being let us just say that there are seven planes which

191

you have to master, planes which are sometimes called the physical, etheric, astral, emotional, vital, mental and spiritual planes. You live on each of these planes even whilst you are present in your physical body. You face challenges and tests on these planes in just the same way that you face them on the physical plane of life. Each of these planes is a different reality, a different World. You visit them in your sleep state but for the most part you do not remember your visits on your return to physical consciousness.

Q: Is there a final existence, a finish? What is the ultimate life?

ZT: Obviously I can only give you my opinion. My understanding of life, and I talk now not just of physical life but of the essence of life, is that although we have been given individualised consciousness by our Creator, we are all unique, at some time in the future our destiny will be to surrender that consciousness back to the whole, to our Creator, and to merge our individuality in the oneness of that great Being. We therefore possess our individuality for only a short time, on a cosmic scale anyway, and then of our own free will we will surrender our individuality back to the source, our Creator. This will not be demanded of us. It will be something that we will want to do, to surrender our individuality for the good and the well-being of the whole. But that is, for most of us, a long time ahead in the future.

Q: In the meantime can we evolve to the point where we ourselves can be the soul of a planet?

ZT: No. That does not lie within your consciousness even though you are indeed creators and have been given the divine gift of creation which is not given to all beings. The Angelic Kingdom, for example, does not possess the ability to reproduce itself as do you. Recognise that you have been given many talents with which to learn and evolve your consciousness, talents which other planetary beings do not possess. You have been given the divine gift of free choice, the right to choose your path, to choose your destiny. It would perhaps surprise you to know that there are many planets whose inhabitants do not possess that gift. Even on this plane of Earth the three other Kingdoms of Matter do not possess free choice. You might regard the Animal, the Vegetable and the Mineral Kingdoms as inanimate matter, subservient to your will, but they all have consciousness and are following an evolutionary path similar to yours.

Q:   Why was Earth singled out as a special planet and the beings upon it given free choice? Why do other planets not have it?

ZT:   One of the things you have to understand is that Humanity, and I use that expression to mean human consciousness both on the physical and the higher levels of life, is a very special species of cosmic being. Humanity's evolutionary path can be likened to an experiment and this experiment is being watched with great interest by many, many great Cosmic Beings from universes beyond your comprehension. Humanity is an experiment in creation by a great Being. To this end you have been given cosmic gifts which very few other beings possess.

This Earth, therefore, is a very special place. You are highly privileged to incarnate on her, to be part of the school of Earth and to advance your spiritual consciousness through the exercise of those cosmic talents. There are many beings on other planets who are not permitted to achieve consciousness in this way. You have been given the supreme gifts of the God-head: Its own divinity, Its own creativity, Its own free choice. You are, in essence, gods in the making and this Earth is a school for gods. You may now see why Earth is looked upon with envy by the other planets in the Solar System for they do not all possess that potential. You have, in fact, the potential and the destiny to outstrip every other plane of consciousness within this Solar Body if only you could but harness your being and direct it with wisdom and love.

This planet, therefore, is watched with interest because it is the scene of a great cosmic experiment. There are some amongst the watchers who would say that the experiment has failed, that Humanity will destroy itself, indeed is already destroying itself, and that Humanity has polluted this Earth beyond the point where she can be saved. I do not believe this to be true, for this Earth has seen many cycles of human evolution, has witnessed the comings and goings of many great civilisations. Earth has produced levels of life far more evolved both technologically and spiritually than that which you demonstrate today. Humanity's evolution appears timeless, but it is controlled by our Creator and Its Spiritual Hierarchy. You are but one minute cog on a vast Cosmic Wheel. When it began or when it will end I cannot say.

Q:   Can I ask what is the path that Humanity should be taking in order to regain its divine destiny?

ZT:   Every one of you is unique. The fact that the very finger-prints on your hands are all different reflects the uniqueness of your spirit. There is no one path to be taken by all Humanity. It is by each one of you walking your own path, fulfilling your own destiny to the highest of your being, that you will unite to fulfil the destiny of Humanity. Most individuals in the World today totally ignore their responsibility for right personal behaviour. They always look outwards to try to put the World right, to change the path on which Humanity is set, rather than look inwards to put themselves right. As I have said many times before, you want peace on Earth but you will never achieve this until you, as individuals, have first established peace within yourselves. If you do not have peace in your hearts there will never be peace on Earth.

What you must do therefore is to be at one with yourself: for you are all divine. You have within you the consciousness of the Godhead if you will but listen to it and use it. In a sense, a world in crisis is, as the first Teacher said, a good place to do this, for is it not true to say that it is only when you are in crisis that you begin to listen, that you begin to seek other Worlds, other understandings. Think back in your own lives to the times when you have been in crisis. Perhaps it is only in such moments that you have turned to whatever God you believe in, to whatever understanding of life you have. Well, your World is now in crisis and that crisis will bring about great learning, a great revival of the cosmic knowledge which is the birthright of Humanity. Behind every dark cloud there is light and that light will soon shine on the plane of Earth.

Q:   How long will it be before that light shines upon the Earth?
ZT:   That depends upon Humanity. You all have free choice. You all create according to your own wills. If everyone in this room tonight were to leave with their wills resolved then the change would become manifest immediately, for as you go forth and contact your fellow human beings so you would be spreading a contagious disease, a disease which would spread rapidly throughout Humanity. Through your own behaviour you would spread the contagious disease of love. Surely the example of all the great Masters, even if you do not recognise them as Masters, has been one of love and when I say love I do not mean romantic or sexual love, I mean divine love. The love of the divine. The love

194

which sacrifices all for the divine, the love that sees the whole before the individual, that will always place the self on the altar of the whole.

Q:  If human life is just a drama on a stage does it really matter what we do?

ZT:  I have talked a great deal about the reality of life and of how, in fact, it is an unreality. You of course consider physical life as the reality of your being, and in the sense that you have to experience it, it is. Recognise that you create that reality. Through your thoughts, your words and your deeds you create the reality of human life. If you would seek to change that reality then change your thoughts, your words and your deeds. It is as simple as that, for you are the masters of creation. You can create whatever you so desire. That is the nature of the divine gift that has been given to you. Remember that with that gift goes great responsibility for you create not only on this plane of life but also on the higher planes as well, and when you pollute this planet you also pollute the other planes of life as well. Therefore your behaviour influences millions and millions of aspects of consciousness. That is indeed a great responsibility. Face up to it!

# THE TRUE NATURE OF ILLNESS

I am going to talk on the true nature of illness. As a teacher dealing with an immensely complex subject I must of necessity abbreviate, make analogies and over-simplify, but if I am to present an awareness of the true nature of illness from my side of life it is necessary that I do this.

I will take as my archetype the Trinity, the Trinity of Creation, and I will suggest to you that Humanity can be divided into the trinity of body, mind and spirit. I will further suggest to you that each of those centres of creativity demands a body of expression: a physical body, of which you are aware, a mental body and a spiritual body. Each of those bodies exists on their different levels and the spiritual body, being a very fine body, obviously exists on a higher level than the physical body. Each of those bodies vibrates at a certain note, at a certain frequency, and so expresses the degree of its soul consciousness. Everything that manifests in the spiritual body, the highest body, must inevitably manifest in the lower bodies as well and therefore a spiritual illness, a soul illness, will also manifest in the mental and the physical bodies. It is quite possible, of course, to have an illness on the physical level which is not the direct result of an illness in the spiritual or mental bodies, but I will come to this in a minute.

I wonder if you recognise that, as far as you are concerned on the physical plane of Earth, you are not your bodies. The real essence of you is your spirit which only temporarily inhabits the physical plane of Earth. Your body belongs not to you but to the Goddess of this Earth who created it in her womb. Recognise that your physical body has consciousness and feeling, has its own individual expression and intelligence with which you can communicate. You can talk to it just as I talk to you now. The concept that you, as beings of spirit, are not your bodies, is not perhaps new to you, but

197

have you ever thought that it is possible to hold a conversation with your body, to ask it questions, to make requests of it, to seek its guidance especially where the healing of illness is concerned.

When you die and your spirit returns to the higher planes of life so your physical body dies too and returns to the womb of the Earth, to the Goddess. Recognise that, just like you, your body has walked a path of evolution gaining consciousness. It has lived a life of meaning and purpose learning lessons just as your spirit has done. Remember that the Solar System in which you live is a body similar to your physical body and that the organs of that body, the planets, function just like the organs of your physical body. You are a microcosm within a macrocosm, you are bodies within bodies, consciousnesses within consciousnesses, evolving and learning. Recognise that your physical body, therefore, given to you in a sacred trust by the Goddess, is an evolving, conscious being, worthy of your respect, your admiration and, above all, your love, for indeed it is love that makes the physical body pulsate and obey the commands of spirit.

Let us now consider the nature of illness. Illness, dis-ease, dis-harmony, can be likened to the Devil, and when I speak of the Devil I talk now not of the Satanic being created by various religions to make their understanding of God more appealing and relevant, but of the real Saturnian influence, the testing influence of the planet Saturn. The Devil, Satan, is nothing more than the testing aspect of Saturn. You are constantly being tested on every level of your being. The Saturnian aspect tests to evolve. It tests to improve. It tests to raise consciousness on every level of your being. It tests even the essence of spirit itself. Life after life after life your spirit returns to dwell in yet another physical body and the soul, which is the memory of spirit, brings with it the consciousness of past lives. It also brings with it the weaknesses of past lives, the lessons that have to be learned, the karma that has to be transmuted. The way that you have treated your physical bodies in the past is reflected in your present physical body. After conception, the spirit, using its soul memory, creates a body of its own choosing within the womb of the mother. That body embodies the soul pattern, the soul memories, of past lives. It will therefore create within that body the weaknesses of past lives. Therefore as you grow to adulthood, to become a mature man or woman, so past weaknesses of the soul will manifest in your body

198

and will present themselves to be faced and mastered once again.

Let it be understood, therefore, that many illnesses, if not indeed most illnesses, exist on a pre-physical level, that is on the mental and the spiritual levels and that before any illness manifests on the physical it can be seen by those that have eyes to see on those higher levels of life. It is quite possible to see an illness before it even manifests on the physical level, and if one can do that then it is obviously quite possible to treat an illness on the higher levels before it even manifests on the physical level of life. Indeed, in some ancient civilisations the healers of those times would do just that. They were primarily concerned with healing on the higher levels so as to prevent illness manifesting on the physical level. To-day, alas, that knowledge is lost and what you have to deal with in your civilisation is physical illness on a physical level. But if you can accept that the causes of illness are not entirely of the physical and that, for the most part, they are initiated by previous experiences, if not in this life then in previous lives, it would help you to understand the root cause of illness.

Let us realise, first and foremost, that all illness comes from within. All illness is caused either by the body, the mind or the spirit. You are the cause of all your illnesses. It might appear that a disease originates outside the body, but you contract a disease only because you permit it to come into your body, because your body is not in perfect harmony. This can either be because you have not treated your body with respect and have not maintained it in a perfect state so that it is immune to all illness, or else because there is some weakness in either your mental or your spiritual bodies which requires that illness to come and test you.

I can feel the question in your minds "Why then do we have these epidemics on the Earth when so many people catch a particular disease and only a few avoid it?". The answer to that is very simple. Many groups of souls incarnate together life after life following similar evolutionary patterns. Therefore many individual souls in a group will tend to exhibit the same weaknesses and will therefore suffer from the same dis-ease, the same illness. But, truly, a person that is living in perfect harmony in body, mind and spirit can, and should, resist all illness. There is no need for you to be ill except when an illness comes to you as a testing experience, to evolve your spiritual consciousness. In all cases illness should be seen as self-generated and for the benefit of the body, the mind and the spirit, for what else is an illness but an evolutionary lesson requiring you to concentrate all your energies on the illness, on the cure and, more particularly, on your physical body which so many of you choose to ignore today.

Your physical body is not unfeeling matter. Those who are closely concerned with illness, the medical profession in particular, are very aware of the majesty of the human form. It is indeed divine. Most of you, however, are unaware of the complex biological functions that the body performs, for the most part, autonomously and automatically, of the way in which it adapts to the challenges of physical life and of the many creative functions which take place within it. If you were to multiply the knowledge of the human body today one hundredfold then you would just be beginning to understand its full capabilities. Today you know so little of what the body can do, of how and why it creates. For example, although the physical process of conception is now understood, the cause and the moment of conception, the level on which that decision takes place, is still unrecognised by most people today.

The body therefore has consciousness and, as such, has the ability to accept or reject a disease, to decide whether or not to learn the lesson of that disease. It is then the responsibility of the spirit that dwells within that body to bring about healing and to transmute the illness. The first step towards the cure of any illness is an acceptance of that illness. You must recognise that the illness has come to you as part of the Divine Plan, as an instrument of evolution. It is not something to be fought against and conquered, to be pushed into the background and ignored, to be regarded as an inconvenience to your daily living. It is an opportunity given to you by your Creator to forward your evolutionary progress. Therefore accept that test in love and with love. Recognise that the test is one which, on another level, you yourself have requested.

Once you have accepted an illness it is then easy to communicate with your body, to recognise the true nature of the illness and to decide on the form of healing which must take place, the treatment that is best suited to your body. Remember that everyone is unique and that a particular form of treatment may bring about a cure in one body but not in another. When considering how to heal an illness always remember the higher bodies which play such an important part in controlling your physical body: the mental and the spiritual. It is the union of those three bodies, of those three energies that brings about the healing process. All of them must be employed.

In the World in which you live today many drugs are available which can effectively banish an illness for the time being and so remove a test. You must choose whether or not to use them. Remember that although you can postpone a test that is placed before you, ultimately, you will have to face that test again at a later stage in your evolution. Remember also that a test that has been postponed or ignored, when presented again, becomes more difficult to handle. This is also true of an illness. An illness postponed will only re-emerge at a later date in a stronger, more virulent form and will be more difficult to heal and transmute. An illness should be faced when it occurs. This, of course, needs time and energy. An illness must be looked at with consciousness. It must be recognised as a malfunction of the physical body that requires consciousness to heal. Talk to your body, talk to the illness, understand the cause of the illness and so bring about the cure yourself. From an understanding of the cure there will come consciousness, there will come understanding of the true nature of life and of the path that you are walking in life.

Every illness that you have, on any level of your being, reflects a weakness in your spirit. Illness reflects either a karmic or a planetary weakness which you have come to master and to learn from. The level on which the weakness manifests differs according to the nature of your being. For the most part you are concerned only with physical illness, but behind every physical illness there lies a deeper and higher meaning which you can discover very easily if you meditate on it, even while you are ill. You can always discover the true cause of an illness.

Obviously your physical body, having its own consciousness and will, can of its own volition become ill. It requires, therefore, that you heal that body in love, that you explain to the body that you as the soul-being dwelling within it cannot fulfil your destiny unless you have a healthy vehicle in which to function. The body must be made aware of the reasons why you are seeking to cure the illness and of the steps that you are taking to bring about healing. The body, respecting the higher consciousness which is you, just as you respect the higher consciousness that is your God, will respond to your demonstrations of love.

Illness, therefore, comes from within, no matter on what level it occurs, no matter what the nature of the person or the nature of the soul. It always comes from within, never from without. Acceptance of the illness, acceptance of the source, leads to a true understanding of the illness. There are obviously many forms and degrees of illness present on the Earth reflecting the many weaknesses of Humanity and the behaviour that has taken place. Remember that you inherit the illnesses of your forebears and that the seeds of illness that you are now sowing will be visited upon your children and upon your children's children, in fact for generations to come. That is why great souls often incarnate on the Earth specifically to accept and to transmute a certain illness and to cleanse the Earth of that illness for the generations to come. One can perhaps see that demonstrated by the life of the Master Jesus. He incarnated to transmute a great deal of past evil and to open the way for Humanity to walk along a new path with fresh motivation and understanding. Any illness, even the common cold, must be seen as an illness to be accepted and transmuted in love and through love.

It is easy when one does not have great spiritual consciousness to be confused, even annoyed, by an illness; to see it as an obstacle to one's enjoyment of life, indeed as an obstacle to one's evolutionary path in life. Nevertheless, it is a fact that until the illness is accepted and cured, until you are restored to perfect health, you will find it hard to function on any level of your being. Remember that mental illnesses have physical counterparts and that spiritual illnesses have counterparts on both the mental and the physical levels. Look therefore to the spirit, to the centre, to the core of your being. Look with honesty and love at what you see there. Talk to your spirit, communicate with it, and from the understanding of that union will come the abolition of illness.

## QUESTIONS AND ANSWERS

Q:  The speaker was saying that one should always seek to cure an illness and not postpone it through the use of drugs, but today the medical profession nearly always uses drugs to restore people to health. The emphasis is always on getting rid of the illness. Is this so wrong?

ZT:  The ultimate test of an illness is that you cure it. Whether you cure it in this life or another life, on the physical level or on another level, is for you to choose. Obviously, as you are only too well aware, there are some illnesses that cannot be cured and from which people die, but one should see that in the context that people die for many reasons not just because of illness or old age but because they have decided to withdraw from physical life, perhaps because they have failed the major test they came to face. People who are apparently in good health can suddenly die after a very short illness. The nature of such an illness is that the soul may decide to withdraw from physical life if certain destined patterns have not been met, if there is a need for that soul to return to the other side of life so as to take stock and to begin again.

Q:  Could you comment for us about illnesses in children? At what level are they learning?
ZT:  Let us remember that within a child's body there can be a very evolved soul and that the age of the physical body does not reflect the age, the point of evolution, of the spirit within it. The spirit that is present within the body of a young child may be very wise and very evolved, but for many reasons that spirit will not be able to express itself, if only because the vehicle of the child has not yet evolved to the point when it can express itself as a mature human being.

Illnesses that manifest in children are very often, but not always, caused by illnesses that are present in their parents. Remember that the elements, the genes, which go into the construction of a child's physical body are taken from both the mother and the father. It should be recognised that even though the child's body is created within the mother's womb that the vibrations and characteristics of the father are present and help to form that child during the nine months of its growth. Therefore weaknesses in either one of the parents can and will repeat themselves in the physical body of the child resulting in illness, perhaps even an illness which the child's spirit does not desire. That is why some young children choose to die, because the body that has been created is not suitable for the destiny they want to follow. Until the age of twelve, when the soul is fully in the body, a child can, and often does, terminate its physical life because the characteristics in life which it sought for its destiny have not been fulfilled. There is, therefore, no such thing as

203

suicide under the age of twelve in a child. Obviously the child does not decide to withdraw on the physical level because it is so young and immature. It is the spirit that makes the decision because the body is ill and is not suitable for the life it wants to lead.

Illness, of course, even in a young child can manifest through the spirit. Illness can be part of a karmic pattern and let us remember that such a karmic pattern is not just of the child but can be of the parents. The test, or illness, which a child faces can often be not for itself but for the parents who have created it. Remember that parents learn as much from the child as the child learns from its parents. The learning process is two ways and a child that dies may have offered to make that sacrifice in order to help the parents, its nurses and doctors, or even society as a whole, to be aware of certain facts of life which the people concerned have to learn.

Illness, therefore, is always an evolutionary process. It always produces growth and understanding on one level or another. Children may appear more deserving of our sympathy because they are young and have not yet fulfilled the potential of their being. That perhaps makes the lesson more poignant, but the principle for a child is just the same as for an adult. The nature of illness and disease is the same for a child as for an adult. You only look at a child with more love than you would do an adult because the personality of the child has not yet sullied its being. You can see the purity of the Godhead more clearly in a child and you therefore feel more compassion for it.

Q: I certainly agree that many, perhaps most, illnesses start within the body and that when the body's resistance is low we can catch whatever it is that is around. But how would you explain something like the 'flu epidemic of 1919, when it seems that a massive infectious disease suddenly arises which our bodies are quite incapable of withstanding? Does not the source of such a disease originate outside the body?

ZT: Indeed, yes. If we take the example of our Solar System, another physical body, we can say that most illnesses of our Solar System originate within the System. We can say that the Earth in particular, one of its major organs, is ill and is spreading disease within our Solar System. We can also say that into our Solar System there will come at times, shall we say, a meteorite, a heavenly body of some import, which is foreign to our Solar

System. Such an event of course, has both meaning and purpose and will present a test, a challenge, to our Solar System. It is also true to say that on the Earth plane as well you can have, using the same analogy, a foreign body invading the Earth, a new form of disease, one which has been created by Humanity. This disease will have a significant impact upon Humanity because Humanity has no response or no resistance to it. It reflects an overall weakness of Humanity at that stage.

Remember that human thought is capable of creating forms of power and energy which in turn can create disease. Your thoughts, ultimately, control your total environment. Your thoughts can create illness and disease. Therefore you can create a form of what you would call 'flu, but that 'flu is really the result of Humanity's thoughts and emotions. Humanity therefore creates its own epidemics. I would also say to you that no matter how many people around you are catching a certain disease if you are in perfect harmony and balance you will not catch it. In just the same way a healthy person can walk among lepers and not catch leprosy, but if a person is run down and depleted of energy and not in perfect health then they will catch that disease.

Q: So the way forward is to concentrate on perfecting our physical bodies and getting our bodies, minds and spirits working in harmony?
ZT: The way forward is through inner perfection and from that inner perfection will come lasting outer perfection. Today you have many examples of people who although they appear to have healthy outer bodies are in fact in total disharmony within. The result is that without that inner harmony the outer perfection soon crumbles.

Q: Are you saying that the development of vaccines to counteract typhoid or smallpox is wrong, because no matter what you say we now live in a world where people no longer suffer or die from these diseases?
ZT: It is self evident that the use of vaccines has effectively prevented the spread and development of many contagious diseases. Such developments are the result of Humanity's physical response to a physical challenge. Any disease, any challenge, any test which Humanity has to face will eventually be surmounted, but

as one test is faced and conquered so another one will present itself. It is, to use a medical analogy, the same disease appearing in a different form. Look at what is happening today. By taking a course of antibiotics you may suppress a particular illness but in spite of, or shall we say because of, that treatment the weakness, the illness, is still present and will manifest in some other way, in some other form, at a later stage.

Q: You have said that Humanity will be afflicted by a disease coming from the Animal Kingdom, one that will be more destructive than a hydrogen bomb. Can you say anything more about that?

ZT: I have said that a disease originating in the Animal Kingdom would be passed on to Humanity and would cause much suffering and death. This disease has been created by Humanity's misuse of the Animal Kingdom. The disease which you call AIDS did indeed originate in the Animal Kingdom but it is only a precursor of a greater disease which will afflict the whole planet. AIDS is but a warning to Humanity to show it what lies ahead and to demonstrate that a disease can arise at very short notice over which Humanity has no control whatsoever. It should serve as a warning to Humanity that only right behaviour towards the physical body can prevent one from being afflicted by such an illness or disease.

Q: Are you saying that it is possible for human beings to achieve such perfection right now and so be able to resist all illness? If so can you say something about how we may bring this about?

ZT: I would qualify your statement by saying that once the individual has grown to an understanding of the true nature of his or her body and the true nature of illness then that being can, and should, live in perfect harmony. The trouble with your society today is that children are not taught about their bodies or right relationships with them and are not made aware of their responsibilities in this matter. Indeed, if anything, they are taught the opposite; namely, that they should rely on drugs and surgery to maintain good health. They are not taught of the importance and significance of correct eating, correct exercise, correct breathing or correct living and so inevitably they will suffer from illness and

206

disease. They therefore restrict the potential of their physical bodies until they have grown into a true understanding of life. But once that understanding has been reached it is possible to achieve perfect harmony and to be immune to all disease. Indeed that is the purpose and the true nature of life.

# THE NATURE OF GROUP ENERGY

The religious dogma of the Trinity is but a small reflection of a great cosmic principle which touches every area of human endeavour. That cosmic principle manifests in many forms, in many ways, reflecting the diversity of Humanity's evolutionary path. You yourselves manifest through the trinity of body, mind and spirit. As we now look at the nature of group energy I would like you to remember that trinity for we do indeed have to consider the body, the mind and the spirit of a group.

The body of a group, the physical manifestation of a group, is of course self-evident. It consists of the human beings who go to make up that group and whose physical presence decides the nature of the group. When even one person is not present then the energy of the group changes. When even one person is absent from the group then that affects the work and the creativity of the group because energy is missing, and when I talk of being absent I do not just mean being absent physically but energy being absent from the total consciousness of the group. This can happen either because of the behaviour of individual members of the group as they experience their own personality problems or because of members of the group pursuing aims which are detrimental to the group. For the purposes of our discussion, though, the physical presence of the group, the physical work which they do, can be considered as the body of the group.

In an ideal group the physical work to be done would be shared equally amongst all the members of the group, but the reality of human expression prevents this happening. People work at different levels, each reflecting their own aspect of consciousness, their own level of vitality, their own capacity for work. So whilst all must work to the highest of their consciousness it must be recognised that the total work of the group will not necessarily be shared

209

equally amongst its members. What is essential, though, is that each member of the group works to the highest of their consciousness and physical ability. Each member works in different ways, at different levels, and this must be recognised as a fact of human existence.

You should not compare one member of the group with another and say that one works harder, that one is more creative or that one gives more to the group than another, for that is just a human physical comparison and does not reflect the total giving of that person, especially on the higher levels of life. The group energy is shared between all the members of the group. Each gives and each takes. On some days you will give more than you will take, on others you will take more than you will give. That is the purpose of group living, of group sharing: to support one another on the physical plane of life. Indeed the energy of the group should make physical living easier. It should make it easier to handle the physical, as well as the higher, burdens of life.

Let us now look at the mind of group energy. Remember that mind comes before body. Your physical body is but the instrument of your mind. Your mind receives the inspiration, the force of intuition, and translates it into human activity which your physical body carries out. Therefore the mind of the group is the source of group creativity. When the minds of the group are in harmony, when they have common purpose, when they are open and intuitive, when they are attuned to the Godhead, then cosmic energy flows down to permit those minds to create on a level hitherto impossible. There is such a thing as a group mind, if you would call it that. Minds linked and united in common purpose can create a force for good on the plane of Humanity, not only within their own group but within the World as a whole as the group sends its energy out. But the mind, in turn, is but the instrument of spirit, of consciousness.

So let us now look at the highest level of the group — the spiritual consciousness of the group. Your consciousness is the innermost part of your being, the spirit, which lives before birth and lives after death. It is this spiritual union, the joining of the individual consciousnesses through meditation and group attunement, that binds the group together. It is this fusion of energy, this linking together on the higher planes of life, which unites the group in a common purpose, in a common cause. Although there may be

210

difficulties on the body and the mind levels, if the spiritual consciousness is one, if the individuals of the group are together on the spiritual level, then only harmony will result. Only good can come from spiritual consciousness working in unison to be of service to the World.

So spirit motivates mind which creates through the body. Each is important. Without the trinity you could not express, you could not create. Therefore recognise the energy present on each of those levels, for they are important. Physical energy is different from mental energy, is different from cosmic or spiritual energy. Each must be recognised and channelled. Each must be aligned with the other energies in the group so that the group may present a united front, a united energy for good in the World. When you come to join a group you are in effect offering your consciousness to the group. You are offering the highest part of yourself to the energy of the group and if union takes place on that level then everything else will fall into place. If a group is operating only on the physical level, on the level of body without the involvement of mind and spirit, then inevitably conflicts will occur. The work will not be of the highest and will not be representative of the true consciousness of the group.

It is essential, therefore, when you join a group that you enter on the level of spiritual consciousness, recognising that there is an energy deep within you that wishes to merge with the energy of the group, that wishes to be a part of that energy, both to give to it and to allow it to permeate your being. If you are open to the energy of the group, listen to it and respect it, then that energy will flow down through you and will allow you to create according to your own consciousness. The energy will manifest differently in each member of the group according to their individualised consciousness. That is the nature of human evolution and the way in which our Creator creates the diversity of life. The one energy will create many aspects, many different facets, each reflecting the individuals of the group.

Group energy should be an important focus for any group. Recognise that it is present and that it can be cultivated. Recognise that you can either give to it or take from it. Remember that one of the purposes of being in a group is to support the other members of the group and that they also can give to you as you can give to them. Remember that how you as individuals behave in thought, word and deed reflects on the consciousness of the group. Everything that you do to the highest of your physical, mental and spiritual abilities affects the group energy and the higher the level of your giving the higher will be the level of that which is given back to you. Indeed the energy that you contribute to the group will be returned ten-fold to you. It is by giving that you shall receive.

One of the major purposes of groups is to help people to place their individualised consciousnesses in a correct perspective and to get them to recognise that they are not alone. They are individualised in consciousness but they are also part of the whole. In a group you learn to give of yourselves not just to the individual members of the group but to the group as a whole and to the energy that manifests through it. You learn you are a part of a whole and that you have to sacrifice your part to the whole knowing that what is right for the whole will also be right for yourself.

So as you work in a group on a day-to-day basis, as you have your ups and downs, as you make your mistakes and achieve your gains in consciousness, remember that there is always support. Remember also that the members of the group are mirrors of consciousness reflecting back to you and that provided that reflection is done in love you will be led into a greater understanding of yourself. It is often the case that within the family unit very little criticism takes place. You tend to accept the weaknesses and failings of the members of the family because they are your family. You therefore form an idealised opinion of yourself and of your abilities, of what you can and cannot do, of what you should and should not do, an opinion which is usually supported by your family life. But when you move into a group relationship and meet people beyond the family so new aspects of your being manifest. It is no longer possible to accept the ideas and opinions you have of yourself. You discover that you have to release some of your cherished concepts in order to be in harmony with the group with whom you live and work. You realise that you have to sacrifice a part of yourself for the good of the whole. You have to recognise that you are no longer an island but just one small aspect in the sea of life. Learning to live in harmony in a small group is but a preparation for living in harmony with the World. If you cannot do it in a group then you cannot do it in the World. The group experience is therefore a preparation for becoming a citizen of the World.

I have been talking of group energy but what is the real nature of that energy? You are aware of many energies even though they are unseen forces. You have all experienced the energies of love, hate and fear. For the most part you are probably only aware of a group energy when it threatens or appears to threaten you. Nevertheless a group energy is around you the whole time. You can attune to that energy at any time of the day when you seek it. It is there, created in those moments of group meditation and attunement when the members of the group link together and offer up their energy and love. There can be no greater sacrifice than to give of your energy, to give of your being, for the use of the group, and from that giving there comes an understanding of what is the purpose of life, of what is the physical reality of human evolution. It is not to be alone. It is not to be one. It is to be the World.


## QUESTIONS AND ANSWERS


Q: The speaker referred to attunement or meditation by a group. Can you say simply what is the purpose of group attunement and what are we actually doing when we attune?

ZT: The purpose of attunement, of course, depends on the motivation of those that are attuning. If you are attuning out of fear or greed, out of habit or hostility, for reasons of self-gratification, if you are attuning not because you want to but because you have to, if you are not giving your energy freely, then you are creating a blockage and are limiting the purpose of attunement. But if you attune openly and consciously, if you link the energy of your being not only with the people with whom you are attuning but with the millions of beings around you on both the physical and the higher levels of life, then you are truly attuning to the Godhead. In true attunement you are opening yourself to the energy of the Godhead to allow It to permeate your being and become a part of you, to reveal Its plan not just for you alone but for the group of which you are a part. In true attunement you are attuning to the Universe. Attunement can be likened to raising an aerial. The nature of your aerial attracts a certain frequency of radio waves to it and what is the aerial but the consciousness, the motivation and the energy that has gone into the attunement.

One of the great mistakes people make with attunement is to

213

enter into it expecting a quick result. We have a problem; therefore we will attune and solve it. Would that life was so simple! Now that is not to say that there cannot be solutions, but that very often you are asking the wrong question. Moreover, the answer that you receive may not be the result of attunement but what another part of your conscious being has drawn down. One should always attune to the Godhead and not to an individual source. One also has to learn to listen rather than to talk and it is hard to listen especially when what you hear may not be to your liking! It is difficult to ask the question if you really do not want to know the answer. Attunement, therefore, requires courage. It requires understanding. It requires commitment, otherwise what is the point of attuning, of asking a question and then ignoring the answer. So be aware that when you attune you are consciously attuning to the Godhead. You are recognising Its presence, Its purpose and Its design for you and are saying that you wish to be a part of that.

Q:  There is obviously no point in people attuning if they do not want to do it, but what should one do in the case of a community in which half like to attune and the other half do not?
ZT:  What happens in such a case is that inevitably a separation grows between those that attune and become at one with the energy flowing down through the community and those who do not. A separation grows which although perhaps not manifest on the physical level slowly becomes more and more manifest on the mental and on the spiritual levels. Gradually there appears a division of purpose, a separation of identity, a dissipation of the energy available for group activities. When such a thing happens inevitably either the community breaks up or, if the community energy is stronger than the individuals, the individuals leave the community.

Q:  We are thinking of starting a group. What is the best way to do it? Have you any suggestions?
ZT:  One of the first signs of an evolving being is the desire to work in a group. It is amazing, you know, how many people find it impossible to work in a group because the basis of all group activity is that you place the group before the self. This means that you give your energy to the group and allow the group to freely use it to fulfil the nature of its being. Groups are coming into existence all

214

over the World today. For many reasons people are banding together to discover new aspects of life, to investigate new teachings and to experience human relationships not readily available in the 'normal' World.

When a group is formed it is essential that it be based around a core group and, from my experience, that core group should consist of three people, five at the most. This core group should form the basis for the larger group and as it meets and sounds its note so others will be attracted to it. It is essential that the selection process be left open and that all those who are attracted to the note are allowed to come to it. There will, of course, inevitably be some who will come for the wrong reasons, but this will become apparent as the group meets and works together. The purpose of the group, of course, should reflect the lesson of the planet which is one of sacrifice, of giving. If a group meets for self-centred reasons, to take from each other, then that group will soon collapse. A group is only strong if the members give of themselves and of their energies for the good of the whole group.

The important thing with a group is that as it meets regularly so the energy builds up and all the members of the group are touched by it. There is therefore a healing process taking place. The energy of the group heals and transforms all who are a part of it. As the group attunes together so in that linking of energies you are transmuting the disharmony of the group. Group attunement, therefore, is a healing process, healing not only the individuals but the planet as a whole. The energy created by a group in meditation reaches hundreds of miles up into the cosmos. Such is the nature of group energy as you come together, mingling the power of your auras, your chakras.

Groups form for many reasons reflecting the nature of those that form them and the work they want to do. A true group forms itself before any of its members even incarnate into physical life. They will have chosen on the higher planes of life to become members of a particular group and to give of their consciousnesses. The core groups of the great esoteric schools of old would always be twelve in number, each person in the group reflecting a different sign of the Zodiac. Nothing is gained by repeating the same energy pattern in a group. The strength of a group comes in its diversity, in the uniqueness of spirit of those that come together to give of their love and energy.

Once the group has been formed it is essential that it meets regularly. Like a young seedling it must be nurtured before it is exposed either to the pressures of new members joining or to challenges from outside which cannot be handled. Only when there is strength and, above all, commitment can the group expand and begin its work. The greatest weakness in group activity that I see on your planet today is lack of commitment. It is so easy to be distracted by the material world. There will always be demands from your families, your jobs, your sports. That is the nature of the World in which you live, but just as some people go to church on Sundays so you should go to your group on the appointed day and dedicate your lives to that activity. It is important and from that commitment grows the power which bonds the group together.

There is so much to be gained from group activities that it is amazing that people still choose to live in isolation in the World. As I have already said, the energy created by a group sustains its members. In times of famine a group can truly feed its members with its energy and where others will starve they will survive. In times of drought it is the same. The energies present in group activities are beyond your understanding, but that is what life is about. When the Human Race as a whole can unite as you all are uniting now, then the evolutionary pattern will have been fulfilled.

Q: Do you feel that we should meet once a month or once a week if that is not enough?

ZT: Obviously the demands of physical life to a great extent restrict the actions of many people. But what, after all, is important? What is the purpose of you being here on the plane of Earth? If there are so many benefits to be had from group activity, if truly this energy can transform your being, the more often you meet, the more often you give and share it, the greater will be the reward. It is unfortunate that you have only one birthday a year. If you could have one each month would you not like it! It is the same with groups. Obviously if you do not live close together then you have to adjust the pattern of meetings according to what is possible, but the more often you meet the better. Moreover once the energy of the group has been established, even if it is not possible to meet together, if you all meditate at an appointed time the energy will still circulate and will still be present even though thousands of miles separate you.

Q: What are the qualities one should look for in prospective members of a group?

ZT: One essential quality is humility; to recognise that you are a small part of the whole and that your feelings, emotions, ideas and wishes should not necessarily have preference over everyone else in the group. Humility implies a recognition of the whole before the individual. It is difficult for the young to be humble because in the first two cycles of life they are usually encouraged to develop their individuality, to become self-centred. During the first twenty years of life they think only of themselves, of their education, their needs, their physical development. The parent helps the child to become an independent adult, but when the child is an adult it then has to learn to release all that self-centredness and to begin to give back to the whole.

Another quality is truth. Truth must be demonstrated within the group in thought, word and deed. Above all you must be true to yourself and true to the other members of the group, for if you cannot speak the truth and share openly with them then there is no group. Very often you cannot see the truth in others because of a falsehood in yourself. Remember that truth does not reside solely within your heart. It is to be found, amazingly enough, within the hearts of others as well! If only you will all recognise that fact you will learn a lot from each other and so contribute to the wholeness of the group.

Another quality is love. Remember that the true energy of a group is love and by love I mean the energy of your Creator freely given to you. Love is the reflection of Its wholeness and Its being. It is that love which gives you life, individuality and freedom. It is that love which touches everybody, expecting no return. It is that love which truly bonds a group together, which creates the consciousness of a group.

Remember that on the physical level you are all different. The group is made up of many parts. Your bodies are different, your birthsigns are different, your personalities are different, your destinies are different. Therefore the group cannot be as one on the physical level. That is a fact of being, something which has to be recognised. The group cannot be regimented into physical wholeness. Indeed the strength of the group is dependent on the strength of the individuals in it. I said earlier that in the perfect group every sign of the Zodiac would be present. So one would expect twelve

217

signs, twelve separate human activities. Every aspect of life would be present and if each person gives of his or her being to the highest then the whole group benefits from that giving. All can take from it as if it was their own.

Q:   In what way can we improve the quality of our group activities? ZT:   You improve the quality of the group only by improving your self-being, by being true to your spirit, by seeking the highest, by trying to manifest the highest, by doing even the humblest household task that has to be done to the highest of your consciousness. For example, you think that housework is drudgery, but do you not realise that there is always someone who will observe the results of that drudgery. In a centre like this where you have so many visitors there is always someone who will appreciate the energy that you have expended. Now do you expend that energy just to receive appreciation and thanks either from the other members of the centre or the visitors, just to make yourself feel good, just because you seek recognition for what you have done, or do you expend that energy, as you should do, simply because you wish to express the highest of yourself in everything that you do?

If you go into a desert and build a beautiful sand-castle very few people will see it. It will probably be destroyed in a few days. So why build it? You build it because you are there and because you want to create. So you build that sand-castle to the highest of your consciousness, you build it for the sheer joy of building it, of using the talents which your Creator has given to you. Now this centre is not a desert and you are not building a sand-castle, but every single thing that you do is observed by somebody if not by the other members of the centre then by the guests. Every single thing that you do is noticed by someone and is a mark of the consciousness of the centre and the standards that it is setting. If people come to this centre and see consciousness they will be affected by it. They will recognise that consciousness, see what consciousness can do and will then try to manifest it in their own lives. Consciousness attracts consciousness which creates consciousness. By working with consciousness, even at a task like polishing a floor, you can change the World.

Q:   Since physical life is so impermanent and we ourselves only live for a short time would it not be better to concentrate our energy on increasing our spiritual consciousness rather than on creating on the physical plane, especially since so many of our creations appear unnecessary?

ZT: Why do you create? Why do you build a house, plant a garden, make a beautiful pie for supper, create a nice dress? What is the purpose of creation, for all of you will die sooner or later and will leave all your physical creations behind when you transition to a higher body. What then of the dress that you created, of the house that you built and so on? Can you remember what you created in Egypt, in Rome, in Greece, in Atlantis, in any of your past lives? Although all your creations are indeed still present on another level of life you cannot recall them. So why do you create? Why, if you knew you were to die tomorrow would you create today? Why expend that energy?

The answer, as you well know, is that what you are creating is consciousness. You build consciousness through the way that you create. This is what this World is concerned about, the gaining of consciousness, for that is what you take with you when you die: consciousness. You come into the World only with consciousness, you leave it only with consciousness. Everything else remains here on the plane of Earth. Physical matter, therefore, can be likened to modelling clay. That is all. You spend your life modelling! It is the energy that you put into that modelling that creates consciousness, the consciousness which makes you divine.

# RECONCILIATION

As you gather here tonight you are already beginning to feel the all-pervasive energy of the Christ-Mass. Indeed your very presence here bears witness to that energy. Over many years I have talked about this energy and have promoted the concept of goodwill, of God's will, being manifest specifically at this time. I have said that when there is goodwill or God's will between all people then there will be peace on the Earth. Part of the essential process of peace which concerns the Earth so greatly at this time, not only in your own individual lives and your relationships with each other but with the World as a whole, as you face the threat of a global conflict leading to a nuclear holocaust, is the principle of reconciliation.

Reconciliation is an essential part of goodwill. You who live on the Earth would see reconciliation as an external force. You would look outwards and would seek to reconcile your views, your opinions and your ideas with those of the people with whom you clash, not only in your family and in your country but in the World as a whole. Indeed, your experience in the World has usually taught you to look outwards, to solve problems externally rather than internally. Nevertheless, I would say to you that the essence of reconciliation is not to look outwards but is to look inwards. It is only when you as individuals reconcile yourselves inwardly that there will be peace on this Earth and that the outward reconciliation can then take place.

You cannot reconcile outwardly until you have reconciled inwardly, for what is it, after all, that you are reconciling? When you consider the threat to the World or even the threat to you as individuals what is it that causes the conflict, the hatred and the division? It is the thoughts that you have created of that other country, of that other person. What is needed, therefore, is the reconciliation of those thoughts, the recognition that they are your thoughts, that they are the creations of your own being. Reconciliation is the balance of the personality with the soul-impulse. It is the recognition of the balance between the two, of the fact that in the world of physical creation there has to be physical thought and analysis but that they are only one aspect of yourselves, the outward part, the outward manifestation of physical life. It is the impulse behind that thought that is the more important if you will but heed it. You therefore need to reconcile the deepest, the most sacred, the most holy part of your being, the essence of your spirit, with that with which you create externally.

Consider the present state of the World and the conflict between the U.S.A. and the U.S.S.R. It is obvious that this conflict will never be resolved on the level at which those countries are now attempting to resolve it, for the character, the personality, the thought-forms of the two ideologies are so ingrained and fixed that they will never be reconciled. The one cannot accept the other because it is so totally diverse and opposite. Reconciliation will only come about by the countries' leaders reaching inwards to the God in them and through that recognising the God in the other, seeing the holiness, the wholeness, of all who dwell on the plane of Earth and recognising their divine responsibility to their Creator.

The principle is just the same on an individual level as you clash with members of your family or with your neighbours. You are all holy. You are all divine. You are all one. How easy it is to see the faults in others. You are all so good at doing that, but how difficult it is to turn that eye inwards and to see your own faults, your own weaknesses, the lessons that you have to learn. It is precisely because you have not learnt those lessons that you experience such difficulty in facing them and in coming to terms with them.

The basis of reconciliation is the practice of right behaviour through the principles of Humility, Divinity and Love. The first principle of the trinity that you need to observe is the principle of Humility, of being humble both with one's self and with others, of recognising that you are all learning, that you are all walking your paths in life and that you all make mistakes. What you all need is love and support, not criticism and hatred. What you all need is encouragement, not scorn. What you all need to recognise is that you are but individual grains of sand on the beach of life. Be humble in that knowledge.

The next principle that you need to observe, one just as important as Humility, is the principle of Divinity. Recognise the divinity of all things from a small blade of grass to an evolved human being, from your God to that which you call the Devil. The Divine is in all things for the Divine has created all things and though you may not recognise the Divinity in everything, that is for you to ponder over and to seek. Treat everything with reverence, for everything is divine. Everything is part of Divine Creation. It is for you to seek understanding of that Divinity through right thought, right speech and right practice. That is your responsibility to your Divinity. If your God were to stand before you now you would not feel separation from It for you would be enveloped by Its Light, Its Creativity and Its Love. Yet when that God is dispersed into millions of beings, into millions of aspects of creation, you can then stand before them and have the right, you feel, to criticise, to ignore, indeed, even to destroy. But that God is still there. It is your recognition of It that is not present. Recognise therefore the principle of Divinity.

The last principle that you must observe is the principle of Love, which is the energy of Creation. Recognise that without love there is no life, that without love there is no creativity, that without love there is no future. Humanity without love becomes a zombie, becomes a force to be battered this way and that by the storms of life, having no direction, no purpose and, above all, no relationship with anything that exists on any plane of life. You are all beings of love, filled with love, energised by love, and that love flows from the source through all who are open to it. Love flows through people such as yourselves and is, in turn, reflected on all those with whom you come in contact, with all those with whom you have a karmic and a moral obligation.

If you are to evolve, if you are to be of service, then, as I have said, there must be reconciliation with one's self. I cannot stress too much that at this time what this World needs above all is light-bearers. It is easy for aged souls, for souls of understanding and wisdom, to be successful in the physical World. You can truly achieve anything that you desire if you put your minds to it. You can make money. You can attain positions of authority and power. You can acquire material possessions. But what good will that do you, for being souls of aged evolution you will soon experience soul disquiet, soul unease. The richest man or woman in the World who does not have a quiet soul remains unfulfilled.

Recognise, therefore, that the most important thing for you, when you look down on this plane of life after death, will be to see that you have truly done something to aid the transformation of this World, that you have grounded an impulse which will leave its mark on the generations to come. You will want to see that you have transformed this World through your physical living, that you have truly been of service and have given freely to the World no matter what the cost. Remember that no sacrifice is ever in vain for you will come back in another body, in another Age, to live again on this plane of Earth and what you sow now you will reap then.

I will end with this thought since all of you have been concerning yourselves with the question of nuclear war and nuclear disarmament. If there was a war, if there was a nuclear conflict, and if one side had actually launched their missiles and the destruction of a large part of the World was thus assured, what should be the response of the other side? Should it be to fire their own missiles back in a futile gesture of revenge or should it be to accept the fact that, even though they viewed the opposing ideology with abhorrence and would not want it to triumph at any cost, they should refrain from firing their own missiles so that human life on the Earth should be allowed to continue on its evolutionary path? Is it not better to sacrifice an ideology in order to ensure the survival of the Human Race and the three other Kingdoms of Matter? That is the real nature of sacrifice: to give one's life even if one knows that one is without fault, without blame, for the good of the whole. There is only one person that can do that. That is the person who is reconciled with themselves and with their Creator.


## QUESTIONS AND ANSWERS


Q:  It seems to me that although talks such as this do give hope for the future, Humanity is walking down a very dark tunnel and that only occasionally is there a flicker of light at the end of that tunnel to guide us on our way.

ZT:  It seems to me that even though the good Lord does put a little light at the end of the tunnel you all expect a great searchlight! You will not get one in your World today because it is so dense and so obscured by evil. The path of Truth in these perilous times is never that well lighted. All that you can do, as you well know, is to take one step forward at a time using the light that is available. You only have to concern yourselves with that one step. Do not worry about the end of the tunnel or your path to it, for you will come to it all too soon. As you well know, at the other end of that tunnel, which is death, there is a light beyond your imagination, a light so bright that every part of your being is illuminated and is seen in its true nature. So do not be afraid either of darkness or of the end of the tunnel.

Q:  I hear what you are saying but the trouble is that we are so mortal.

ZT:  You are mortal and will be mortal until the day you die. This is true of all life, but your mortality, to a large extent, is controlled by your Creator. You will not attract unto yourself any thing that you have not chosen. Your World is in the state that it is today because it *has* chosen. It is an act of learning, an act of being. The World lives in fear of a nuclear holocaust because it has chosen to do so. In the final analysis Humanity must decide whether it wants to sacrifice the planet for the sake of an ideology or a religion. Have the two major nations of this World the right to destroy all the other nations because of their political differences. They are acting as 'God', but as a 'God' without love, without compassion. You might well be fearful when the fate of your World is placed in the hands of such a 'God'.

Finally, consider which culture or nation is the greater, the one which triumphs or the one which sacrifices? Perhaps this is the ultimate test now facing the two great ideologies, Communism and Capitalism. Perhaps they are being presented by their Creator with this challenge for a very definite purpose. Perhaps it is a test to decide the nature of the next Age and of the next Root Race. Which is the greater civilisation, the one that would sacrifice itself for the World or the one that would fight and would destroy much of the World on which it lives in order to win? Can one glory in a victory which involves so much destruction? Can there be any glory in such a victory?

Q:  Surely, until we learn to be humble, to accept what other people say or do, there is not much chance of us co-operating together any more than we do now? Humanity cannot unite until it begins to accept every aspect of itself in humility.

ZT: One of the interesting things about the Human Race, when viewed from our side of life, is that you as individuals always think that you are right when so often you are wrong! Even when you have been proved wrong on many occasions, the next time you still think that you are right in your opinions, in your ideas, your values, your concepts. Of course if you do not think that you are right who else would! But why such certainty? Why are you so certain that what you say about somebody must be right, that your opinion on this subject must be correct just because you thought of it? Here, of course, comes the quality of humility.

Q: I think the salvation of the Human race is that it has a sense of humour.

ZT: Would that salvation was that simple! Consider that on the one hand you have some general sitting in his airborne flight-command post with his finger poised above a red button waiting to receive an order to exterminate a large part of the World and yet on the other hand you have someone like Mother Theresa going round the streets of Calcutta collecting people who are dying in order to ease their passing from life. What a contrast, and yet both ways of life are valid, both are an expression of Humanity in its uniqueness. What you have to do is to encompass those two extremes and view them both in love, to see that they both have meaning and purpose. What is important therefore is neither the general nor Mother Theresa but you as individuals, for how you view them decides your view of the World. The World is what you think of it, what you make it.

Q: Can you please tell us about destiny and what does it mean to us on the plane of Earth?

ZT: The subject of destiny is very complex as is the whole question of whether it is fixed or whether you can avoid it. Either you are the master of your destiny or destiny is the master of you. More than a few evolved souls have spent many hours trying to explain this both to themselves and to Humanity. I will try to present an abbreviated explanation.

The first thing you have to consider with destiny is that there is no such thing as time. There is earthly time, of course, the time of which you are well aware, but that time does not play a part in destiny except in the abstract sense that the only choice that you have is the time that you choose to face your destiny! By that, obviously, I mean physical time not just in this life but in lives to come as well as in lives that have passed. In that sense you have a choice. You may choose when you wish to incarnate and pursue a certain destiny. Perhaps at this point we had better look at the choice of one's destiny because it has so many implications.

Aged souls choose their own destiny. If you are a young soul your destiny is mostly chosen for you by great Spiritual Beings who in their wisdom know what you need to experience on the physical plane of Earth and the best time to experience it. But those of you who are aged souls choose your destiny yourselves, and when I say destiny I mean destiny as a broad pattern of events. Destiny is not a narrow path unless you are a very evolved soul like Jesus or the Buddha who incarnate to fulfil a very specific task, but even in a destiny like that there are choices and tests which the great Masters have to face and resolve. Even they can change their destinies.

So it would be true to say that if one has chosen a destiny one should follow it and that if one does not one is creating blockages. Obviously if one has elected to follow a certain destiny then one should follow that pattern of events and learn something from them. If you decide to avoid that pattern then all that you are doing is postponing that pattern of events to another life, another incarnation, another moment in spiritual time. It is not being avoided, it is just being postponed. Very often you can incarnate on Earth with a very strong destiny to fulfil and because of a series of events in early physical life which perhaps were not destined, for whatever reasons, the pressure of physical life can become so strong that it is not possible for that soul to experience that destiny. So of its own accord the soul decides to change its destiny realising that the task it had set itself is impossible. In this case one's destiny becomes changed in mid-life, in mid-stream. This happens on many occasions.

Remember that everyone has both destiny and choice. You may be destined, for example, to meet someone and accomplish something with them but if that other person changes their mind and chooses some other path then that will affect you. "Ah", you would say to me, "Surely all this was known in the vast plan and is not that too a part of destiny?" Without wishing to complicate

227

matters, yes! So destiny is not a simple matter! When one has choices, even those choices are recognised, are taken into consideration in the greater pattern.

Obviously, if one is an aged soul the restriction on one's destiny becomes very limiting for there is no point in reincarnating to repeat what one has learnt before. One only incarnates to learn something new, to discharge past karma and to give of oneself to the Earth. Therefore there is no point in changing that destiny and finding oneself in a position where one cannot give, where one cannot serve, where one cannot fulfil the potential of one's being. So the more aged one becomes in soul evolution the more limiting becomes the pattern and, above all, the stronger becomes the impulse to seek that destiny, to follow it and to fulfil it. So the stronger the impulse, the stronger the soul, the stronger the calling and, above all, the stronger the receptivity.

Let us think about this. If one is receptive, one listens. One is receptive to many sources, many impulses, not just from the physical World with which one comes into contact and which sometimes is called universal feed-back, but also from the guidance and the wisdom which is pouring down from the Higher Realms. Every soul incarnates on Earth with a destiny to fulfil but once the personality gets in charge of the physical vehicle it can block the soul impulse and can reject that destiny path. No matter what guidance or wisdom is sent down the personality remains impervious to it because it does not like what it has to do. There are many in the World who do this. But this rejection is not forever. It can be changed and, sometimes, dramatically, especially if one has constantly rejected one's destiny in past lives.

I am always quoting to you the transformation of Saul into Paul mentioned in the Bible. I am not saying that Paul was any better than Saul. They both had their faults. But we all know that this transformation involved a shift of consciousness from one extreme to the other. This is often the case when one changes one's destiny or when one catches up with one's destiny. One can resist for just so long and then eventually one comes to terms with the fact that one must get down to doing what one came to do. One is always being guided back to one's destiny path. One is always being given guidance but the question is whether or not one hears what is said to one.

Young souls can change their destiny frequently because everything for them is a learning experience, but older souls are more restricted because they do not wish to repeat what they have already learnt. Nevertheless, within that broad framework there is also the learning experience of changing one's destiny because that in itself is a learning process. When one comes down with a strong destiny impulse and then chooses to ignore it, to reject it or to change it, that in itself is a great learning experience, and if there is pain or suffering because of it, then the next time one incarnates one listens more clearly. One is more responsive to the force of destiny.

Having said all that, the great transforming feature of destiny is that one *is* linked to the Godhead Which is the source of all destiny, all love, all wisdom, all power. So no matter what one does, no matter what the motivation in one's life for changing or avoiding one's destiny, for not even seeking one's destiny, if one goes down on one's knees before one's Creator and in love and humility recognises what one has done and asks that one's life be reshaped and redestined to achieve what one has previously denied, then that will always be done. So one is never lost. One never loses one's destiny. One is never off one's path if one is attuned to the Godhead.

So let us not make destiny into too much of a hang-up. The concept is important, is significant. There is a Divine Plan for this Earth and I use the word Plan in your Earthly terminology although the cosmic concept is very different. The Beings who rule and govern this Earth are working to a Plan. There is an evolutionary cycle that is being fulfilled and you are part of that cycle, you are part of that Plan. Therefore there is a part that you have to play, a role that you have agreed to play in that Plan. There are lessons that have to be learnt. I am talking now of the Spiritual Hierarchy, of Inter-Planetary Masters, of Galactic Government, of great Beings of whom you have no concept. I am talking now of spiritual forms around you in their thousands who you cannot see but who are also a part of that Plan. So be humble in the insignificance of your individual destiny and yet recognise that your destiny is significant as is everything in the Cosmos.

Q: Thank you. I liked your explanation and I appreciate the love behind it.
ZT: It is the same love that you have. I am no different to you except that I have no physical form. What an advantage! Yet you

have so much more potential than me for I can stand and talk to you but that does not change your World. I can inspire you, I can motivate you, I can talk to you, but that is all that I can do, whereas you have the physical ability to transform your World. You can create with your hands, motivated by your hearts.

You are in one of the greatest schools of learning in the Universe. One could say that a single life on the plane of Earth is worth a thousand on the higher planes. The Earth is one of the greatest schools of learning perhaps because there is the greatest evil and one needs the greatest evil to appreciate the greatest good.

# A PERSPECTIVE OF OUR WORLD TODAY

You live in a World in crisis. In every country people live in fear, if not fear of a nuclear holocaust then fear of natural disaster, fear of losing money or social status, fear of disease and so on, and where there is fear there cannot be love. Those of you who are trying to lead God-centred lives, who are trying to change the pattern of human behaviour on this planet, are sometimes overcome by doubt and concern. You become dispirited and wonder if the struggle is really worth it, if the benefits to be gained from righteous living will indeed ever manifest on this plane of Earth. Even souls of aged evolution are beginning to fall by the wayside faced by such crises around them. I would therefore like to give you a perspective from our side of life of the World in which you live today and ask you to keep faith, to trust the Plan for this Earth and the great Being who created it and watches over it.

I will begin with a story. Whether the story is true is for you to decide. You can regard it as a legend, as a myth, if you so desire. Hundreds of thousands of years ago there was a planet within the solar system centred on the star which you call Sirius and living on that planet were many races all fulfilling the evolutionary pattern of the God whose spirit was in that star Sirius. Those races lived through many cycles of evolution developing their consciousness and moving upwards on the evolutionary spiral of that solar system. There was, however, one race on that planet which, in spite of the cosmic talents that it had been given, could not and would not use them for the good of the whole. This race of people became more and more self-centred and used their God-given talents to create power and wealth for themselves. They rarely respected the wishes and the needs of their own race, let alone those of the other races or the planet as a whole.

Because the other beings of that solar system gave freely in love,

231

because they did not oppose the desires of this evolving race, so the evolutionary cycle of the planet became unbalanced and the Lord of that system was faced with the decision of what to do with this race of people. The choice was either to remove it from the planet, to await another cycle, another time, when it could evolve, or else to follow the request of one of the great beings of that race who asked that the race should be given another chance. That being asked that the race should be removed to another solar system where it could evolve and grow more aware of its divinity, where it could more properly use the cosmic talents which it had been given. The Lord of Sirius acceded to this request and it was decided to reincarnate this race of people on another planet where the wheat could be sorted from the chaff, where those who did indeed recognise their divine responsibility for right creation, who could live by and obey God's Law, who could ground and demonstrate it, would be selected to go forward into the next evolutionary cycle.

So it came to pass that that planet in the solar body of Sirius was dissolved and the souls of that race migrated to the solar system in which you now dwell. They were placed upon the planet Earth to fulfil a divine plan. Let us remember that at this stage, before the coming of Humanity, Earth was a planet of perfection. It had been created by the Goddess of Earth to fulfil her divine plan. The three Kingdoms of Matter that were present on the Earth lived in harmony and balance. The Animal Kingdom, in particular, was not as you know it today, for all the different species lived in harmony with each other. It was truly a place of paradise, demonstrating the wisdom and the love of the Goddess. It was on this planet of perfection that the race of Humanity was placed. It was seen as the ideal situation in which Humanity could further evolve.

So over many milleniums of years Humanity has lived and evolved impelled by the patterns of successive astrological influences. Most people today look at the history of Humanity and think that it has lasted for only thirty thousand years or so, but they do not know of Atlantis, of Lemuria and of Cordemia. They do not know of other civilisations which have come and gone, of other cycles of human evolution which do not form part of the history and knowledge of Humanity today. The Human Race has been evolving upon this planet for a long time, nevertheless, as I look at it today, I can see that relatively few souls have grasped a true understanding of life. I have seen only a few great Teachers or

Masters come from amongst you, only a few who have returned to the planet to try to change the pattern of human evolution, only a few who have tried to lead Humanity into an understanding that the essence of life is sacrifice. Humanity must recognise its divinity and the source that created it, the source that controls it. Above all, it must recognise why that divinity was dispersed into millions of individuals. It is this fact which the Human Race would not recognise on its former planet.

As you approach a time of great crisis, everywhere I see that Humanity is ruled by fear. Both individuals and countries live in fear of each other and where there is fear there cannot be love and love is the divine energy of your Creator. Where the energy of love is lacking then darkness and evil will be present. No part of the planet today is free from fear. Even in a civilised country such as Britain this fear manifests in the form of envy, greed, hatred, mistrust, prejudice and so on. Why can you not see that you are all one, rejoice in the diversity which appears in the Human Race and recognise that as a great strength? To be alike is weakness, to be different is strength and to be unique as you all are is divine. You are all unique spiritual beings for not one of you is the same, and in that uniqueness lies the greatness of the Human Race. For you are not clones, you are not robots, you are not as beings on many other planets: you are individual God-centred beings with the potential to become a god.

Above all, you possess the divine gift of free choice, freely given to you, but where has that free choice led the Human Race today: to the point of self-destruction, to the point where perhaps one of the great nations of this World would kill millions of people, indeed would destroy the World rather than allow another nation to win an ideological battle. Is that the act of God-centred beings, beings of sacrifice and love? Has not the demonstration of all the great Masters that have evolved from this planetary system been one of sacrifice and love? Did not the Master Jesus himself demonstrate this by his death on the cross, a sacrifice to save the race of Humanity that came after him. But even when that divinity is demonstrated it is not readily accepted. It falls, for the most part, on deaf ears. But there are a few who hear that message, who recognise their divinity, and it is to you that I speak now.

I ask you to take heart. I ask you to be strong in the resolution of your spirit, in that still, quiet voice which speaks within you. I ask you to follow that inner light and to be true to it. I can reassure you that there is a Plan for this Earth, that there is a great Being overseeing that Plan and that no evil thing can touch you if you are but true to yourself. Though many may suffer around you, though many may perish, though there may be droughts and floods, earthquakes and cataclysms, those who are true to that spirit within will survive and by survive I do not necessarily mean the survival of the physical body but the survival of the spirit on the higher planes of life. For the Day of Judgement is coming, the time when the wheat must be sorted from the chaff if this planetary system is to move upward on the evolutionary spiral. Now that does not mean that those who are not chosen are faced with extermination. It merely means that they will return to what could be called a Group Energy and will allow those who have earned the right to individuality, who have recognised the divinity of their being, to progress further along their evolutionary paths and so fulfil their potential.

I therefore say to those of you who feel threatened by the World in which you live today, take heart. There is a great Being watching over you. Every sacrifice that you make is noticed. Every act of love, every act of service that you make on this plane of Earth, is recorded. Everything that you do to help your fellow human beings is noted for such is the true nature of Humanity. The act of a conscious human, a person acting with humanity, is to give freely no matter what the cost. It is to give of oneself as one has never given before. It is to recognise the divinity of every aspect of the World in which you live. Above all, it is to recognise the divinity of the planet on which you dwell.

As I said earlier, you are not of this planet. This planet is but a school of life in which you learn your lessons. It is a school of great beauty offered to you in a sacred trust by the Goddess, whose body is this Earth, as an act of sacrifice to this race of beings which has been placed upon her. Over the milleniums she has watched the human race pollute her body and use her creations for its own ends, failing to recognise either the wholeness, the holiness, of the Earth or the very presence of her being and her part in the evolutionary pattern. Nevertheless, there are some today who are becoming aware of the presence of the Goddess and of her power. There is a recognition growing that the Goddess is as important as the God, that the feminine is just as important as the

234

masculine and that it is the energy and the potential of the two in balance that is the source of divine creativity.

Do not be dragged down by the World in which you live. Do not allow the suffering and the lessons of others to become your suffering, your lessons. Observe with compassion but recognise that their path is not for you. You are here to ground and demonstrate your spiritual potential in your everyday living as you come into contact with the three Kingdoms of Matter and with your fellow human beings. Live life with consciousness and awareness. This is the greatest opportunity for evolution that you have ever had. Recognise it and use it, use it to attain the breakthrough in consciousness that will make you realised beings. In that way, as the Aquarian Age comes into being, you will be part of that select band of Humanity which is sowing the seeds of the millenium of peace and plenty. The Aquarian Age will be an Age where Humanity will truly represent itself on this plane of Earth, where beings from other planets will come and sit at Humanity's feet in order to learn of its consciousness and divinity.

You are gods in the making but in any learning process there will inevitably be pain and suffering, not so much on the physical as on the mental level. You will make mistakes, that is to be expected, but the purpose of mistakes is to learn from them, not to repeat them. Above all, recognise that everything on the plane of Earth is one. The person who sits next to you now, even if you have not seen them before, is your brother and probably has been in another life. The person who you meet tomorrow is your sister and probably has been in another life. You are all one on this plane of Earth. There is no separation except the separation which you create with your thoughts and your fears. Where there is love, unconditional love, without judgements, where there is the recognition of a fellow-soul evolving on the path of life, then the divinity and the blessing of life is present.

Recognise this energy as you gather here tonight. Let that feeling of love grow from within you. Let it go forth and descend upon this troubled planet. Recognise that a group such as this, joined together in common purpose, in common design, in the unity of the power of love, can indeed save this World. That is the potential of your divinity. Recognise it and use it.

Q:   Can you give us some practical advice on how we can best help the planet at this critical time through the way in which we live our daily lives.

ZT:   The practical steps which can be taken are threefold. Firstly, there is the recognition of the presence of the Goddess who controls and governs this planet. I wonder how many of you in your prayers ever thank the Goddess for the gift of her being, this beautiful planet on which you dwell. As a mother or a father knows, although they do not expect it, is it not nice to be thanked occasionally by your children? It is essential to give energy back to the source. It completes the cycle. So in your prayers and meditations send energy to the Goddess and link with her. Appreciate the sacrifice that she is making, the freedom she is giving to Humanity to use her Being, her Body, as they so desire.

Secondly, there is right relationship with the creations of the Goddess, according to the highest of your consciousness, through the way you treat the flowers, the animals, the very ground on which you walk, how you contact them, attune to and align with them. They are all part of the living force which to a great extent controls your life even if you are not aware of it. How many of you, when standing by a plant, for example, are aware that that plant is communicating with you, obviously not through physical speech but in the sense that it is either giving to you or even taking something from you.

Finally, there is what I would call public accountability, which is every day to try and preserve the holiness, the wholeness of this planet. That means standing up and being counted when evil people try to use this planet for selfish or ideological ends. Recognise that it is necessary to oppose the forces of darkness and by oppose I do not mean take up physical arms and fight, I mean oppose with your pure energies, with your pure thought-forms. It is necessary to offer your energies up to the higher levels of life to be used by the great Beings. This is needed so badly at this time if we are to save the planet. But so many do not care. So many feel that no change can come about. So many feel that the path of Humanity cannot be changed. But it can. In these three ways you can begin to change the pattern not only of your life but of those around you.

Q: In the talk the word sacrifice was used several times. To me sacrifice means denial. Could you tell us what you mean by sacrifice.
ZT: It has been said that the lesson of this planet is sacrificial service through love, love being the energy of your Creator. Sacrifice and service: the two go together. You would probably think that the greatest sacrifice you could make would be to give your life that another may live. To surrender one's life is seen as the greatest sacrifice because of the way that Humanity views its mortality but, in truth, there are many sacrifices greater than giving up one's life. The essence of any sacrifice is consciousness or spiritual understanding. The nature of the sacrifice, on any level, depends on the understanding and the motivation behind it. If you are sacrificing something which you still want then it is not a true sacrifice. An unwilling sacrifice greatly diminishes the effect of the sacrifice. A sacrifice must be a willing one. It must be freely given, it must be free of all thought forms and attachments.

In the World in which you live today life is a continual sacrifice. The lesser point of evolution is constantly sacrificing to the higher. For example, you need food to sustain yourselves. For many of you this involves the sacrifice of the Animal Kingdom. That Kingdom is constantly sacrificing itself to you to aid your evolution. Many in the World today do not even recognise or appreciate this sacrifice. Communication forms an essential part of any sacrifice. If some being has sacrificed itself for you there should be communication between you to establish an understanding of why the sacrifice is being taken. Any act of sacrifice demands an understanding on the higher levels of life as to why the sacrifice is being asked for and why it is being given.

Consciousness therefore plays a large part in any act of sacrifice. Constantly the lower evolution sacrifices to the higher even on the planetary level and beyond. Sacrifice is an essential part of life, a necessary lesson, but just as you, as an individual, would demand purpose and reason for your sacrifice and, perhaps, above all, would like recognition of the sacrifice that you had made, so be aware that this is true of all levels of life. The energy behind all sacrifice should be the energy of your Creator, which is love. Where there is no true love there is no true sacrifice. If you cannot love the person to whom you are making the sacrifice it is better not to make it at all for a false sacrifice is of very little value. The energy of love must be present in any sacrifice.

Q: Although many of us here have only met for the first time tonight there is a very strong group energy present. Would you comment on this?

ZT: The people here tonight come from many countries, from many continents, from many walks of life and yet, at the appointed time, at the appointed place, you have all come together to form this group. Everyone of you that is present is meant to be here. If just one of you were missing tonight this group would not be complete. Such is the nature of the Plan of your Creator. Each one of you has something to give to the energy of the whole and, in return, has something to receive. This reflects the pattern of life. Can you now recognise the stupidity of those who would exterminate large numbers of Humanity in a nuclear war in order to gain an ideological victory, for if large numbers of Humanity were destroyed the Race would become imbalanced and would lack wholeness. Humanity would no longer be a complete group. The ideology that 'won' a nuclear war would have sown the seeds of its own destruction because Humanity would have become so imbalanced.

There is great strength in the diversity of Humanity. Rejoice in the differences of the peoples and the races. See that as a strength. Recognise that all beings are complementary and go to make up the whole. Recognise that all you as an individual can do is to give of your highest to Humanity just as you have given to this group tonight. As you have been touched by the energy of this group, as it has uplifted and moved you, as seeds have been sown which will come to fruition in the days to come, so recognise that this should happen on a planetary level as well.

What Humanity needs above all at this time is wholeness: wholeness of body, mind and spirit. There is no division except where Humanity creates it. Let us pray that the division, the self-centredness, which destroyed that planet in the system of Sirius aeons of time ago will not do the same thing here on Earth. Let us pray that there are souls amongst you who will stand forth for this wholeness, who will recognise that through the group, through the whole, is the path to both individual and planetary transformation. Now that does not mean that you should not have your moments of solitude when you go within yourself. That is part of the essential balance of life. But there must also be times of sharing with your fellow human beings, times when you give of your being. In as

238

much as you serve just one of your fellow human beings you are serving your God, you are worshipping your God. In as much as you ignore or do evil to any one of your fellow human beings recognise that you are doing that to your God. There is only one God. There is only one Race: the Human Race.

# THE ESSENTIAL QUESTION

I wonder, as you listen to me talking now through this instrument, who you think I really am and even if you knew, and my name was familiar to you, would that necessarily lead you to believe in what I am saying to any great extent? Does my voice speaking to you from another level of life really have meaning? Does what I say to you have purpose? Why should I seek to talk to you and why should you want to listen to me? What is it that I can tell you which you cannot discover for yourselves? So much has been spoken through this channel and, indeed, through other channels all over the World and yet so much has been ignored. That, of course, reflects the nature of Humanity's divine birthright and we of the Spiritual Hierarchy would not want it otherwise. It is for us to touch your hearts but it is for you to respond. If you do not respond then there is little that we can do.

To help you to understand why I am talking to you now let us, for a moment, reverse the roles. Let us suppose that you are the source of the wisdom and that you wish to speak to me, a discarnate being, who is planning to incarnate on the Earth. You, with your wisdom and your experience of physical life, would want to help me to prepare for my life on Earth. You would want me to have an understanding of the nature of physical life and of how best to prepare myself for my physical incarnation. You would therefore seek to advise me through a channel such as this.

Let us consider another case. Let us suppose that you were to die and then incarnate on my plane of life. Having only recently been separated from your friends and loved ones, what would be more natural than that you would want to help those who you had recently left behind on the physical plane. Now that you are free from your body of clay and are dwelling in one of your higher bodies, with the freedom that that gives, what would be more

241

natural than that you should try to help your friends in your new found consciousness. You would therefore seek to advise your friends through a channel such as this.

Recognise that the power which links us together at this time has been created over many lives. We have worked together on the physical as well as on the higher planes of life. We have long served each other on the various planes of our spiritual existence. We are bonded for eternity. I serve you therefore as a brother would serve a sister, as a husband would serve a wife: in love. I give of myself, to help you, out of love. I give my love to you without requiring a response. I offer my wisdom to you no matter whether you accept or reject it. I give freely of my being as an act of love to help you on the plane of Earth just as you, if you were on my plane of life, would do the same for me, for we are all part of the Race of Humanity.

Now you must also understand that what I say to you and what you would say to me is restricted not only by the nature of the channel, not only by the Law of the Cosmos which carefully defines the degree to which one can intervene on other planes of life, but also by the restrictions of our consciousness in the understanding of time and destiny. You can now begin to appreciate why you would want to contact those with whom you are linked on the Earth plane. You would come to a sanctuary such as this and would sit amongst your friends, just as I do now, and from a higher body, a body invisible to the human eye, you would seek to contact those friends. You would try to talk to them and yet you would not be able to make an impression on them for you would be talking on a different frequency to them. You would be trying to advise them, you would be trying to warn them of events to come, and yet they would not be able to hear you for the only means of communication between the different planes of life is mind to mind, even when talking through a channel as I do now. That is the only level which is open to us.

Many of you listening to me now are aged souls. If you were to grade the consciousness of Humanity I wonder where you would place yourselves. Would it surprise you to know that many of you are in the top ten per cent of human consciousness! You represent the peak of achieved human consciousness and yet you know only too well how much you still have to learn. You know only too well how often you make mistakes, especially in these difficult times

242

in which you live. We for our part, therefore, are trying to guide and to help you in these difficult times, but if our wisdom is rejected, if the advice we give is ignored, if our warnings for the future are not heeded, then there is little that we can do for it is you, and you alone, that is responsible for the pattern and direction of human evolution.

If you now, as individuals, were to ask in your meditation what it is that you want out of life, what it is that you value above all else, that you seek the most as a free kindred spirit, it would not be an earthly, a physical thing, would it? It would not be the acquisition of wealth and material possessions for yourself, nor would it be the advancement of your family or even the happiness of the ones you loved most dearly. Would it not be true to say that what you seek above all else is an understanding of life, the certain knowledge of why you are here, of what you are doing and of what is the purpose of life on this planet on which you dwell?

If you have this aim, as I believe many of you do, then is this not the ultimate quest that you should set your heart on? Is this not the Holy Grail that you should seek as did the knights of King Arthur's Round Table and which, once found, is capable of enlightening you beyond all human understanding? Have you realised that once you have found this Holy Grail the whole meaning of life changes? The impact that you will have on this planet will magnify tenfold. It is by your understanding of that question, by your search and your answer, that you become a realised human being capable of helping others. Yet as I look into your auras and see the problems that you, as individuals, are facing in your lives I realise that you are but a reflection of Humanity as a whole. Humanity is suffering just as you, to varying degrees, are suffering. You are suffering because you do not see the holiness of life that is around you. You are suffering because you are not God-centred, because you do not see this Earth, this Cosmos, as being God-centred. If you believed it to be so then you would place your destiny, your body, mind and spirit in the hands of that God.

For many of you today has been the usual day of conflict and tension, a day of trying to balance the material aspects of your lives, the desire for personal aggrandisement and money, for individual advancement, with the desire for peace of mind and harmony in the World. You have been struggling to balance your many desires, emotions and thought-forms, all the factors that

243

create imbalance in your being and which, ultimately, are the cause of a world in conflict, a world which is in disharmony in almost every aspect of its living simply because it has lost sight of the divinity of life. Consider, therefore, that if you really believe that you are divine beings, then, are you not joined to the Godhead, are you not a part of It? Furthermore, if you are a part of that Godhead and are able to communicate with It and invoke Its energy, then, the Godhead must have full knowledge of your total being and of all its needs.

Consider the words of the Master Jesus, who said that every hair on your head is counted. The full implication of that statement is incredible. It means that every thought that you create, every word that you speak, every act that you perform, is noted, accepted and recorded by the Godhead. It means that that Being is conscious of everything that you do, of everything that you need, of everything that you truly seek in your heart. You therefore want for nothing. Moreover, if you are the children of that divine Being, then, just as you guard and watch over your children, does not that greater Being guard and watch over you, with equal, if not greater care? If you consider how, even at your level of consciousness, you guide and protect your children, then, when you consider the consciousness of your God, a consciousness a million times greater than yours, you may realise how that consciousness can guide and protect you.

Everything that I have said so far has been but a preparation for one essential question. I ask you to look into your hearts and to say "Am I truly God-centred?" Do you really believe that there is a God, a God that is not just an intellectual creation about which you postulate and discuss, a God that is not just to be found in the Bible and other holy books of this World, a God that is not just a Being about Whom I and the other Masters talk, a God that is not just an image that people invoke and worship, but a God that truly dwells in your own hearts and is unique to you? Do you really believe there is such a God and, if so, what do you in your hearts believe to be the power, the majesty and the glory of such a Being? What do you think are Its limitations, if any? What do you think is Its purpose for you? I wonder how many of you have ever invoked the energy of your Creator, have ever asked for anything and have recognised both in the asking and in the receiving, when it comes, the real nature of the link that is between you and your Creator: a divine, unbreakable, eternal link.

244

How many of you are aware of the presence of God in your everyday lives? How many of you are aware of the meaning of life, of the nature of sacrifice, of the one-ness of all life, of the existence of other planes, of other spiritual kingdoms? You must recognise that Humanity today is suffering because of the nature of its society which is Godless, a society which creates in its own image rather than in the image of its Creator. Such a society creates in division and separation and seeks only to forward itself and not the whole. Where there is self-interest, inevitably, there will be conflict and where there is conflict there will be violence of thought, word and deed. Such violence almost always leads to war.

However let me make it quite clear that you do not have to walk that path. You can be in the World but not of it. That, above all, is what I and the other Masters have been trying to make clear to you. You need not be touched by all that is happening and is going to happen on this plane of Earth. I say this not as a promise of escape but as the reality of what life is about. But first you have to take one important step. You have to make one act of surrender. You have to recognise not only the God in yourself but the God in each and everyone around you. You have to take that first step, a step which for some will be a step taken in faith, a step into apparent darkness. You have to say that you will put your hand in the hand of your Creator and that you will follow Its path. That is the surrender that you have to make.

You must recognise your Creator as the source of all that you need for your life and know that if you work for that Divinity to the highest of your being then all your needs will be met. It must be apparent, as you look round the World today, that Humanity cannot meet its own needs. Millions are starving. Millions are oppressed both physically, financially and religiously. Millions live in fear. There is very little unconditional love in your World. There is very little compassion. Humanity has failed to recognise and demonstrate its inherent divinity and the result of that failure is soon to manifest as a scourge across the face of the Earth. You can avoid that scourge only if you are at one with the source of all life, your God.

I therefore ask you all to consider most deeply, at this critical time in the Earth's evolution, where you stand. It is essential that you do this for the days are numbered until the time when you will be assessed and judged. You must make your decision. You must uphold what you know to be true. You must say that this is what I am, this is what I believe, this is what I hold to be my understanding of life and by this I will live or die. Such is the nature of the World in which you live. It is a World where the wheat will be sorted from the chaff. It is a World where only the most evolved consciousness will survive physically.

I therefore ask you to go within yourselves. Consider the question that I have posed on many occasions: what is the purpose of physical life? When you return to Earth in your next incarnation what will you want to bring with you? It will not be the physical possessions of this life. It will not be the pain and the suffering that you have experienced in it. It will be the spiritual consciousness that will enable you to lead your next life with greater understanding. Recognise that every jump in consciousness that you make is a step up the evolutionary ladder not just for yourselves but for Humanity as a whole, for as you learn and demonstrate so you uplift the greater mass of Humanity. The chosen ones are watched. The chosen ones demonstrations are noted. That is the responsibility of evolution.

There are many Masters on the plane of Earth at this time who are seeking, each according to their own unique note and vibration, to bring Humanity into a greater awareness of God. They are trying to lead Humanity into an understanding of the fact that God is in all things, in all people, in all religions, in all races, in every field of human endeavour. They are teaching that God is universal, beyond your understanding, beyond your comprehension, that God has an infinite number of aspects, is many-faceted, that you are but one aspect of millions and yet you are divine.

So on this day go forth and consider: where do you stand? Is all that has been given to you, not only through this channel but through all the Masters who have touched human consciousness, to be treated as a detective novel and regarded simply as a source of amusement and interest, or is it Truth? If it is Truth, and if it has meaning and purpose, then must it not become a part of your being? Consider why we should talk to you, of what is our purpose. Are we not one in our understanding of the purpose of life and the purpose of Humanity? Are we not working for one thing? In all things there can be only one answer.

Q: The Master has reaffirmed for me the decision that I have made recently, the details of which will no doubt become clearer. However it does seem to me that I am taking a step into darkness.
ZT: You may choose to call it darkness, but what you are talking about is the future, in your Earth-time anyway. So what you are saying is that the future is darkness. What is wrong with darkness? Is darkness evil? Is darkness to be feared? When you go out at night it is dark, but that is not necessarily a source of fear. Indeed, it can be a source of wonderment if the sky is clear and you can see the stars. There will always be stars in your darkness and, you know, when you look back on your decision in the years to come, to you it will be like someone who has walked with a heavy burden all his life suddenly taking it off his back and wondering why he had not done it sooner!

Q: You have spoken about the need for individuals to become more God-centred but is this not also true of groups and communities?
ZT: Of course, yes. If you have a group of people who are God-centred then the nature of that union is assured. The group is, so to speak, rather like a marriage. No matter what the husband or wife does, because of their bond of love they will look compassionately at each others faults and weaknesses. The one recognises that the other is merely revealing an aspect of themselves that they still have to master in life. The same is true of a God-centred group or community. If an awareness of the divine impulse is there, no matter what the personality of the group may display, because the members recognise the note and the soul quality of the group so they can accept in love the imperfections and weaknesses of other members of the group.

Q: Several of us are thinking of living together as a community. Can you say anything about the timing of this?
ZT: It is no good coming together on a personality level, out of fear or expectation, out of weakness or desire. It must be a recognition from the God-centre within you that both the timing and the consciousness is right. It can usually be said that there is a correct

247

time for beginning such a venture, a time before which it would have been wrong because of many factors. In just the same way that you do not normally marry until you are over twenty so there is also a time that is best suited for you to come together in your group, but that decision must come from the God-centre within. It must be motivated by the force of spirit not by the force of personality.

Q: I have spent a good many years being somebody's wife and several other people's mother. I've lost sight of who I am. In two weeks I am going away on a holiday and for a short time I am not going to be anybody's wife or anybody's mother. I would like your help to guide my thoughts as to what I should be doing with myself. Everybody else seems to have some great spiritual quest but I don't know what I should be doing at all.

ZT: It is difficult, because of the way in which society is structured today, for a mother of children to do anything but survive, or so it would appear. The demands of young children are great, indeed, can swamp not only the mother but the whole family as well. This is not just because of the way in which the family unit is structured and society lives today but also because of the demands of modern life and the way in which life is lived today. Many factors combine to place an unnatural burden on the person who runs the home. Normally this is the woman, but sometimes it can be the man. It is an unnatural burden and therefore it is only natural that at times you or any other woman should ask that question.

In actual fact, if you did but know it, you are fulfilling one of the greatest roles that you could play, for no matter what other people are doing with their individual talents, what you are doing is being responsible for creation and for the continuation of the human species on the plane of Earth. The nurturing of a baby, the overseeing of a child's adolescence, the development of a young person's spirituality to the point when they are able to stand by themselves in harmony and balance and contribute to the upward path of human evolution is surely one of the most important, if not the most important, task that a human being can perform.

At times a mother can lose sight of what she is really doing. The everyday demands of physical life do not permit her to have time for herself or for considering the spiritual aspects of life. But you should remember that Woman is created in the image of the

Goddess. Out of your wombs comes the creativity of the World. Through your hands passes all human life. You are the mothers of creation. It is an immense and awesome responsibility. The greatest thing that you can give to this World, that you can give to your Creator, is to present your child at twenty-one a balanced, sane, educated, aware, loving person. There will be a time in your life for other things, for fulfilling what your heart desires, a time when you will have the freedom to bring out your creativity in other fields. For the moment, though, this is not possible either for you or many other mothers, but recognise that this in no way inhibits your spiritual growth, for you are exemplifying the lesson of this planet, sacrificial service through love.

So when you are on your holiday I would ask you to consider the relationship between health and divinity, between health and consciousness, between what one does and what one is. Go back to your roots within, to your seed-thoughts, your seed-forms, to the primaeval energy within you. Touch into that energy and come back renewed, having bathed in the energy of the Goddess, for you are at one with her. Above all, remember that it matters not what anyone else is doing. They have different paths to walk, they have different tasks to do. They have their own destinies, their own challenges, to fulfil. It might appear that some are more active, that some are evolving more than you, but that is only seeing things with the outward eye. It is what one sees with the inner eye that is the more important. So think highly of yourself.

# PEOPLE

Human society today is primarily concerned about the relationships of people, of race to race, ideology to ideology, religion to religion, husband to wife, brother to sister and so on. You are concerned about relationships because you see the people around you as representing either the greatest support or the greatest threat to your happiness in life. Other people's thoughts, words and deeds are the primary cause of your worries, are the primary cause of your fears on this plane of life. There are only a very few people who can have a meaningful relationship with the Animal, Vegetable and Mineral Kingdoms, who can communicate with these Kingdoms on the higher levels of life. Most people in the World today ignore the feelings and the divinity of the three Kingdoms of Matter and for them it is the relationship between people that is of the prime importance. I would therefore like to discuss that relationship with you and to put forward a few ideas for you to consider in the days to come.

I will begin by stating a fact, a fact which is ignored by most people in the World today, namely, that every human being that incarnates on the plane of Earth is divine. Every human being has the spark of divinity within them, the spirit. Every human being is linked to the Godhead, is a son or daughter of God and is fulfilling a specific purpose in the evolutionary pattern of Humanity and of the Earth. Every human being, therefore, has a part to play in the evolutionary cycle, be it large or small. Moreover, since I am aware of the Plan for this Earth, I can state that that part is a destined part. Therefore every human being whom you meet comes in contact with you because of that Plan and because of the magnetic emanation of your being. You create that emanation by your thoughts, words and deeds and by the vibratory note of your spirit. There can be no day, no night, when you meet someone by chance, when the person who stands before you does not have meaning and purpose for you. Therefore recognise that you are all magnetic beings capable of attracting or repelling the energies of other human beings into or out of your aura.

Most of your time is taken up by your relationships with other people: you either like or dislike somebody, you are either trying to help or hinder them, you are either trying to be an example to them as they walk along their evolutionary path or are trying to mislead them. People cannot be ignored. They are for most of you the purpose of life: a husband for a wife, parents for children, brothers for sisters, neighbours for neighbours and so on. How you all relate together is of primary importance since it determines the nature of your life. Indeed, in times like this when the World is apparently subsiding into chaos, when even someone living in a civilised country like Britain feels threatened by the violence and the conflict of society around them, it is only natural that you should look most carefully at the people around you, at the note that they are sounding, at the consciousness that they are exemplifying.

Though you may find this fact hard to accept, the Divine Plan knows no error. Even in this World of ever increasing conflict and violence no one dies, no one is murdered, no one is raped, no one is mugged, no one is abused physically unless there is a reason for it. That person, either through their actions in past lives and the karma they have created or through their actions in this life, has drawn that event to them. That is the nature of Cosmic Law and if you will but examine that Law in your hearts and meditate on it, it will be a source of understanding and wonderment to you. You will grow in awareness of the forces that affect your World and of how protected you are if you are indeed pure in body, mind and spirit. Though you walk amongst the greatest evil on the plane of Earth if you are pure in spirit you will not be touched. The forces of evil cannot come into your aura unless you permit them to.

In a World where violence has become an everyday occurrence it is only natural that you should be suspicious of strangers. The openness of past societies has perhaps gone for good. You live in a World where people are suspicious of those who come from a different class, country or culture, are critical of what they say or do, are sceptical of their mental and physical abilities. People are constantly questioning whether strangers can be trusted, whether they can be allowed into their society or family. There is, therefore, a constant process of analysis and judgement going on in your minds. You judge everyone that comes before you according to your understanding of life. But what is the source of that judgement? Let us consider.

Would it not be true to say that you like the people who feel and think as you do but dislike those who oppose you? Do you not regard people who feel and think like you as your friends and those who do not as your enemies? But what is the reality of that judgement? Why should one be a friend and the other be an enemy when all they are doing is reflecting their individual and unique consciousnesses? Have you ever thought that perhaps you can learn more from your enemies than from your friends? If you relate only to those people who support your opinions and judgements because they are of your level of consciousness and evolution, if you relate only to those people who support you in your weaknesses, then you are restricting your own growth and evolution. If you shut out anyone who would hold a mirror to you simply because you do not like what they are saying or doing, then, maybe, you are rejecting the very person who has been sent to present an important lesson to you.

What is the source of your likes and dislikes? What is the source of the judgement that either accepts or rejects the person who stands before you? Are you conditioned by class? Are you conditioned by accent? Are you conditioned by your job and social position? Are you conditioned by sickness and health? Are you conditioned by the colour of a person's skin? Are you conditioned by religion and creed? Are you conditioned by sex? And so the list could go on. All of you, to varying degrees, are conditioned by the society in which you live. Some of you, however, are beginning to put aside your conditioning and are beginning to recognise the factors that have created your views and your opinions. Because of this you are exhibiting more openness and acceptance towards the oneness of life. You are beginning to respect the individuality of all people, their divine right to be what they have chosen to be, to express what they are according to their unique soul note. If you are affected by what people say or do then recognise that that is merely reflecting something in you which you as an individual still have to learn and come to terms with.

People who you meet are attracted to you by your magnetic aura. They always come to you for a purpose: to test you, to present a lesson to you, to bring you a message, to give you guidance, to help you along your path in life. Be aware that the humble person who comes to your door dressed in ragged clothes, seeking a glass of water and three or four minutes of your precious time, may be a great Master with the key to open the door to the next stage of your spiritual evolution. Everyone that comes into your aura is worthy of your complete attention and consideration, but so few of you are prepared to give it because you do not recognise that what is present before you in that person is the divinity of your Creator. You do not recognise that the being standing before you was created by your Creator to give of Its energy. How many of you today are prepared to look with attention and to give of your total energy to the people whom you meet. If you all would do that then the relationship, the cycle, would be completed so much more quickly. Many relationships exist today simply because there has not been a complete exchange of energy, eye to eye, heart to heart, soul to soul. If that energy was given, if you gave your complete attention to the people that you met and really looked and saw and felt what they were, then, that relationship would be completed. The information that had to be passed would be passed, the lesson that had to be learnt from the relationship would come forward, true communication would take place on all levels and you would both then be free to go on your individual ways.

Very often a person with whom you apparently have great conflict can be the bearer of an important message or lesson for you. But because you erect barriers around people you dislike, because you restrict what they can say or express to you, you shut out the very lesson for which you have perhaps been waiting in order to move forward onto a new level of consciousness and spiritual understanding. Conflict in relationship is an evolutionary tool and it presents you with the opportunity to learn and to be tested at this critical stage of your lives. So recognise that every person with whom you establish a relationship, who is attracted to you, is of divine importance, is an opportunity presented to you for learning and evolving. You should welcome them as bearing the message of your Creator to help you along your evolutionary path. Learn from them. Learn from the aspect of the Divine which is before you. That is the purpose of life. Recognise that what stands before you is the mirror of your Creator. If you fulfil and complete that relationship then you will quickly pass beyond it, but if you resist, if you create hatred, if you create all the emotions which link you either positively or negatively with that person, then you are creating burdens which will be with you for years, even lives, to come.

I would say that any person who you dislike strongly in this life you have probably disliked in many past lives as well and will continue to do so until you break that chain of continuity. Liking or disliking is a personality trait. How can you like or dislike your Creator? Your Creator is the power of love being channelled and grounded through every human being. You may not recognise the purpose of every human being's life, you may not see the purpose in what they are doing, you may not understand the relationship which comes from a meeting, but realise that it is part of the Divine Plan. It is not for you to question that Divinity but to accept it humbly in the knowledge that that is the nature of your evolutionary path. Recognise that you have something to learn from that relationship otherwise you would not have been there at that moment in time.

So as you meet people recognise these facts. It is not for you to love or to hate, to like or to dislike. Do you love or do you hate the reflection you see in the mirror each morning? Either is a wasted emotion for that mirror is but a reflection of yourself and as such reflects the divine. Recognise this fact as you look at the people around you. Consider all the energy which you waste in wrong relationships. Consider all the energy which you expend in creating burdens that will wear you down for lives to come. As you witness the so-called tragic events in life around you, as you see people suffering, recognise that that is not blind chance, that is not fate. Every action happens for a reason. Every person attracts every aspect of life unto them be it violence or peace. The fact that so much tragedy happens in your world today is because the vibratory rate of the planet is being speeded up, karma is being repaid and many lessons are being learnt at this critical time in the Earth's evolution.

It has not always been like this. You live in difficult times. You live in times when unless you recognise that all is divine, that all has purpose, that all is part of a plan even though you cannot recognise it, even though you are not aware of it, then you will not be able to stay balanced and harmonious. Greet each person therefore as you would greet yourself. Do unto others, greet others, as you would greet yourself, eye to eye, heart to heart, hands out-stretched, a smile on your face. Though the person in front of you might repel your personality he or she is divine. Can you repel the divine?

I would like to finish by referring to the story in the Bible of the lady who touched the aura of the Master Jesus and, through her faith, was healed. That lady had been sick for many years and had experienced much suffering. Her relationships with other people would have been deeply affected by her suffering. She had probably walked many, many miles that day, perhaps at great sacrifice, just to wait at a certain point on the road along which the Master Jesus was to walk. In that split second of time, surrounded by many people, she touched his aura with belief and understanding and was healed. The Master Jesus was aware of this act in spite of the crowd and turmoil and all that was going on in his life that day. He was aware of that moment, recognised its significance and acted with love. The woman then departed never to see that Master again. There you have the example of what is people in relationship, of what is love, of what is divinity and of what is the plan for Humanity.

# "DO UNTO OTHERS"

A great cosmic principle was grounded and demonstrated to Humanity two thousand years ago and is recorded in the Bible as that well-known saying "Do unto others as you would have others do unto you". That saying reflects a great cosmic law. As you now enter the Age of Aquarius that law could perhaps be developed a little further and with greater application to the times in which you live. I would state that law now as "Do unto others as you would have others do unto you; for it matters not what others do and say to you, it is only what you do and say that is recorded".

You live in a World of ever increasing division and oppression, a world of pestilence and natural disaster, all of which signal the very beginning of Armageddon. You are only too well aware of the pressure of World events upon you. It would seem that almost everywhere on the planet today nations and individuals, races and religions, are forever persecuting each other and if they are not doing that then they are abusing the three other Kingdoms of Matter. It would seem that this is a time, above all, for those of consciousness to take action, to combat evil forces to the ultimate of their being, to fight what they know to be wrong. It is difficult at such a time to know what is the appropriate thing to do when faced with such events, but I am going to invite you in this talk to consider the second part of that law: that it matters not what others do and say to you for it is only what you do and say that is recorded.

It matters not what others do and say to you. In this World today there are always people who are doing and saying things against you either consciously or unconsciously. There are always people wishing evil against you or against the society in which you live, for they believe that what they are doing is right and appropriate for the whole Human Race or, more particularly, for the race to which they belong and they regard that race as being the whole Human

Race. But those of you who have walked a little further along the path of human evolution are becoming aware of the Universal Whole. You are beginning to recognise that every race that walks this planet forms an essential and vital part of the Human Race, with a consciousness that is significant to the whole human evolutionary life-stream. You are realising that every individual has been given the freedom to walk his or her own path, to experience the concepts which they wish to ground and bring forward.

It is inevitable, because of this, that there will be clashes. It is inevitable that there will be conflicts and as the vibratory rate of the Earth quickens, as time speeds up, as this planet proceeds towards its apocalyptic moment of transformation and transmutation, so we will see an increase in these conflicts. Therefore now is the time to recognise that you can only be responsible for yourself. It is the recognition of that responsibility that will help you to face these times of trouble and distress. Now that does not mean that you are not all part of the same race, that you should be selfish, that you should not help your fellow brothers and sisters. I am asking you to consider what is the best way of helping those brothers and sisters? How are you to uplift them in their time of need? How are you to change human consciousness?

There are many people today who with the best of intentions give talks, write books, establish spiritual centres and try to change the world according to their consciousness. But in so many cases these endeavours have become playgrounds for the ego, the personality. What we are witnessing is unbalanced people trying to ground unbalanced principles. You must realise that it is only that which is in perfect balance and harmony, that which is grounded with perfect purity, that is capable of having real influence and meaning upon Humanity. Only that which is perfection transforms. You, as individualised beings, in perfection can touch and change the World by your example.

What we of the Spiritual Hierarchy are therefore concerned with at this time is to raise the perfection of the individual to the highest of his or her soul-consciousness. Do not worry what others do and say to you. That is their karma, that is their evolutionary lesson, that is their destiny. If you live in harmony they cannot touch you: your aura is the protection of your being. If you yourself are in perfect harmony and radiance no force, no power, be it nuclear or physical, mental or emotional, can enter and harm your being for the protector of those in perfection is Infinite Perfection Itself. To change this World you must change yourself. You must change by example and that example is your soul note, is your light, shining forth to the highest of your being for all to see.

Consider in your everyday lives what it is that deeply touches and affects you, and I talk now not of the perfection of Nature, of the beauty of a sunset, of an animal, of a tree, but of the beauty of Humanity. Is it not true to say that what touches you the deepest is an outpouring of unconditional love demonstrated by one of your fellow human beings? You cannot avoid being touched and transformed by that love-energy and, afterwards, encouraged by that transforming power you then go on your way trying to shine your perfection. When you see a true act of sacrifice, when you see a true act of giving, when you see a true act of service, then you are seeing the love of your Creator grounded and manifested on this plane of Earth. It is the recognition of that love that touches you. You love not the person, not the personality that grounds that love, but the love itself, for you recognise the presence of your Creator, that force of Spirit which shines and pulsates within you.

You are approaching times of great change. You will see, in the not too distant future, a world that you have never seen before and, perhaps, will hope never to see again. In such times what is to be your Saviour? How are you to cope with such changes? How are you to watch suffering and persecution without it entering into your being and dragging you down? Should you try to oppose evil on a physical level? Should you make war against it? Should you invoke higher powers to defeat or destroy those who threaten you? Remember: do unto others as you would have others do unto you. Recognition of that Law implies acceptance of Divine Will, of Divine Control. Only those that know it in their hearts can accept it. If you do not know in your hearts that there is a God of Love and that that Divinity protects you down to the least hair on your head then you cannot live life in freedom, you cannot live life to the full, with a proper understanding of the meaning and purpose of life.

You are responsible only for your own evolution, for your own point of consciousness, and what the Human Race needs now, above all else, is individualised consciousness in balance and perfection. Even if you are to die, as did the Master Jesus upon the cross, until the hour of your death that perfection shines forth, illuminates, converts, changes the consciousness of Humanity. What is death? It is the spectre that haunts the unconscious, those who do not know of the reality of life and the immortality of the soul, those who truly fear what others do unto them. If you live in that fear then you are part of the fear of Humanity and of the problems which Humanity is now facing and having to come to terms with.

Be aware, therefore, that how you live each day, how you sound your note, how you manifest your perfection, how you give of your soul-consciousness, changes the World. All the fine speeches, all the fine thoughts in the World, will do nothing if right action does not come from them. You must live the truth of your understanding. You must demonstrate it and in that demonstration you will change the World more than you can imagine. When you go to church or to a lecture and hear an inspired speaker talk, in that moment of transformation, as you are uplifted beyond time and space, you feel that divine energy, that feeling of oneness with all life. You are so touched by it that when you go forth from that place you carry that energy with you. It has left its mark on you. You go forth a disciple of that energy. You remember not the man or the woman who gave the talk, although you might regard them with affection. You take with you a part of the energy that has been grounded. It is just the same with you as an individual as you live your life each day.

You can, and should, be disciples of the Light and what the World needs at this time is Light. Let the Light shine forth in your being. Remember the last part of that saying: it is only what you say and do that is recorded, that is held in your karmic pattern, that you carry forward to your next life, that you have to face again, that you have to transmute. Many of you worry so much about the evil of others that you have little time to reflect on your own evil, yet if there was more concern with your own behaviour, with how you act towards others rather than how others act towards you, how great would be your evolutionary progress. Do not worry about what others say and do. That is their burden. Let it not become yours. Go forth in the light of your spirit. Hold to your consciousness. Be true to your understanding of life. Shine your light and be a being of transformation.

It will be difficult in the years to come for even an evolved soul to reach an understanding of the true purpose of life for you will see many events that will shock you. Even now as you read your papers and watch your television you see a World behaving in a manner that you cannot understand. Every day the degradation of Humanity becomes worse. Humanity seems to become inhuman. Do not let it touch you. This is the time of Armageddon. This is the time of the sorting of the wheat from the chaff. If you are wheat, do not take heed for the chaff for the wind of evolution will blow it away. Only the wheat will remain, but that wheat must be pure, must be healthy, must be strong. What we need now is such strength, is such example, is such consciousness. Therefore be true to yourselves. Be true to that light within and live it. Let it shine as if your life depended upon it for, truly, it does.

## QUESTIONS AND ANSWERS

Q:   I am thinking of starting a Spiritual Centre. Is there any advice you could give me about doing this?

ZT:   The word 'Centre' today has as wide a range of meanings as does the word 'love'. You have Meditation Centres, Teachers of Wisdom Centres, Community Centres, Alternative life-style Centres and so on. The implication of the word today is that if you start a Centre, that is a spiritual act, a good thing to do, because starting a Centre or working in a Centre is regarded as being part of the so-called New Age movement. Unfortunately many Centres are very Old Age, not New Age at all. Let us recognise that each one of us is a Centre. Each one of us grounds our energy and light and shares it. When you try to form a Centre, if you are to be the focaliser of the Centre, then you must be in balance and harmony otherwise that which you create will be in imbalance. If your motivation is not pure then you will attract impurity. The note that you sound decides those who are attracted to your Centre.

I therefore feel that, in your case, a little bit more growth has to take place, a little bit more understanding of life before you yourself would want to say I am a Centre, let people come and learn from the note that I sound and send forth. Now many people want to come together and work in a small community, to grow together in understanding, to be of service to each other, to share the journey along the path of life. That is good, for you all need support and understanding in these troubled times. Unfortunately the word Centre has so many connotations today that I would be very careful how you name and sound your note. I would suggest that you allow it to grow organically, in its own time, at its own pace, rather than to force it as in a greenhouse. Sow your seed in your beautiful land of America but let it grow in its own time. Do not try to run before you can walk.

# TO BE A PILGRIM

*Who would true valour see,*
  *Let him come hither;*
*One here will constant be,*
  *Come wind, come weather.*
*There's no discouragement*
*Shall make him once relent*
*His first avowed intent*
  *To be a pilgrim.*

*Who so beset him round*
  *With dismal stories,*
*Do but themselves confound;*
  *His strength the more is.*
*No lion can him fright,*
*He'll with a giant fight,*
*But he will have a right*
  *To be a pilgrim.*

*Hobgoblin nor foul fiend*
  *Can daunt his spirit:*
*He knows he at the end*
  *Shall life inherit.*
*Then fancies fly away,*
*He'll fear not what men say,*
*He'll labour night and day*
  *To be a pilgrim.*

Those inspiring words, written over three hundred years ago by
John Bunyan, are as true today as they were then. They will be just

as true three hundred years from now. Humanity is on a pilgrimage. You, as individuals, are pilgrims. Each life that you lead can be regarded as a pilgrimage and, as many of you will appreciate, during that lifetime of pilgrimage you will embark upon certain specific pilgrimages. Those pilgrimages can be regarded as a microcosm of your whole life. They symbolise for you the whole nature and purpose of your life. A pilgrimage, therefore, is an instrument of vision to enable you to see more clearly the true nature of your being and the path that lies ahead of you.

Throughout the Ages men and women have gone on pilgrimages. The followers of every religion, every creed, every race, have embarked upon them. In olden days pilgrimages usually involved travel of a hazardous nature and sometimes could last for months. They often involved great personal sacrifice. People did not go on pilgrimages as a social event. There was always deep purpose and spiritual intent in a pilgrimage. It represented the individual embarking on a quest to seek the higher aspect of themselves which, once found, they would then ground and manifest upon the physical plane of Earth.

Recognise that there are many levels to a pilgrimage. Although you travel on the physical level to your place of pilgrimage you also travel on many other levels as well. The pilgrims of old, as they visited the holy shrines and temples, as they visited the places made sacred by holy men and women, went there not just to kiss the sacred stone, to look at the sacred relic, in the hope of witnessing some psychic manifestation, to be healed of some major illness, but because they were attracted to the energy which vibrated and pulsated there. They went there to experience and to place themselves in a vortex of spiritual energy. The pilgrims were, in fact, on a higher level of life, creating lines of etheric power as they travelled. They were creating a web of light and energy. Moreover, when they departed from the place of pilgrimage, because they had connected themselves to that source of power, they were forever linked with that energy and could draw upon it whenever they so desired.

You have come on a pilgrimage to Glastonbury, a centre of great power and antiquity. Recognise that you are tapping into an energy as old as the Earth herself and that when you go forth from this place you will be forever linked to it. The energy of Glastonbury is yours to use whenever you close your eyes in meditation and go inwards to the spirit within. It can be a source of help in times of need. It can provide energy and inspiration as you face the challenges and the tests of the World in which you live. So when you go on a pilgrimage you fulfil two functions: you give as well as you receive. You give of your energy to the source and you take from the energy of the source in return and in that mingling of energies you are fulfilling two functions. You are like the bees of the Animal Kingdom. Bees do not just take pollen from the flowers they visit. By the very act of going from flower to flower they are helping to fertilise the flowers they visit. You are human bees, giving and taking, and so fulfilling the purpose of your life. That is the true symbology of the pilgrimage.

You have all embarked upon a pilgrimage of Light. You have come not only to find yourselves but, truly, to seek the Holy Grail, for what is the quest for the Holy Grail but a pilgrimage. You seek that Light, you seek that wholeness or holiness, that understanding of life, in just the same way as did the pilgrims of old. They, too, raised themselves above the level of the everyday affairs of life, went forth upon their inner quests and became pilgrims. Whilst on their pilgrimages they experienced fears and doubts just like any other human being, just as you do in your lives today. They had to contend with dangers along the way. They had to face their doubts and their fears as to what they would discover when they reached the goal of their pilgrimage. Would it all have been in vain? Would they find what they sought and would it be available to them? Would they reach their goal in time and so on? Their questions are merely a reflection of yours. Do you too not question the purpose of your being, the purpose of your life on this Earth? Do you too not worry about what lies ahead for you in the future? Are you not searching for your Holy Grail and do you not wonder whether you will find it within your lifetime?

A pilgrimage, therefore, is an act of commitment, an act of spiritual commitment. It is a time of spiritual upliftment, a time when individuals go forth to seek their destinies knowing that the microcosm of the pilgrimage is but a reflection of the macrocosm of their whole lives and, indeed, of the planet on which they dwell. Every pilgrim that comes and touches into the energy that is Glastonbury will experience something different for they are all unique. That power will touch them and will uplift them each according to their individual consciousness, their commitment and,

265

above all, their surrender, for surrender is indeed an essential part of pilgrimage. The pilgrim must be humble before the source of pilgrimage. In olden days pilgrims prayed upon their knees or prostrated themselves upon the ground before the sacred shrine or altar. They surrendered everything in order to receive from the source. You live in times when the greater mass of Humanity denies the source of life and as such there is no wholeness, no holiness, in many people's lives. There is no recognition of the divinity that is present not only in themselves and all Humanity but in every aspect of the physical World in which they live.

This year, 1984, is a year of karmic resolution and as such is a year very suited for pilgrimage, a year when those of you who are prepared to commit yourselves, who are prepared to walk that path, should indeed humbly seek your Holy Grail. Recognise that the path of the pilgrim is not an easy one. It is one which requires sacrifice. It is one which requires surrender. It is one which requires self-will and self-motivation. There will be many who will not, who cannot, walk that path. There will be many who will seek to obstruct you. There will be many material possessions to distract you from the path, for at no time in the World's history has the technology of Humanity been such a distraction to its spirituality. Those of you who live in the Western World are surrounded by an abundance of life, an abundance of technological and material possessions which very often you do not use wisely or with respect. For many people this abundance has become a consuming interest, a consuming passion, to the exclusion of the reality of Nature and the World around them and of the holiness that lies within them.

You have come on a pilgrimage to Glastonbury, the centre of the Holy Spirit, the third aspect of the Trinity of our Creator which is sometimes known as Father, Son and Holy Spirit. You are seeking to contact the power of the Holy Spirit, the power of initiation and transformation, whose mystical symbol is the phoenix. Like the phoenix you too must place yourselves in the cosmic fire in order to come forth renewed. It was this power that touched the disciples of Jesus and transformed them from followers into disciples. It is this power that will transform you too if you will but seek it, not on an outer but on an inner level. All can experience an initiation in this place and leave with a commitment to transform not only themselves but the World as a whole.

Why is this so important at this time? Because the World itself is shortly to undergo a baptism of cosmic fire. There will be destruction and death. There will be plagues, droughts and earthquakes. There will be much suffering and transmutation of karma. There will be a dramatic change in Nature as the Goddess restores the holiness to her Kingdoms. From this cataclysmic transformation there will come a new race of men and women, a race of people who are attuned to the Godhead, who have made that act of transformation and have prepared themselves both inwardly and outwardly for the New Age. Those that have attuned to the God within, to that still small voice, will know what is to happen. They will know where to go and what duties they have to perform.

Many pilgrims have come throughout the Ages to this great power centre of Glastonbury. They have invoked the energy here and have attempted to transform themselves. Many have succeeded but, equally so, many have failed, for they have used the power to further themselves rather than to create a better World, to further the evolution of the Human Race. That choice lies before you now, but in that you have truly made the commitment to pilgrimage, in that you have truly made the commitment to sacrifice and service, then you will have begun to place your feet upon the path to your Holy Grail. I ask you therefore to honour that commitment, for there can be no greater destiny at this time than to lead Humanity along a new path, than to shine your light and to let it touch the place where evil dwells. Go forth as pilgrims that others may witness your light all over the face of this World.

Many of you have travelled from all over the World to come to this centre of power. Although you are different in race, colour and creed yet you are one in your desire to be of service and to manifest the spirit that lies within you. Share this moment of timelessness when the personality self is dimmed, when the worries of the World are forgotten, when only the true you is present and listening. Recognise that force of spirit within you. Recognise that it is divine, that it is linked to the Divine and, above all, that it is protected by the Divine. No harm will befall you when you are attuned to that force of Spirit for the very aura of your being protects you at all times even in the face of the greatest danger. That is what the pilgrims of old recognised and knew within.

As you go forth from this place I give you my blessing. May you be worthy of the many feet that have walked this path of pilgrimage. May you remember, just as John Bunyan did three hundred years ago, when he wrote those famous words, that there can be no greater intent than to be a pilgrim.

## QUESTIONS AND ANSWERS

Q:   Can you tell us a little more about the energy of the Holy Spirit and the energy of the Goddess and how they are linked to Glastonbury?

ZT:   Let us begin by understanding that when we talk of the Goddess we are talking of Mother Earth. The three Kingdoms of Matter on Earth are the creations of the Goddess. Your planet, therefore, is female in energy. Now when I say female I do not want you to think in terms of the male and the female in the physical sense but rather of positive and negative, male and female in energy. The form of the Earth is of course far removed from the recognisable female shape, nevertheless, it is female. The Goddess gives you your physical bodies, the matter of which belongs to her. Therefore when you dishonour your bodies you are dishonouring the Goddess, for your physical bodies are sacred to her.

When we consider the energy, the impulse, of what is called the Holy Spirit it should be recognised as being an impulse coming from beyond this Earth. In the Bible the Trinity of Creation is referred to as Father, Son and Holy Ghost or Holy Spirit. These three aspects of cosmic power are grounded on the Earth through three mounts of Power: one in Northern Mongolia which grounds the Father, one in the Holy Land, Palestine, which grounds the Son, and that was why the Master Jesus was called the Son of God, and one in Britain, in this centre of Glastonbury, which grounds the Holy Spirit. These three aspects of the God of this Solar System in which we dwell are grounded in the cyclic pattern of the Solar Ages to fulfil the evolutionary cycle of Humanity. Four thousand years ago the birth of the Age of Aries saw the grounding of the Father aspect, two thousand years ago the birth of the Age of Pisces saw the grounding of the Son aspect and now we have the beginning of the two thousand year cycle of Aquarius which will see the grounding of the Holy Spirit aspect.

So here in Glastonbury we have a blending of the energies and powers of the Goddess and the Holy Spirit. The Goddess, like you, is subject to the influence of the Holy Spirit for that Spirit touches all life within our Creator's Body, our Solar System. Many people confuse the energy and presence of the Goddess, that being who rules over the Earth and the Kingdoms of Matter, with God. Many forces that are attributed to God are in fact the power and the work of the Goddess. Indeed, the Christ impulse of which you are aware was born out of the union of our God and the Goddess. The Christ is an energy that was created to bring about changes in human consciousness. It was a supreme sacrifice by our God and the Goddess to bring about a spiritual transformation in Humanity which had fallen from grace.

Q:   You have said that Glastonbury is a major point for the energy of the Holy Spirit but are there not other points elsewhere and, if so, are any to be found in the U.S.A?

ZT:   When we talk of energies and power centres you must also consider the timespan of human evolution. Although you may find this hard to accept, America's moment of destiny, her time of greatness, has not yet come for even though she is a major power in the World America is still very young. Above all, she is young spiritually. Nevertheless, the Western part of America is destined to be the Eden of the New Age when it dawns. The power which is to be grounded here will in a sense be a vehicle of transportation from the old to the new Age. The energy grounded here, in Glastonbury, will spread forth all over the planet. Glastonbury is what you might call a cosmic aerial transmitting energy over the whole Earth plane. It is, though, the only aerial for that energy, but it is a universal aerial that transmits the power all over the Earth for all to experience. I can also say that the next impulse of the Trinity will indeed be in America in two thousand years time.

Q:   The Master spoke of the time of tribulation in which much upheaval will occur and advised that we should listen to that voice within that will guide us to safety during that time. What is the best way to stay in tune with that voice all the time?

ZT:   If you were in tune with your inner voice all the time you would be a great Master! So whilst you might aim for that perfection also recognise that most of you will not be able to achieve it. Obviously, when you meditate, which should be in the morning and in the evening, at those times when you shut out the outside World and go into the inner one, you should be able to communicate with your inner voice. But you should also recognise that if you are close to Mother Nature then she can tell you as much as your intuitive channel. For example, you know very well that before there is a great natural disaster many animals flee to safety. There is a silence before the storm. On this level Nature is at one with the will of the Goddess and knows what is to happen. That is why the ancient priests watched the forces of Nature so closely. Here in Britain the Druids, in particular, knew that by observing the Animal Kingdom they could predict exactly what was to happen to the Earth as a whole or to the very place where they lived. So watch Mother Nature. Be at one with her, for she controls the forces which are to be unleashed. At any time, if you are open to that energy, it can touch you. In the twinkling of an eye you will know.

Q: You said that the Druids were aware of the natural world and were in tune with it. Was this also not true of the American Indians? Is there any connection between the Druids and the American Indians?

ZT: There once was, as many of you know, the great continent of Atlantis between America and Europe. Before Atlantis went down some of the great priests went forth to other continents to take with them the seeds of Atlantis. Those seeds went to America as well as to Britain. The roots of Druidism and of the tribes known as the North American Indians are indeed the same. Their manifestation differs according to the land and the race, but their understanding of Nature and their approach to life are very similar. It can also be said that the stirring of the desire here in England to obtain a greater understanding of Druidism is reflected in the desires of some people in America to seek a greater understanding of the traditions and culture of the North American Indians.

There is so much technology in America today. There is so much intellect but very little wisdom and appreciation of Mother Nature, the Goddess. America must restore balance to its evolutionary pattern and respect the natural rhythms of the so-called primitive peoples of its continent. Who, indeed, is the healthier and the saner person: the high powered executive creating wealth in his high-rise building in New York or the Indian sitting on the ground in his tepee on a reservation? At the end of their physical lives who will have gained greater consciousness, a greater understanding of the

270

purpose of life. Technology has its place in human evolution but only when it is balanced by wisdom. Intellect without the wisdom to use it is as nothing.

Q: So many have said, as the Master said today, that by living truth and becoming it others will be changed. But it is very difficult to see how others are changed by living truth. Could you explain how this takes place just by living?

ZT: If you think back in your own life to when you last saw an act of love, an act of kindness, an act of spirit, performed by a person who was probably not even aware that you were watching them, by a person who was acting as a spiritual being, then you will remember just how that act touched you, for your eyes are the windows of your soul. Even though you might have a trying day ahead of you, even though you might be beset by physical problems, the very fact of witnessing that act of consciousness changes the day for you. You have been touched by the power of love. Consider the example of Mother Theresa of Calcutta. No matter what are the personality aspects of that lady her demonstration touches people all over the World. The manifestation of her being touches people not just because of her humanity and her love, not just because of the people that she heals and helps, but because her expression of love is a true reflection of the Creator. People are touched by her example.

A demonstration of love touches you because you are beings of love, created by love, in love and with love. A demonstration of love touches all people and although some may deny it, although some may be hostile to it at the time, they have been touched by that energy and in the days and months to come it will become a part of their being. So ground and demonstrate your true being and you will change the World, and where there was one there is now two and that two becomes four and that four soon becomes one hundred and forty four. Never underestimate the power of your influence for you are gods in the making. You are spiritual beings. You are beings of creativity. Every thought that you create positively reaches out to everyone in the Universe and has the power to transform and transmute.

Q: But surely right thinking is not enough, is it? You have to have right action?

ZT: I was not talking solely of thinking. There is too much thinking in the World today. What we need is more feeling. We have just

271

experienced a cycle of patriarchal evolution where Man has been in control of government, of religion, of medicine, of every field of human endeavour and Man, a being of intellect rather than wisdom, has tended to impose his intellect on every sphere of human activity. Humanity today has to redress the balance and that is why we are now seeing the re-emergence of the feminine aspect, the re-emergence of Wisdom to balance the Power of the male. That is the source of what you call Woman's Liberation. It is to be regretted that many in this movement today are trying to establish the female aspect of Creation in a masculine way.

Q: The Master spoke of plagues. In America and in other major cities of the World there is a disease called AIDS. Can you comment on this?

ZT: AIDS is the first of the seven plagues from which Humanity will suffer. It comes about basically because of Humanity's abuse of the Animal Kingdom. The source of AIDS is the Animal Kingdom. The disease began in animals and was transmitted to humans. Now you must understand that the purpose of disease is not to punish: it is to bring about transformation. Disease is a great tool of evolution and all disease should be seen in this way. AIDS, of course, is a disease which is usually transmitted sexually. The greatest disease of the Human Race today is its abuse of sexuality. With AIDS, therefore, you have a disease which demands sexual responsibility. AIDS can be likened to a genetic timebomb, because ultimately only the pure in body, mind and spirit will survive it. This is indeed the beginning of the sorting of the wheat from the chaff.

Q: When you speak of disease and of sorting the wheat from the chaff I find that very emotive because it is often those who are the poorest and the weakest in our society that are the most prone to disease. Does that mean that those who die from malnutrition or disease are the chaff, and who decides who is the wheat and who is the chaff anyway?

ZT: You are associating chaff with illness and disease. That is wrong. Because a person is ill, because a person is deformed, because a person is starving, that does not mean that they are chaff. Indeed, sometimes, you can have a very great soul in a deformed body. Remember that the lessons of disease are learnt as much by

272

those that watch as by those that suffer. Let us be quite clear that when I talk of the sorting of the wheat from the chaff, to use that biblical expression, I am talking of consciousness not of physical attributes. I am saying that in the millenium which is to come only souls of a certain consciousness will be allowed to come back to this Earth and to live on it. There will be two thousand years of only evolved consciousness living on the Earth and then gradually there will be a re-introduction of lesser consciousness. At present there is a great imbalance on the Earth. There are so many unevolved souls on the plane of Earth that they swamp the evolved ones. If I may use the analogy of the balance of the dough and the yeast in a loaf of bread, there is not enough yeast, not enough soul evolution, to raise the dough, the mass of Humanity. What we are seeking to do is to restore the balance so that there is the right proportion of yeast to dough.

Q: What will happen to these young souls while they wait to come back?
ZT: They will dwell on other levels of life. One does not stop learning and evolving just because one dies. One lives and learns on many different planes of life, where one experiences other facets, other aspects of cosmic knowledge and law. The restriction will simply be on incarnating onto the physical plane of Earth. You may be interested to hear that there is a race of people who dwell under the Moon's surface who formerly evolved on the Earth and who are awaiting their time to return to Earth.

Q: When will this cycle begin and where on the Earth will it manifest?
ZT: That is, perhaps, the most leading question that has been asked tonight! It implies knowledge of what is going to happen to the race of Humanity, of which continents will be in existence, of whether or not the Earth is going to upright on its axis, of which nations will survive and so on and so on. I think that even if I knew these facts and could tell you I would not wish to do so! Many people, I know, have prophesied of such events. All I would say is that there is to be a transformation of the planet. Some continents will sink, others will rise. There will be a great movement of the Earth's surface as has happened in the past. For example, this power centre of Glastonbury came from Atlantis. It was thrown off

from that continent when Atlantis went down and impinged itself upon the British land mass. The Hawaiian Islands, as you call them, were the sacred mountains of the great civilisation of Lemuria. So let us just say that great events are coming and that from the experience of these events will come a great surge in human evolution.

Q: So many people fear these events though.

ZT: The people who fear these events are the people who fear death, for it is the same fear, the same emotion. If you do not understand death and its purpose then you will see no purpose in a cataclysm but, truly, the evolved and aware soul, whilst being aware of the fear of death, chooses not to experience it. When one is fighting in war death is always present, but if one lives in the shadow of the fear of death then it is impossible to live, to be a living human being. Fear totally consumes one's being. But if one is truly living in the moment then there is no fear, for there is no future. The way to come to terms with what is to happen is by living each moment now to the fullest and from that living will come an understanding of the events to come.

Q: You have talked about how these Earth changes will be a catalyst for evolution. Can you tell us if there are forces working against evolution, forces such as nuclear war, industrial pollution, ideological distortions of human consciousness, false messiahs and so on? How can these be counteracted and who are the beings that are behind them?

ZT: One of the things that you must realise is that as you approach the time of what I will call 'maximum salvation' you will also have a time of 'maximum temptation'. The two go hand in hand. The present World situation can be likened to a melting pot. As you melt gold or silver so all the impurities come to the surface in the heat of the pot. The World is going through this process now and all the impurities, all the imperfections of Humanity, on many levels, are coming to the surface. Therefore there are present on the Earth today many, what you would call, evil forces. Remember that evil is just live spelt backwards. Either you live or you are evil. These evil forces are sent here to further the human evolutionary cycle. Humanity must choose between 'living' and 'evil living'.

274

There is much evil coming to the surface at this time because the vibratory rate of the Earth has been quickened in order to preserve its stability. Humanity therefore is faced with many tests, many choices, not only in terms of nuclear war, of the pollution of the planet, of the false messiahs who will appear, of the financial decisions facing the World's institutions, but of every aspect of human endeavour. For every side or opinion that is present there will be another side or opinion to oppose it. This therefore requires that you exercise the great gift of discrimination. It is how you choose, and your motivation for choosing, that in essence represents the sorting of the wheat from the chaff. There will be many who will follow the path of evil, but remember that you can walk to the gates of Hell and still turn back. You follow a path only for as long as you wish to. There will be much suffering in the World but no more than Humanity can bear and understand. Many will not be touched by the plagues. For example, if you are a vegetarian and a great disease strikes the Animal Kingdom destroying and polluting the animals that many choose to eat for food, then you will not be touched by it. If you live a life of sexual purity you will not be touched by AIDS. If you are pure in body, mind and spirit you will not be touched by much of what is to walk the face of this Earth.

Q:  I am involved in helping people with terminal illnesses like AIDS. Can you give any guidance on how to help them?
ZT:   There are many ways of helping such people. The help they want, of course, is to be cured, but that is not possible. So they must be helped into an understanding of the nature of their illness and, above all, of the acceptance of it. So many people who are ill today will not accept that they are the cause of their illness. They will not accept that they, and they alone, are totally responsible for everything that they suffer. So it is perhaps in the acceptance of their disease, in the understanding of the nature of death and the evolutionary opportunities that come from it, that you can best help these people.

I must here inject a note of caution. At another time I have talked about drug abuse and I have said that many of those who take hard drugs are really suffering from spiritual arrogance. They know that such drugs harm their bodies yet still they take them. They know that they are abusing the sacred temple of their spirit yet still they do it, even to the point of death. They are in effect deliberately challenging their Creator. They are destroying the divinity of their body as an open act of defiance to their Creator. That is why they are doing it. It is difficult to help such people until they are humble, until they have opened themselves up to the power of love.

Q: Some people with terminal illnesses have been cured. Surely there is a cure for everything including cancer through transmutation of that disease by understanding the nature of the disease that they have?
ZT: There is a cure for everything and I am not talking now about medical cures. Each one of you has within your body the capability of complete self-transformation, to heal anything that afflicts your body. You can heal yourself of anything.

Q: It is often the case that many people, especially those who are ill, feel alone. How can we help such people?
ZT: You are never alone. If you are alone it is because you choose to be so. Remember that in the unity of spirit you are all one. At this very moment in time, as you sit in this room, no matter what your race, your religion or your sex you are one and in the one-ness of this energy, in the oneness of this expression, you represent the Human Race. This is what the Human Race should be: a great force for good, a great manifestation of divine love for all the Universe to see. There are many planets that do not possess your divinity, that do not possess your potential. There are many that do not have free choice, that do not have the divine gift of creativity. You are special beings on a very special planet. Respect that great gift.

# TRAGEDY

You live in a World of ever increasing violence, of violence not only between individuals and between countries, but also of violence towards the other Kingdoms who share this plane of Earth with you. Today violence is even shown on the television and in the cinema as a form of entertainment. Children are permitted to watch violence in order to condition them to the nature of human life and the realities of the World in which they live. All over the planet Humanity is at war and is in conflict on either a physical, an ideological, a religious or a financial level. Because of this there often occur acts of great tragedy, or what you would call tragedy, and it is on the subject of tragedy that I wish to talk now.

The word tragedy in your modern language comes, of course, from the Greek. Initially it was applied to a drama enacted on the stage in which the actors played their roles revealing a deep inner meaning, a prophetic meaning, to the lives of the people they portrayed. Implicit in the drama was the presence and intervention of the ancient gods. Indeed both the players and the audience tended to regard themselves as puppets with the gods pulling the strings perhaps for their own amusement, perhaps for the evolution of the participants. However, when you think of tragedy today it is interesting to note that the concept of divine intervention has been lost. You see tragedy only with earthly, physical eyes and you have forgotten about the concept of divine intervention which the ancient Greeks recognised.

So I will begin by stating that there is no such thing as a tragedy by chance, as a tragedy by accident, as a tragedy created by human intention. Everything that happens on the plane of Earth has reason, has purpose. You live in a World in which many people apparently experience great tragedies. You live in a World which itself is entering into a time of great tragedy, a time when many millions

277

of people will suffer, and unless you have an understanding of tragedy, of what controls it and of what purpose it has, then you will be swamped by the energies of what you will witness.

The first point that I wish to make is that tragedy is an individual perception. Whilst many people might agree and view a particular act as tragic, that perception is rarely universal. Let me use an example from the last World War. If a bomb had gone off and had killed Winston Churchill and his cabinet, here in England that would have been regarded as a tragic act. But if a bomb had gone off killing Adolf Hitler and his generals that would not have been regarded as tragic but rather would have been seen as evil men getting their just deserts. But that opinion would only represent the British and not the German standpoint. So you can see that one's assessment of what is or is not a tragedy depends on one's own beliefs, on one's concepts of life and death and of how one views the purpose of life and what is taking place on the plane of Earth.

In your World today millions of people are dying in distressing circumstances. You are aware of the wars in the Far East and the Middle East, of the clashes between the followers of the major religions, of the massacres taking place. You are aware of the droughts in the equatorial regions where thousands die each day of starvation. But do you regard these events as tragedies if they occur in some far off country and you are not personally involved in them? Are not events always more tragic at home than abroad, more tragic in your own family than in society at large?

What causes a tragedy? What is the essence of a tragedy? How should you react when faced with tragedy? Again I refer you to the drama, to the famous words of Shakespeare when he wrote "All the World's a stage and all the men and women merely players. They have their exits and their entrances and one man in his time plays many parts, his acts being seven ages." Those are wise words. You are indeed all playing roles and the length of your role is seven ages, seven cycles or three score years and ten. When you leave that stage at death, which many regard as the greatest tragedy that they will ever have to face, you have a completely different perspective of tragedy.

As you read this now, what do you feel is the greatest tragedy which could befall you: the death of your husband or wife, your child, someone who is close to you, your mother or your father, the loss of your house, your money, the loss of your health and so on

278

and so on? All these things are involved with the word loss, with a physical removal, whether it be of individuals, material possessions or life itself. Either something is being taken away from you or some limitation is being imposed upon you. But do you see this limitation as being divinely imposed? Are you aware of the Lords of Karma and of the fact that there is indeed a divine system of justice which balances out everything in Creation? Are you aware that every human action initiates a divine response?

Recognise, therefore, that any individual who suffers such a tragedy has attracted that tragedy to them. They initiated and sent out the energy which attracted that tragedy, that limitation to them. Tragedy comes to people either because they chose it for their destiny path or because it will present them with a lesson in life which they have yet to learn. It is inevitable, when you observe incidents of apparent tragedy and see people suffering, that you will feel compassion for those who are suffering because you yourself will probably have experienced those lessons in previous lives. You too will have experienced similar moments of tragedy and it is from that experience that there comes both the compassion and the understanding of the need for what you call tragedy. You know that the inner pain has to be experienced in order that those who are experiencing it may grow to a higher point of soul evolution.

There are many, for example, who would say that the death of the Master Jesus was a tragedy. Here was a man who, if he so chose, could have saved the World on a physical level anyway. Here was a man who could have transformed human society if he had but lived his full lifespan. If he had touched every corner of the planet and demonstrated his point of consciousness how great would have been the revelation! Yet he was removed from the plane of Earth and, moveover, we are told that that was part of the Divine Plan. Many inspired books reveal that his life and death were prophesied long before his actual birth. Jesus's life was divinely planned and both the time and the nature of his death were known a thousand years before he incarnated. Perhaps Shakespeare was right: you are but actors upon the stage of life playing out a role you know not why. All that you do know is that you have been placed here to act and that acting is the blood of life that flows within you.

Many people cannot face a particular tragedy because they have not yet learned the lesson of that tragedy. If the lesson of tragedy

279

has not become part of their consciousness then they will never accept the true purpose of tragedy. They are condemned to experience all tragedy, to learn from it and, indeed, to suffer from it, for that is the plight of all those who partake of tragedy: to suffer with those who are suffering. No one suffers on this plane of Earth without reason. No one suffers on this plane of Earth unless they have drawn it down upon themselves either in this life or in past lives through karmic behaviour. When you witness the acts of great tragedy in the World today be it in Ireland, the Middle East or Africa, and you see people dying under terrible conditions, experiencing great pain and suffering, have you ever considered what is to be the karma of the people who are creating that pain and suffering, what is to be their lesson in their next lives? What is to be their tragedy, their lesson in life?

It is difficult to be detached in the face of tragedy, but that is what you must be. See tragedy, as did the ancient Greeks, for what it is: an act of divine intervention, a grounding of the force of karma for a reason you may not understand or recognise at the time, but having meaning and purpose. Recognise the hand of the Divine in all tragedy and look for the evolutionary lesson behind it. All can learn from tragedy, no matter where it occurs, especially those who are of the consciousness to recognise the hand of the Divine. The true role of the priest is to explain tragedy to the people. It is to show them why such events happen and to let them know the reason and the purpose behind it as did the prophets of the Old Testament.

You would say to me that if millions of people are dying of starvation in Africa, what is the lesson of that for me? Such a tragedy may not be caused solely by the acts of the people who live there and the way they have cultivated or abused the land. It can be caused by a society thousands of miles away, through the way they are living and abusing their environment. Perhaps the greatest tragedy of all, if you could but see it, is that of failing to recognise that you are all one, that this planet is a whole and that all who dwell upon its surface are linked not only on the physical level but also on the higher levels of life, through their divine spirit, to the Godhead. How you act and behave in this country of Britain does affect the millions dying of starvation in the drought belts of Central Africa. It is not solely their fault, for you are all responsible for the maintenance and harmony of this planet on which you live. Finally, remember that whilst at this moment you may not be experiencing their tragedy, even now, in the style of the ancient Greek drama, you may be sowing the seeds for a tragedy of your own making.

I therefore ask you to consider tragedy in a new light. Look upon those who experience tragedy with compassion and understanding. Learn from their experience. See tragedy not as most people see it, with fear and hatred, as something to be avoided, as the vengeance of a cruel and unjust God upon Its people, but as a divine evolutionary tool. Recognise that that tool is used only in love and that everything that manifests on the plane of Earth is an aspect of your Creator's love. Recognise that it is through your understanding of that love, igniting the intuitive force within you, that you will come to an understanding of the true meaning of tragedy.


## QUESTIONS AND ANSWERS


Q:   I am not sure, even after hearing that talk, that I would be able to cope with a tragedy in my own life. What advice can you give us on handling a personal tragedy?

ZT:   I would like you to imagine what would be the greatest tragedy that could happen to you at this moment in time. Now that does not mean that you are invoking that tragedy upon yourself but, rather, that you are just playing a little mental game. Having done that, now consider why it is a tragedy.

If you have been honest with yourself, you will have projected your life forward into the future and will have created some event which you would consider to be tragic. Now many of you are coming to an understanding of death. You no longer fear death and are seeing it in a correct perspective. You are recognising it as a moment of transition, a moment of rebirth. Perhaps you will be able to think of tragedy in the same way. As you consider your example of tragedy ask whether it is a tragedy just for you alone or whether it is a tragedy for others beside yourself? Will others share that tragedy with you or is it a personal, individual event? Consider how your point of spiritual consciousness affects your opinion, your concept of tragedy. Would a more evolved soul see greater or less tragedy in life than you? Is the concept of tragedy therefore in any way linked to soul evolution? Are you, the observer, a part of that tragedy? Consider, also, is it possible to avoid tragedy? Is it possible to avoid that which you have created as your tragedy? Can one invoke divine power and protection in one's prayers. Can one, so to speak, employ divine protection against tragedy?

The analogy I like to give when talking of tragedy is to consider the Colosseum in ancient Rome with two gladiators fighting in the arena. One of them will win and one of them will die. Their energies and attentions are focussed completely on their struggle. The spectators watching that fight will have come for reasons of enjoyment and the death of one of those gladiators is a part of that enjoyment. Now you, observing that fight, would perhaps view it as a tragedy. But is it a tragedy for those who fight or for those who watch?

Q: Are you suggesting, using your analogy of the gladiators, that it is not tragic for the people who die, only for the people who are watching that event?
ZT: I am asking whether it is a tragedy for the gladiators or for those who watch the gladiators?

Q1: It is a tragedy for those who watch. It is not a tragedy for those who are fighting because they are so involved in what they are doing that very often they do not even know that they are about to be killed. The tragedy, if it is a tragedy at all, is with the parents, the wives, the friends of the gladiators who are fighting. Often those who are involved in a tragedy are so involved in trying to survive that they seem to be quite resigned to what they are having to go through.
Q2: But if you are a soldier and you go off to fight a war there is a very good chance that you will be killed. That is the nature of war. If you are the wife of a soldier and your husband goes off to war whilst you hope that it will not happen there is an expectation on your part that as such things happen in war it could happen. So when it does happen is it an act of tragedy?
Q3: If you had wanted to be a soldier and did not mind dying for your country, if you understood the process of death, it would not be a tragedy. Moreover, if your wife is evolved enough to recognise that as well and does not hold on to you in sadness and misery but carries on with her life in a useful way, then, there is no tragedy for her either.

282

Q4:   Yes. Normally, when a loved one dies, you are more concerned about your suffering than their suffering, your loss not their loss. So is there such a thing as tragedy? Is that what you are trying to say? Surely there is a link between tragedy and soul evolution. The more evolved and the more aware you become the less tragedy there is, because you see meaning and purpose in everything. It seems that a tragedy is only a tragedy if we accept the events as tragic. If we do not accept them as tragic then they are not.

ZT:   We have here the very important word 'acceptance'. Let us consider acceptance and with it the word understanding. Can there be tragedy with acceptance?

Q:   No. Because if you accept it, it is no longer a tragedy.

ZT:   So if you learn from events and take understanding from them then there is no tragedy. Tragedy occurs only when the lesson is not learnt, when there is no acceptance, when there is hostility to what has taken place, when one is still in conflict inside one.

Q1:   Human nature being what it is we so often react to what we consider to be a tragedy by feeling resentful and bitter.

Q2:   Perhaps we could take it a step further than that and say that if we totally accept events in our lives and see them as the will of God, and release them, then there is no tragedy.

Q3:   A plane crash is almost universally regarded as a tragedy, especially when it is caused by human error. Are you saying that that is the will of God?

ZT:   In a plane crash many people are killed instantly, usually in a moment of great destruction. No matter what your religion, race or social position if you die in an aircraft accident it is regarded as tragic. Yet is it not true to say that some people sense that an accident is going to happen before it even happens. There are intuitive people who know that something is going to happen and so they don't get on that aeroplane or change to another flight. So, as Shakespeare said, 'Is life but a drama being played out on the stage of Earth?'. Can you therefore choose whether or not you wish to play in that drama? Can you avoid that aircraft accident if you were meant to be in it? The answer to that is that you have the free choice to change the route by which you are going to walk your destiny path, but your ultimate destiny you cannot change.

In conclusion, perhaps the most important thing that can be said of tragedy, rather like the tragedy of the Greek plays, is that it brings an aspect of life into focus under the microscope, no matter whether it be the high point of the play or the high point of your life. You focus all your energy on that tragedy. In times of tragedy do not people become more loving and generous towards each other? Even in war the opposing sides can become less hostile and more loving in the face of great tragedy. A sailor who sees an enemy ship being sunk knows that he too might die that way and so is full of compassion for those who are dying. Tragedy, therefore, demands concentration and from that concentration great learning can come forth by the way that you as individuals respond to that tragedy.

Let me give you one final example. You can perhaps remember the incident of the British politician who was recently assassinated by a car bomb, yet the behaviour of his wife at that time of tragedy, her complete unwillingness to condemn those that had done it, even less to demand the death penalty for what they had done and, indeed, to openly forgive them for what they had done, made that particular tragedy a point of learning for millions of people. Any tragedy therefore is a lesson to be understood. Whether it applies to you as a participant or as an onlooker it presents you with an opportunity for soul searching. You react according to how you see that tragedy, how you understand it, and from that understanding will come the strength for the day when you face your tragedy, for truly all of you at some stage in your lives will be touched by tragedy especially in the Age in which you now live.

Above all, let us get tragedy in perspective. Obviously our perception of tragedy is individual and unique but let us consider the tragedy of the whole, the tragedy of the planet and of the Kingdoms and beings that form life on its surface. Surely the greatest tragedy of all is that Humanity having been given a Divinity on which to live and evolve has seen fit to desecrate that Divinity.

# THE VIRGIN PRINCIPLE

It would be true to say that the way a society honours or dishonours the Virgin Principle is an accurate reflection of its point of consciousness and spiritual evolution. I therefore speak to you now to lead you into a greater understanding of what that Principle means and of how it can affect your lives. Today, in western society, the Virgin Principle is an object of ridicule. The term virgin is considered to apply only to the female of the species and is regarded as having only a sexual connotation. However that viewpoint merely reflects the sexual attitudes and customs of the society in which you live. Truly, a virgin can be male or female and the aspect of the virgin that I wish to talk about now has little to do with sexuality. That is not to say that sexuality does not play a part in it but only one of little importance.

Whereas today to be a virgin is of little significance and, indeed, is often thought of as a manifestation of personality weakness, in ancient societies that quality was regarded as being essential if one was to become awakened in consciousness. It is a fact that the priests of the ancient religions were always virgin, be they male or female. They were virgin through choice, they were virgin through consciousness. It was not a discipline thrust upon them which they struggled to observe. They were virgin because of their inherent understanding of what was implied in that Principle and of what they were striving to attain and to ground on the plane of Earth.

That the term virgin is applied mainly to the female of the species today is simply a reflection of the imbalance present in the World as a whole. Many of Humanity's problems are directly attributable to the fact that Woman has fallen from her pedestal. In the patriarchal societies which have existed over the last two thousand years Woman has been suppressed, seduced and distracted from her true nature. It is, therefore, inevitable that the sexuality which she represents is held up to ridicule today. What Humanity desperately needs at this time is for Woman to climb back onto her pedestal and once more to exhibit her true virginity: the virginity of the priestess, the virginity of the Goddess. In similar fashion, Man, too, should strive to exemplify the virgin principle of his being.

The virgin birth plays an important role in the dogma of the Christian Churches. It is believed that the Master Jesus was born of a virgin. Although I have said on several occasions that that belief is incorrect, that the Master Jesus was not born of a virgin, nevertheless the Christian concept of the virgin birth is but a reflection of a natural function of Cosmic Law. The virgin birth represents the grounding of a pulse of cosmic energy of great purity. When one is a virgin, when one is totally pure in thought, word and deed, in body, mind and spirit, then one no longer creates physically, one creates cosmically. One no longer creates through one's physical organs but through one's cosmic organs. When one has attained that state of virginity, a state that you would call Christ-consciousness, then one can create in ways beyond your comprehension. That is the nature of a truly awakened soul, the virgin aspect of creation.

To be a virgin is not the destiny of all people, is not the destiny of all souls. Only a few annointed and chosen ones will seek to walk that path. Nevertheless, you should all respect those who are trying to walk that path and should strive to the utmost of your beings to uphold the Virgin Principle in your own everyday lives. The true virgin, therefore, is a person awakened in self-realisation, one who strives through purity, on every level, to harmonise their beings with the divine flow of the Universe. Such a person has surrendered their individualised self and has become a vessel for that universal energy. They are allowing the energy of cosmic creativity, what you would call the energy of the cosmic Christ, to flow through them and to manifest on the plane of Earth. A true virgin, therefore, creates cosmically and not physically. Woman today creates physically, produces her children physically. This reflects the nature of human evolution and of Woman's individual status in it. But birth can be a cosmic act. It does not have to be through the physical process of which you are aware. Recognise that cosmic birth does exist upon the plane of Earth today and is practised by certain chosen beings.

You should all strive, especially at this time of the Moon entering Virgo, to consider the virgin aspect in yourself, your purity, and to see if you are allowing that cosmic energy to flow through you. Remember what is implied by your standing on the pedestal of the Virgin Principle. It will mean scorn and mockery. It will mean stones being thrown at you, both physically and mentally, because you are standing out from your fellow human beings. You are a mirror to what they are not. You are demonstrating something that they have not yet achieved even though they know in their inner-most hearts that that is the path upon which they are set. To be a virgin therefore is to stand forth, is to stand alone.

Consider the lives of all the great beings who have walked this Earth, who have truly manifested cosmic consciousness. They have always walked alone. They have always been virgins, be they male or female. They have risen above human sexuality as you know it today. They have walked in purity of thought, word and deed and have grounded their consciousnesses to be a light for all Humanity to follow. You, like them, should not despise those who are caught up in the web of human sexuality, who are impure in thought, word and deed for that is a lesson which they are learning, that is but a reflection of their point of consciousness at this moment in time. They will in time evolve beyond that level. You are responsible only for yourself. Concern yourself only with the virgin aspect of your own being.

What the planet needs most at this time is the virgin. If you are a woman and have had a child do not think that you cannot be the virgin, for you can. All of you must manifest and ground the Virgin Principle in everything that you think, say and do. Above all, if your thoughts are not pure then you cannot create physically in purity. You must begin with your thoughts for they are the source of all action. As you meet with your fellow human beings recognise that the way you manifest your aspect of the Virgin Principle decides the nature of the relationship and its creations. The true virgin acts as a mirror to people around them. The true virgin causes people to look at themselves, to recognise the virgin in themselves, to see how much of the virgin they have attained, how far they have yet to go. Each of you can, and should, strive to develop your own virgin aspect, to place yourself on the pedestal of the Virgin Principle and by striving for that purity you will be inviting the energy of the Cosmos to flow down through you.

When you are pure, when you are virginal, you are beyond physical energy. You have become a cosmic being capable of

287

creating cosmically on the plane of Earth. The way to save Humanity and this planet is by becoming virgins, is by allowing that virgin cosmic energy to flow down through you and to manifest upon the plane of Earth on which you dwell. The virgin, therefore, is the leader. The virgin is the principle which others worship and follow. The virgin is the initiator of change. The virgin is the pattern of the future. The virgins of Aquarius are, therefore, being called to account. Their creativity will change the World. Their creativity will give birth to the Age of Aquarius. From their wombs, both literally and figuratively, will come the children of the Aquarian Age. What they create now in purity will determine the nature of that cycle.

Consider, therefore, the virtue of being a virgin. Look within yourselves and recognise that aspect of your beings. Regard the Virgin Principle with honour and respect and when you see it manifesting in others pay respect to it, for in essence the virgin reflects the purity of the Goddess on which you dwell, that being who not only gives you your physical bodies but also gives you the expression of life. The Goddess is a supreme example of the Virgin Principle and so reflects that purity in her energy. Seek the purity of her being. Let it be a light to lighten your darkness. Go forth in the knowledge of what the Virgin requires of you. There can be no greater calling, there can be no greater path, than to be a virgin.


## QUESTIONS AND ANSWERS


Q:   If we were all virgins Humanity would cease to exist! Human reproduction through the sexual act is a natural process intended for the survival of the species. How then do you equate the sexual act with the virginity of the Virgin Principle?

ZT:   You live in a society that has distorted the meaning and purpose of the sexual act beyond all recognition. Indeed you are so conditioned by the sexuality of your World, a sexuality which invades almost every aspect of physical life, that it is difficult for you to discern the true purpose of the sexual act: you cannot, in fact, see the wood for the trees! If we look at another creative energy — magic — you may, because you are less influenced by your conditioned thought, perhaps see the true purpose of the sexual act. There are three kinds of magic: black, white and pure. Black and white are the same. They are forms of magic used by Humanity for good or evil according to Humanity's motivation and inspiration. The only true form of magic is pure magic, that is magic that is used for the sake of the principle itself. This means that the magic is invoked but the effect is left to the power of the principle. May God's will be done. That is the natural process, the process of Nature.

The sexual act should be a natural act of reproduction. Indeed, are not the sexual organs known medically as the reproductive organs? That is their natural function. In Nature, in the Animal Kingdom, where thought does not intrude, the sexual organs are used solely for reproduction. The Animal Kingdom is linked to the Godhead, has no free choice and so creates in a natural rhythm. Sexual intercourse is only desired, only takes place, when reproduction of the species is desired. But Humanity has free choice and a developed brain which is capable of creating psychological thought and the desire for pleasure. Humanity today, for the most part, bases its living on the pursuit of pleasure, on self gratification, and that is how it approaches the sexual act no matter whether it be out of lust or some so-called spiritual 'purpose' like raising the kundalini which, incidentally, is black magic.

If Humanity today was without contraception it would look at the sexual act in a very different light, for if you knew that every time you performed the sexual act you might create a child, you would look more closely at what you were doing. You would be more conscious of the divinity of creation and, indeed, of your responsibility for it. Every time you commit the sexual act you create, if not on the physical level then on the higher levels of life. People who use contraception are not only denying their responsibility for creation on the physical level but, by the very thought forms involved, on the etheric levels as well. Nevertheless, in spite of contraception, they have still created and will have to face their etheric children after death.

You are gods in the making. You are learning to be gods of creation. Understanding the act of creation involves understanding being a god, becoming the virgin. Consider the god-like beings who have walked and still walk amongst you even now. Have the great Masters ever taught that the sexual act should be practised solely for pleasure? Have they ever advocated its use simply for raising

289

consciousness? Or was it not the case that they had risen above sex, that they were truly celibate beings? What is the value of celibacy? It allows the creative energy to be used in other fields, in fields more suited to human evolution and potential.

An aware person living in the moment, attuned to the Godhead, leads a life full of joy, a life in which desire, or self indulgence has no part. The sexual act, if it takes place at all, only takes place when inspired by the Godhead, to conceive a destined child. That is the true and only purpose of the sexual act — to fulfil the plan of the Creator — and in that one is doing that then one is being virginal, pure in thought word and deed. The Goddess, the ultimate symbol of the virgin, has always been associated with fertility and reproduction. That is the role of Woman, to be the womb of creation. Few people in the World today are capable of the true virgin birth, of creating using their cosmic rather than their physical reproductive organs. For most people human reproduction comes about through the sexual act, but is one's motivation for that act driven by divine destiny or by one's desire for self gratification? Is one creating in God's image, according to the Virgin Principle, or in self-image, according to one's own inner needs and desires? That is the question you must answer.

Q:  How do we know when we are being virginal?
ZT:  Purity and virginity are qualities very much like spirituality. As you go about your everyday living you do not, for the most part, recognise when you are being pure, when you are being virginal or when you are being spiritual, for they are acts of being. However what you do know, only too well, is when you are not being pure, virginal or spiritual. So perhaps it could be said that if you recognise the impure aspects of yourselves, and correct them, that that would then create that force for good which you seek. None of you are perfect. All of you have many facets of your diamond to polish, but from the small beginning, from the first steps that you make towards the recognition of your impurities, there comes the understanding and the transmutation of them. It is that act that leads one to a greater recognition and awareness of the Virgin Principle in oneself.

I would therefore ask each of you to concentrate on one aspect of your being that is not of the virgin, something which deep down you know should be banished from your being, and resolve that in

the days to come you will come to terms with it, face it and understand it. You will come to recognise that there is no need for that
aspect and see that it is simply restricting your true being. Through
that very act, through that invocation of the cosmic energy which
flows through you, you will be able to say with pride that you have
helped to put the virgin in yourself back on its pedestal.

# THE HEALING TOUCH

Since so many of you here are on the healing vibration I would like to talk to you about the healing touch, but before we can consider the nature of healing and the healing techniques that are present on the Earth today we must first look at the nature of disease, that which necessitates healing. Most people today regard disease as the visitation on a healthy body by a foreign object. Disease is considered to be an invasion from outside the body and, as such, can be healed in a similar fashion. In the World today few people understand that every illness is self-created and that the seeds of any illness always lie within the human body. The medical profession today, with its practice of treating the symptoms and not the cause of disease, tends to support the view that illness can best be treated from outside the body and then only by qualified practitioners. As a result of this attitude the individual's responsibility for health at this time has perhaps never been lower. Although you live in a World of great technological achievement, a World where Science, Humanity's Science, is indeed becoming a god, few people today really understand the true nature of disease or recognise the divinity of the human body.

You must understand a disease before you can heal it. You must recognise that every human being is a magnetic being, a being capable of attracting unto itself according to the nature of its own creations in thought, word and deed. The note that you send out, the vibrations that you emanate, come back to you no matter what the level of life on which you dwell. You have within you a magnetic power with the potential for good or for evil. It is the note which you sound that attracts the corresponding vibrations of the Cosmos to you, there being in the Cosmos an equal potential for good and for evil. It is how you choose to use that cosmic power that brings about evolution. According to the way you live your life

293

so you attract into your being the corresponding vibrations of the Cosmos and these affect the various elements within your body which can lead to disease.

If we take something that is so prevalent in the World today, the smoking of cigarettes and the diseases associated with it, it is easy to see how the one action leads to the others. However, many diseases in your World today are what you would call psychosomatic and are created on a different level: they are the creations of the mind and are not solely the result of physical actions. Such diseases are created in the first place by the individual on the higher levels of life and then manifest later on the physical level. Any person with the necessary psychic powers can see an illness on the higher levels before it manifests on the physical plane of life.

Humanity has to learn that it must take responsibility for everything that it creates within the divinity of its body. Every disease, every illness, including the disease of cancer, is self-originating. It is created by the individual human being. The fact that you have plagues or epidemics when a large number of people die from a certain disease merely represents the collective thought forms, the collective energies of the people in that society. A healthy body can resist any plague, any illness. Disease, therefore, in the broadest sense can be seen as being karmic. That which you have sown you attract unto yourselves.

As we look at the nature of healing it is essential that you remember the source of disease. The medical profession today with its allopathic medicine and surgical practices does not encourage sick people to be responsible for their own healing. Moreover, for the most part, sick people offer their bodies to the doctors and the surgeons and allow themselves to be drugged and operated upon without questioning what is the short term or the long term effects of a drug or an operation. They expect the doctors and the surgeons to be god, to remove the disease in their body and to restore them to perfect health. In the medical profession today there is scant regard for the divinity of life and for the wholeness or holiness of the physical body. For the most part, the doctor is not concerned either in discovering the cause of a disease or in educating the person that suffers from a disease as to how to prevent it in the future. Disease is seen simply as a foreign body to be removed as quickly as possible and the patient to be allowed to return to his or her former lifestyle afterwards.

294

You live in an Age when more than ever before people are beginning to search for and experiment with forms of treatment neither recognised nor accepted by the medical profession. A growing number of people are using forms of treatment which recognise the divinity of the physical body and, above all, which regard themselves as instruments of healing. Now that is not to say that there are not surgeons and doctors who do not regard the human body as a divine creation and try to attune to it when they operate and try to heal. There are some who do this, but one only has to look at the nature of many surgical operations today to see that for many surgery has become an intellectual exercise devoid of feeling, a game of physical skill played at the expense of the human body with its only objective to fulfil the will of the surgeon or the doctor. Compare this with those who heal through the healing touch, through the laying on of hands, through the invocation of higher energies, through prayer and absent healing. Here you will see a recognition of the part that the Divinity plays in the healing process, an acceptance of the fact that every individual is a channel of divine energy.

It is essential, therefore, for those who heal through the healing touch that they ensure that the person who is being healed is aware of the part that the Divinity plays in the healing process. For the patient to lie in front of the healer and to expect the healer to heal them is no better than the patient lying on the operating table and expecting the surgeon's knife to work a miracle. The patient must understand what is the nature of healing and, above all, the responsibilities inherent in healing. The patient must realise that healing energy has to be invoked and that there has to be a flow of energy to them through the healing touch. They should always be conscious of, and invoke, that energy.

Healing is not just a process of one person giving energy to another. Rather it is the process of one person acting as a channel to another, of positive energy to negative receptivity. There has to be a transference of energy for the healing to take place. This is the point of the story in the Bible of the woman in the crowd who touched the hem of Jesus's cloak as he passed by and was subsequently healed. Both felt the transference of energy but it was the woman's faith in the power of that Master and her invocation of the healing energy that created the flow and resulted in her being healed.

In the World today, where the Divinity is hardly ever recognised, the essential role of the healer is to teach as well as to heal. The healer should teach the patient as to the source of the healing energy, which is the Creator of all life. Therefore every act of healing should be seen as an act of worship. Every healer should demonstrate the fact that they are simply channels for that divine energy and that it is the source of the energy that should be invoked and thanked, not the healer. It should be made clear that the healing process is initiated from the higher planes, not from the physical plane of life.

It must also be clearly understood that the Divinity, knowing the destiny of Humanity and the cause of an individual's disease, does not always heal. Some people expect that if they go down on their knees and ask for healing that they will always be healed and, what is more, in the way that they expect. It must be clearly understood that the Lords of Karma, the great beings who control and maintain the balance of human life and creativity on the Earth, judge without emotion. They see only the spiritual reality of what an individual has created and, therefore, what that individual must attract back to himself or herself. It is the nature and destiny of some people to suffer. It is the nature and destiny of some people to be ill. That must be recognised.

Humanity must realise that illness is an evolutionary lesson. It is not something to be scorned, to be pushed under the carpet and ignored. There is always purpose in illness. There is always purpose in disease. They are essential parts of Humanity's evolutionary pattern. They are acts of evolution. It is essential that both the healer and the person to be healed recognise this fact. Inevitably education must come before healing. The role of the healer is not just to channel energy but is to hold a mirror. It is to stand before the person and to enable them to see why they are ill. The person who is ill must then take action, after consultation with the healer, to ensure that the lesson of that illness, that dis-ease within the body, has been understood.

In the World in which you live today, where so many are sick, inevitably the healer will have to choose who to heal. You cannot heal everyone. It is not desirable, or even physically possible, for you as healers to continually channel the healing energy that flows through you. You cannot always be healing. You must keep your physical body in balance. You must respect the nature of your

296

being. Therefore you must choose those who you are to heal. You must select those who will benefit from your healing touch. This inevitably comes down to a feeling within you, to the intuitive force of your being listening and responding to the people who come to you. Intuitively you will know those who you can help and heal. Recognise that there are different healers for different illnesses. Only the great Masters such as the Master Jesus can heal universally. Only they have the cosmic healing touch, the power to raise from the dead. Such power belongs only to those who understand the purpose of creation, and above all, who recognise the workings of the Law of Karma.

Many people in your World today are beginning to feel that they have the potential to be healers. Many are discovering that they are succeeding where the medical profession is failing. There is no longer a clear division between, shall we say, the doctor and the faith healer. People are beginning to recognise that anyone can heal once they have an understanding of the purpose of life and the true nature of disease. Indeed, the role of the healer will once more return to the priest, to the divinely motivated and spiritually grounded person, as was the case in the days of old. Jesus was both priest and healer and that is the ideal to which you should all aim. A true healer shoulders great responsibility, for to heal without reason or purpose is to question the nature of disease and the reason for karma.

It is distressing to see people suffering but the healer must not allow himself or herself to be dragged down by that suffering. The essential quality of any healer, therefore, is detachment. If you are not detached you cannot heal or, rather, you cannot heal to the best of your ability. The healer must always view the patient with detachment: compassion, yes, but always with detachment. The healer must see clearly as he or she looks into their patient's eyes the nature of their soul being. The healer must see clearly the source of their disease, the nature of their inner being, and should always strive to heal not just the outer disease but the inner cause. It is the wise healer that looks first to the cause and then to the disease.

In an Age which is witnessing so many new beginnings, do not be afraid to try to heal. In as much as you are all divine instruments and you align yourselves with the healing flow of the Cosmos you are fulfilling the true purpose of your beings. Many new techniques of healing will soon be discovered and the ways of the old will gradually begin to disappear. They will be regarded as outdated by the people of the New Age. Now that is not to say that all medicine in the World today is wrong, that all surgery is unnecessary, for it has shown that it is capable of great acts of healing in many fields. Nevertheless, the main stream of medicine today has become detached from the divinity of life. It does not recognise the source of life. It does not recognise the divinity of the human body or of the soul that dwells within it. For a true healer, that must always come first.

So as I leave you I would ask those of you who are thinking of becoming healers to consider carefully. There can be no greater role in life. All the great Masters who have walked the physical plane of life have been healers. They have been healers because the World has always been sick. The World has always been in dis-ease, has always been divided. That is the path of human destiny. While Humanity has choice, while there is goodness and evil, inevitably some will choose evil. Some will choose the learning process of illness and disease, and to those I would say, greet that illness just as you would greet health. Recognise that you are carrying forward not just your evolution but the evolution of the whole human race.


## QUESTIONS AND ANSWERS


Q: How does fear relate to disease. Would you consider it to be a cause or an effect?
ZT: There are many levels of fear. Presumably you are talking about fear of disease?

Q: I was meaning fear as an emotion not just fear of a specific disease.
ZT: If one looks beyond the emotion of fear and considers the divine energy of life coming down through each one of you as an individual, it can be said that when you are not at one with that divine flow, which is the love of your Creator, then fear is present. You live in fear only when you are not in the divine flow. Therefore whenever you are not in the divine flow, whenever you are not in harmony with it, there is an opportunity for disease and disharmony to manifest which can lead to illness. Fear manifests when

298

love is not present on every level. So fear can be considered as a lack of understanding of the true divinity of life and this in turn can generate, depending on the degree of fear, conditions within the physical body which can indeed lead to disease.

Q: Do you consider operations like heart and liver transplants necessary even though without them, presumably, the patient would die?

ZT: When one looks at the whole question of organ transplants it cannot be taken in isolation from the attitudes of the medical profession as a whole. Loosely it can be said that the vow of the medical profession is to preserve life. That, in itself, is a noble ideal but in reality that decision to preserve life is based on a fear or a misunderstanding of the role of death. This, of course, reflects for the most part how Humanity feels today. Humanity does not like death because it does not understand it, because it fears it. Therefore any means to prolong life is gratefully sought. Indeed, even you, with your evolved concepts of life and death, would think very carefully of what you would do if you were to be placed on the operating table faced with such a choice. It is easy to say that you do not fear death and are happy to die but if, for example, you are a mother leaving behind young children, you would think very carefully of your responsibilities and commitments. You see yourself as the protector of your children. You would wish to live not for yourself but for your children's sake. There are therefore many factors that can influence your decision but, ultimately, it is the individual who reconciles himself or herself with death.

The medical profession is becoming more and more adept at organ transplants. It has had limited success in some fields, greater success in others. It has, in particular, not experienced a great deal of success in the field of heart transplants. At another time we have said that it is in the field of heart transplants that the greatest danger lies to the human race because the spirit of your being lies within the left ventricle of the heart. Therefore when you have a heart transplant you are removing the seat of the spirit and are creating a zombie. In most cases of organ transplant the body tries to reject any organ which is foreign to it. It is in the nature of the body to do so and because of this massive doses of drugs have to be used in order to accommodate the new organ in the body. This creates disharmony in other parts of the body and I think it would be true to say that anyone who has suffered such an operation never attains perfect health again.

It can be said, therefore, that transplants work only in the sense that they prolong life. They prolong life for varying amounts of years depending upon the success of the operation and the individual health of both the donor and the recipient. Ultimately you as individuals have to decide whether or not you wish to be the recipient or the donor of organs for transplants. It requires deep thought and great consciousness to understand what truly is involved in this process. Is one giving life? Is one preserving life? Is one affecting another person's destiny? What does the person achieve with their life after they have had a transplant? It would be interesting to hold a survey of all the people who have had organ transplants and to objectively assess the quality of their lives after the operation, to see what they have really gained apart from the joy of being alive and of being able to share life a little longer with their loved ones.

It is not for me to say that such operations are right or wrong. They simply represent another step along the present path of human scientific evolution. As always, it is human consciousness that will decide whether or not to use that technology just as it does, for example, with the use of nuclear weapons. The technology is there; it is for the individual to decide whether or not to use it. The choice is all part of the evolutionary lesson. Undoubtedly one is faced with a major choice when one decides whether or not to accept transplants, whether or not to give one's organs for transplants. It is really a question of individual consciousness and of how one views the nature of illness and the purpose of life.

Q: I am thinking of establishing a centre for my own particular form of healing treatment. Can you give me any advice?
ZT: When one embarks on a venture such as yours one must remember that one is judged more critically because one is outside the medical profession than because one is in it. The surgeon can perform a difficult operation but if his patient dies that is accepted as being part of the risk of surgery. Provided there was no malpractice then he will not be blamed for the death. This generosity does not apply to those who are not part of the medical profession. You will truly be pilloried publically if for any reason whatsoever it is

deemed that you have caused suffering through your treatments. This reflects the nature of the World in which you live. I say this not to put fear in your heart or to try and stop you from doing what you want to do. However, it is obvious that before your form of healing treatment becomes publically or medically accepted there must be documented proof of its effectiveness. Moreover, those who advocate and practise such a form of treatment must themselves be holistic beings who recognise the divine healing energy flowing down through them.

So often in the World in which you live today people begin to practise a new form of healing treatment before they have perfected it. But to advance a new treatment and then to have it ridiculed and denounced just because of one or two weaknesses is to risk everything. I think, therefore, that the two of you have a further period of growth to experience in relation to your treatment in order to develop greater public understanding and faith in it. You must establish a common standard, a common code of practice, but one which on the other hand does not rule out the individuality of the energies of those people who use the treatment for healing.

It is unfortunate that in the World in which you live today individuality is frowned upon. Individual healing methods and treatments are not seen for what they really are, a reflection of the uniqueness of Creation. Because there are so many false prophets, so many what you would call cranks, all outside the medical profession are tarred with the same brush. Thus for a system to succeed and to be generally accepted it must be seen as being beyond reproach. So far better that in the beginning you proceed slowly and let the treatment gather momentum naturally rather than expand it too rapidly and run the risk of outgrowing itself like a forced flower. What we are concerned about with any new healing treatment is not the next twenty years but the next two hundred years.

# PEACE

In the World at this moment in time there is a great threat of war mainly because of the nature of Humanity's political and financial empires. Much of the struggle that takes place between these empires is hidden from the public view. As ordinary individuals living your lives you are far removed from the machinations of those who control these empires. Indeed, you have very little idea of the plans that have been made and are ready to be implemented should the decision be made to go to war on any level.

Throughout the known history of Humanity there has always been war. Hardly a decade has gone by without one country or tribe fighting another country or tribe either to acquire a piece of land, to protect its boundaries and sphere of influence or to gain an advantage that was not held previously. The fact that there has not been a major war for the last forty years is only because the major powers of the World cannot see a way of achieving victory without great loss to themselves. If a victory without too great a loss could have been achieved then there would have been war. You are, however, approaching a time of planetary resolution, a time when cosmic factors from beyond the plane of Earth will impel the major powers of this World to make far-reaching decisions, a time when the separatism of the past will have to go, either to be surrendered consciously and willingly or else to be removed forcibly from the plane of Earth.

All over the World today there are many who seek peace. They seek it in many ways: through peace movements, through writing and journalism, through marching and demonstration, through religion and prayer. But will they achieve peace in this way? Why has peace always eluded Humanity? Many people see peace simply as the absence of war but, as you well know, that is not true peace, for that form of peace is but an extension of war, especially if you

303

are still plotting and planning to make war. Peace is not the interval between wars. Can there indeed ever be peace while acts of mental aggression are taking place and weapons of mass destruction are being made? Can one achieve peace simply by getting rid of nuclear weapons or by stating that one is not prepared to use them unless one is oneself threatened by extinction?

The answer to all these questions is something which you as individuals are being forced to consider at this time because of the nature of international politics. But before you can do this you first have to decide the nature of your own peace, what you are prepared to accept or reject, to stand up and fight for or to surrender. I think it would be true to say that most people today seek peace externally. They feel that peace is something which has to be achieved through negotiation, through agreement, through reconciliation, but peace has never come to the plane of Earth through such methods. Although a compromise may be agreed upon and the conflict of interests reconciled, after a few years the old enmities return since the desire for victory is still there. Even though the older generations may remember the scourge of war, there are still politicians who are prepared once again to resort to war as an instrument of national or tribal policy.

Can you not see, therefore, that peace is an inward expression. There cannot be peace outwardly unless there is peace inwardly. Moreover, it is the nature of your own inner peace that will decide your fate in the conflicts that are to come, for if you are at peace inwardly then the nature of the energy that you create and send out will attract peace unto you. You are all magnetic beings, attracting unto yourself according to the note that you send out, and though others may be at war you will be at peace. Though others may be engaged in war, though you may be surrounded by war, you need not be a part of it. At this very moment in time consider how much of your World is in a state of war. Hundreds of thousands of human beings are killing themselves each year and yet you are not a part of that suffering and that slaughter. That is soon to change. Pressures will soon come upon the Western Civilisation that will stretch the peace alliances to breaking point. Pressures will come not only from without but also from within. Therefore you, as individuals, at this time of resolution should resolve within your own hearts what is the nature of your own peace.

When can it be said that you are truly at peace? You are in a state of peace when you are at one with your Creator's Will. When you are in tune with the Infinite you are at peace, and in order to be in tune with the Infinite you have to be self-less, you have to become part of the one-ness of all life, you have to become at one with the Godhead. If Humanity would but recognise its one-ness, its wholeness or holiness, there would be no need for war. If there were no political, financial or racial divisions there would be no war. Recognise that it is the divisions which Humanity creates that are the seeds of discontent, the seeds which lead to war. Consider in your own lives how often you are at war in your everyday relationships, not only with the people around you but with the other Kingdoms of Matter. Be aware of how often you are not at one with the Infinite, of how often you make war to get what you want, what you desire, what you wish to achieve, no matter what the cost to those around, to those who sacrifice to you.

As you look back at Humanity's past wars you can see that little has actually been gained though millions of people have died. Outwardly it may seem that one country has been prevented from taking over another country, a financial interest has been defended, an ideology has been preserved, but what of that country, that financial interest, that ideology, fifty years later? The countries that initiated the last World War have achieved many of the aims they sought militarily through other means. The countries which were your enemies forty years ago are now your friends, those which were your friends are now your enemies. It is obvious, therefore, that the sides which oppose each other in war, the power structures which conflict with each other, are human, temporal creations. It is not a question of right or wrong, of goodness or evil, of one side being for God and the other being against God, for all is of God. Those that make war are, therefore, in a sense, fulfilling the Divine Plan.

It must, of course, be said that God Itself does not desire or initiate war directly as a lesson for Humanity. War is a lesson which Humanity creates of its own choice. Nevertheless, it also cannot be denied that in the act of war great growth and evolution takes place for Humanity. Is it not strange how in a country at war people unite together as never before. The little differences which formerly separated them are forgotten in the hour of crisis. As people are faced with the suffering and the loss of war, as they discover the frailty of human existence, so they come to terms with the reality and purpose of life and death and recognise that they take place every minute of the day. That understanding of life, of course, is there for you to grasp whether there is war or not, but in time of war many people achieve great evolutionary breakthroughs in consciousness.

I ask you, therefore, in this year of resolution to go deeply within yourselves and to seek your peace for, truly, that peace is the only peace that endures. If you do not have peace in your hearts then you do not have peace in your thoughts, your words or your deeds. You cannot achieve peace by war. You cannot achieve peace by violent action, by aggression. You cannot achieve peace by the destruction of that which threatens peace. If you have destroyed an enemy that threatens you, you may have removed that enemy from the physical plane of Earth but what of the thought-forms and the energies that you have created? What of the energies of hatred and revenge that you have released? What of the beings who will come back and inherit the mantle of those thought-forms and energies?

Peace, therefore, involves the quality of humility, of personal surrender. If someone wishes to fight you and you refuse to fight, where is the victory? Though that person may achieve that which they desire they will not be fulfilled by their 'victory' if there has been no struggle to achieve it, if it has been given to them freely with love. What is the real nature of surrender? All of you as individuals find it so difficult to surrender, yet the example of all the great Masters has been just that: the release of the physical in loving surrender and from that act of release comes great strength. If you consider some of the people of this Earth who have stood for peace, who by their very demonstration have shunned war, if you consider the impact that they have had on Humanity you will see that their example is remembered far more than the example of the generals and the soldiers who achieved peace through war. Peace can be achieved for only a short time through war. That form of peace never lasts. The everlasting peace is the peace that you create with your hearts, with the love that comes from within.

Peace is an individual creation. It begins with one person then spreads to two and then to four and so on. Peace is an energy of wholeness which begins individually and then expands. Peace cannot be imposed from above. Peace cannot be imposed by any greater country, by any greater force. Is it not strange that with so many other beings in our Solar Body, with so many other evolved life-forms in our Galaxy, no one seeks to wage war on you? If there are these highly evolved beings from other planets, who visit the Earth in their space ships, with the cosmic power that they possess they could easily establish dominion over this planet and over Humanity as a whole. But they do not do that, rather they seek only to help Humanity along its evolutionary path. There perhaps is the lesson that you should observe. When you have the power, when you have the consciousness, when you have the ability to impose dominion, you do not use it for self aggrandisement. Your space brothers respect your individuality, allow you the freedom to be what you want to be, to evolve at your own pace, to walk your own path and seek your own destiny. You too should give that freedom and that choice to all those around you.

So during these critical years, when so much is being decided on the plane of Earth, be strong in yourselves. Know that there is a force that protects you, a power that is greater than any weapon that Humanity will ever create: Divine Love. Recognise that Divine Will controls all things on your plane of life. The note which you sound, the understanding of life which you exhibit, they are your protection. Inner peace is reflected in outer harmony and even though you are faced by energies of extreme disharmony they will not affect you.

Therefore seek that inner peace, seek that inner wisdom. Know it as the one-ness of your Creator, know it as the one-ness of life. Seek that one-ness in all things and you will find that peace, the peace that passes all understanding. Do not think that it is beyond your comprehension, beyond your attainment. Do not think that it can only be obtained through long periods of meditation and prayer and soul-searching. It can be obtained in the twinkling of an eye, in the understanding of the divinity in one's self, in one's purpose, in one's destiny. That is the lesson of these divisive times, the nature of the choice that faces you all, for there are days coming when there will be war, there are days coming when there will be destruction and death. You must choose now whether you are to be a part of it or to rise above it.

# QUESTIONS AND ANSWERS

Q:  It is easy to talk about peace of mind and at times we do all experience it, but it is not easy to maintain that peace for any length of time.

ZT:  If you were to be at peace the whole time you would be a great Master! You are always in conflict, on differing levels, to varying degrees. There will always be moments in your daily living when you will feel conflict arising, a test presenting itself to you, not that you physically want to make war against anyone but that you are not at one with them in the flow of life. Sometimes you invoke your emotional bodies and bring your emotions into play which causes you to feel very deeply and strongly about the conflict. It is at such times that you have the opportunity of seeing what is peace and what is war within yourselves, for on that level it is just the same as on the international level when countries go to war. You should examine very closely what you are doing and why you are doing it and begin to practise that act of surrender a little more often. Many of you, of course, consider surrender as an act of weakness not as an act of strength.

Q:  You surely must distinguish between situations, between what is important just to you and what is important to life here on Earth. To surrender and so allow a lot of people to suffer would surely be wrong? I was faced with a situation the other day where if I had surrendered my pupils would have suffered. I was told that I was to teach in a classroom which was totally unsuitable. Now if I had surrendered to that I would have had to teach my pupils for a whole year in an unsuitable classroom, but I challenged the authority and got the room changed. I am sure that I was correct to make a stand over that issue.

ZT:  Am I to suppose, from your example, that there were two teachers competing for a more desirable classroom and that the one who didn't get it had to use this 'unsuitable' room?

Q:  Yes. That is correct.

ZT:  So two teachers are competing for one classroom, both trying to justify their position in order to get that classroom, knowing full well that whichever one gets it the other has to have the 'unsuitable' classroom. In that situation you were indeed faced with the decision of whether or not to surrender. Now you have said that it would have been wrong to surrender because you would have ended up teaching in an 'unsuitable' classroom for a whole year, but you have to realise that the act of surrender is not an ending but a beginning. You have to realise what can be achieved by an act of surrender. What, indeed, did the Master Jesus, for example, achieve by his act of surrender? Was his death an ending or a beginning? Did not his death give birth to many creative energies? Therefore you must look very carefully at what you create by surrender, at the energy that you create, bearing in mind that you create on many levels. If you send such an impulse out into the Cosmos then what will come back to you: perhaps something greater than you ever first desired.

You all know the story of Saint George and the dragon. On the one hand there is the story of Saint George slaying the dragon and all the associated mythology that goes with that act, but on the other hand there is the story of Saint George allowing himself to be killed and eaten by the dragon in order to be at one with the dragon and to transform that dragon from within. Which act would achieve the more lasting result and would more greatly affect the generations of Humanity to come, still faced by that dragon? If you think about it, you are at war now because of the acts of past generations who have fought wars. You are experiencing the seeds sown by your forefathers. Perhaps it does require one great act of surrender to transmute that dragon of war.

Q: In the Christmas story in the Bible the angels say to the shepherds "Let there be peace and goodwill between men". What part does goodwill play in peace?
ZT: The angels were saying that true peace between people will only come about when goodwill is present and what is goodwill but God's will. There will be peace on Earth only when God's will exists on Earth, when Humanity recognises God's will. When you as individuals are acting in harmony with God's will then you are at peace with yourselves. When you are manifesting God's will then you have inner peace and there must be inner peace before there can be outer peace. You must be at peace with yourselves before you can be at peace with the World. If you are at war with yourselves then you are at war with the World. That must ever be

309

so. Therefore begin with goodwill or God's will towards yourselves as individuals. Think of the God in you, of the divine spirit which uplifts you at all times. Then when you have inner peace reflect your goodwill on Humanity around you, do to others as you would have others do to you.

Q:  Jesus was surely a man of peace but look what happened to him — a violent death on the cross. Were you not implying that if you were a being of peace you would be protected from death through war or persecution?

ZT:  If you see peace in that light then you have not understood the real meaning of peace, for if you are at peace with yourself that does not mean that you will not be involved in conflict and war, that you will not have to face death. When you truly possess inner peace you have no fear of things physical. Death is no longer regarded as a tragedy, as something to be feared, for with inner peace comes understanding and acceptance. That is why Jesus could die on the cross and forgive those that had put him there: the peace that passes human understanding.

Q:  There seems to be a big gulf between the ordinary man in the street and the government and the military who hold the reins of power. How can we make the governments of the World more peaceful, to reflect the true feelings of those they govern?

ZT:  The politicians and the generals view the current conflict as a struggle for survival in which they are solely responsible for the survival of their country, their religion, their ideology and so on. They believe that they are the sole defenders of their people. It is this egoism which poses the greatest threat to World peace. They are, of course, acting with the best of intentions, with the highest motivation in some cases, but their view of the World and Humanity is blinkered. They take no account of God's will. The ultimate defence, the ultimate deterrent, can only be God's will. Government attitudes and policies will only be changed when God's will is demonstrated by the people they govern. To live and demonstrate peace and goodwill today invites persecution — just as it did two thousand years ago — but that demonstration ultimately will lead to a great transformation of human consciousness. Sow the seeds of peace now, if not for yourself, then for your children. Recognise God's will and there will be peace on Earth.

# THE CREATIVE MARRIAGE

You live in a World that has distorted the reality of almost every human endeavour. It is difficult, even for evolved souls, to recognise the true purpose and meaning of almost any physical act and nowhere is this more true than of the union of marriage. If you were to ask most people today what was the creative purpose of a marriage almost inevitably they would say "Children", because most people today view marriage as the socially acceptable way of having children. Having children is a purpose, but not the purpose, of marriage, for having children is but one aspect of the creative energy that can be grounded in a marriage. Many people that marry should not have children and yet in that union should be able to manifest completely the creative energy of their God.

Recognise, therefore, that the purpose of marriage lies far beyond that of conceiving and rearing children. In order to consider the true purpose of marriage we must go back to the very beginning of human creation, to that moment in cosmic time when you, as individuals, were created. At that moment of cosmic creation your spirit was split into two aspects, into the duality of positive and negative, or male and female. This duality was necessary because at that particular stage in human evolution it had been decreed that Humanity should evolve through the use of the divine gift of free choice. So the purpose of life on Earth is to learn through exercising your free choice when faced with opposites, for by experiencing light you will know darkness and by knowing darkness you will recognise light. It is in the expression and the manifestation of both aspects that the evolutionary process takes place.

So you must realise, even when you are manifesting the highest aspect of your consciousness, that you can only manifest one half of the creative energy. Though you be the most realised person that has walked the face of this Earth you can manifest only one half of the energy of creation. It can be said, therefore, that your destiny over many, many lives is to evolve the male or the female aspect of your being and to that end, as you live each life, you enter into many relationships, you face many tests, you are forced to look at yourself and to learn many lessons. Eventually, after many cycles of evolution, the moment will come when you will merge your spirit, your being, with its other half, its affinity, to become the perfected one, the realised one, the Christed one, a whole balanced aspect of energy capable of being a god, of creating in wholeness, in holiness.

Marriage therefore is an evolutionary tool. It is a tool that is intended to reflect not just the opposites of human sexuality, but the opposites of spiritual energy. Marriage can be likened to a mirror that constantly reflects to both partners the nature of the creative energy that is the opposite of theirs. It is through this reflection that one learns of one's self. There is this belief in your world today that compatibility is the basis of a good marriage, that when two think as one, that when two become one, merging in mutual sympathy and understanding, that the perfect union has been achieved. But I would say that such marriages do not always lead to spiritual evolution and very often can lead to spiritual apathy and soul dissatisfaction. Now that is not to say that marriage should be a seat of argument and conflict, but that there can be love in conflict, that there can be love in argument. Let me also remind you that it is that which produces momentary conflict in your minds that leads to spiritual growth and evolution.

It should be recognised that the creative energy is present in a marriage long before the birth of a child and that a husband and wife can create on many levels before they actually physically conceive and give birth to their children. There are so many levels of life on which a husband and wife can create and those who are not destined to have children have the potential to create in every field of human endeavour and to influence every aspect of physical life. It is through the merging of their inner, spiritual energies that a husband and wife truly create on the physical plane of life. If they do not create children then they will create in some other field: in the arts, in science, in business, in government, in human welfare and so on and so on. A husband and wife create through the merging of their positive and negative energies and through their

312

creations they are grounding the Energy of Creation. Above all, evolved souls should recognise that it is in the field of creative thought that a husband and wife can create so much for good on the physical plane of life. Two evolved souls, living together in a marriage of harmony and balance, can truly transform and transmute much evil on the plane of Earth by their harmonious thoughts and energies. Moreover, through their example and creativity they will help many less-evolved souls to bring about a transformation in their beings.

Marriage, therefore, carries with it a great creative responsibility. You incarnate on the Earth to create both individually and collectively. When you live in isolation you can create only in your own image, you can create only according to your own consciousness and, as such, you can reflect only one half of Creation be it male or female. But when you are living in a balanced marriage, when you have the other half of Creation living with you, exemplifying their aspect of the Godhead, then it is the merging of those two creative energies in harmony and balance that completes the whole and leads to the trinity of Creation. It is through this creative experience, through experiencing the evolutionary process of marriage, that you rise onto another level of life, onto a higher plane of being, and so return to the Source. The two creates the three and so returns to the One.

As you look at the nature of marriage on the Earth today you can see that most people marry for reasons far removed from those of service and holistic creativity. Marriage, for most people, is an act of personal gratification. One marries to fulfil the desires of one's personality, to avoid loneliness, to have someone to confide in and share life's problems with, to conform to social morality and so on, but none of these fulfil the true purpose of marriage. The true purpose of marriage is, and always will be, a spiritual one. There are many, of course, who never recognise that spiritual purpose. That is simply a reflection of their point of consciousness. That is the level at which they enter into marriage and, usually, leave it. But for those of a higher consciousness, for those who are aware of the divinity of all life, of the purpose and meaning of every single human activity, marriage is seen as a holy sacrament. It is a contract made by two divine sparks of life with their Creator. It represents a surrender by the individuals back to the Source. Marriage is an act of service, of sacrifical service, to the other aspect of creation and through that service one creates a bond of divine love which uplifts not just the marriage but the planet as a whole. To do this requires that you recognise that the purpose of marriage is greater than even the wills and desires of the two partners involved. To achieve this purpose, therefore, requires surrender and, above all, humility.

Many times we have spoken of the importance of balance in marriage. Balance can be achieved only by both the partners being prepared to sacrifice their individual wills and desires to the greater force of the marriage, to recognise that the two is more important than the one. Nevertheless, if the individuals develop their divine talents and evolve their beings to the highest of their potential then that is done to the glory of their partner as much as it is done to the glory of their Creator. Rejoice in each others strengths. Rejoice in the uniqueness of each others point of consciousness. Rejoice in the divinity of the talents which you bring to this Earth and recognise that the greatest gift that you can give to your partner is to be a pure channel for the creative energy flowing through you. Marriage is a mirror to your point of evolution, to your point of consciousness. Marriage is a lesson that you have chosen on another level of life. So many people today, when a marriage is beset with problems and tests, tend to blame their partner for the conflict that ensues, but so many people today only look at their partners' weaknesses and not at their strengths. So many people today forget that marriage is a mirror for their own weaknesses as well as their own strengths.

Marriage is one of the great evolutionary tools of physical life and was designed as such by your Creator. Marriage will produce conflict between the two partners even in the most perfect of marriages, but remember that momentary conflict brings about growth and evolution. Do not think that the path of marriage is always destined to run smoothly. Do not think that the power of love will remove all conflicts, all differences. It is not so. Remember that it is through sacrifice to your marriage partner that there comes an opportunity to realise a greater potential for the marriage, a greater creativity. Therefore consider your marriage partner not as an individual to be liked or disliked for their personal characteristics, for the soul aspects that they manifest in physical form, but as a source of Divine Creativity, as an aspect of the Godhead complementary to you in every way. It is by merging those higher aspects that you can create a force for good on many levels of life. What your World needs at this time, above all, is balanced and harmonious creation in thought, word and deed, and through that creativity will be grounded a new child, a new being, one that will truly transform this planet and create a new race of Humanity.

## QUESTIONS AND ANSWERS

Q: What did he mean in that last statement about creating a new child? Was he talking about a physical child?

ZT: No. You are aware that every time you commit the sexual act even though you do not create a physical child you create a child form on the higher levels of life. You create a child energy, a spiritual essence, which exists for eternity. There are therefore many spiritual energies, some good, some bad, depending on the motivation behind their creation, whirling about on the ether. Now in the union of marriage evolved souls should rise above what I will call the sexual act and should create in another way, on a higher level. In a marriage of evolved souls it is possible to create on a level that is more beneficial to the World in which you live. Now that does not mean that the sexual act becomes unnecessary and is no longer needed for the reproductive process, but that evolved souls can create on a higher level if they so choose. I would ask you to look at the principle of the virgin birth and to recognise that it is possible to create without going through the physical act of which you are aware.

Q: Are you talking now about an energy?

ZT: Yes. Have you ever considered what happens when a husband and wife pray or meditate together? The energy that they create on the higher levels of life could, for example, create a thunderstorm.

Q: Yes. I am sure that is true.

ZT: So the perfect union can control the physical World in which you live. You can be the Masters of Matter. You do have dominion over the other Kingdoms of Matter on this Earth. It is here that we

315

touch the force of magic, a force that is much misunderstood on your plane of Earth, and when I say magic I do not mean black or white magic but clear magic about which I have spoken at another time.

Q: I would like to know a little bit more about the purpose of sexuality in marriage.

ZT: Just as there are many levels of human evolution so there are many levels of human sexuality. Each of you approaches the subject of sexuality according to your own point of consciousness and so what is correct for one will prove incorrect for another. It must be recognised, therefore, that the field of sexual energy is as wide as is the spectrum of human evolution. It ranges from the sexual energy of the Animal Kingdom who exercise it naturally, in response to Nature, to that of a great Master who exercises it in a cosmic way, beyond your understanding.

For most of you sexual energy has the connotation of the sexual act. You cannot separate the act from the energy and that largely reflects the attitudes of the society in which you live. However I would like to make it clear that sexual energy is different to the energy created by the sexual act. Obviously the basic attraction in any marriage is what I will call sexual, and by sexual I mean pertaining to the energy of the sexes, but when you recognise that energy as a creative energy and not as a sexual energy you can then see that how you use it affects Creation as a whole. How you create affects the World in which you live. If you create in imbalance, if you create out of lower motivation, then that creativity will be reflected in the World around you.

The sexuality of a man and a woman is capable of creating in every field of human activity and, equally so, it can lead to the creativity of a child. But what has happened today is that the true purpose of sexual energy has been completely reversed. Sexual energy has become not a means of service, not a means of giving to Creation, not a means of creating in the image of the source, but of creating in one's own image, of satisfying the desires of one's lower self. For many people the sexual act has become an act of selfish gratification not an act of service, and that is reflected in the nature of the World in which you live. People are selfish, they live only for themselves. They live only to satisfy their own needs, their own desires. They do not recognise the

316

wholeness of life or the wholeness of the energy that flows through them.

Q: But is it not true to say that the sexual act can be an act of love and that provided one uses contraception and does not conceive a child such an expression can only benefit the people concerned and, therefore, the World as a whole?

ZT: As I have said many times before, the primary purpose of the sexual act is to reproduce the human species. You live in a World which enjoys the so-called benefits of contraception. If there was no such thing as contraception, if every time that the sexual act was committed there was a likelihood of a child being conceived, then people, and particularly the female of the species, would adopt a totally different attitude towards the sexual act.

Q: Speaking as a woman I can say "How true that is"!

ZT: Without contraception one is forced to acknowledge the primary purpose of the sexual act and if one did not want to create, if one did not want a child, then one would not perform that act. But you live in a world which seeks pleasure and what is pleasure but the repetition of something that you have already experienced.

Now I have spoken before of the difference between pleasure and joy. I have said that pleasure is based on memory whereas joy is based on living in the moment. Pleasure is something which you create and, if you enjoy it, try to reproduce, but joy cannot be reproduced, cannot be recreated. It is something which comes in the moment through an inner awareness of the World around you. Joy is that first look at one's child, that moment of spiritual ecstasy as one learns and knows a great cosmic truth, that experience of a beautiful sunset and so on. All those things occur in the moment and then disappear. You cannot live in a state of constant joy unless you are a supreme being. Therefore a vacuum exists between your moments of joy which you feel the need to fill. So into that vacuum you seek to put pleasure seeing it as a form of joy but, truly, it is not, and if you were only more open to the moment you would experience joy more frequently, for the joy of life, the joy of living, is yours to experience.

For most of you the sexual act has become not a creative act but an expression of yourself. You are trying to express yourself through that act regardless of what the act creates on any other

317

level of life. For most people, therefore, the sexual act has become a selfish form of expression. In a natural state man and woman would have sexual relations only when they intended to create a child. Humanity, however, possesses the creative power of rational thought. It has been given the divine gift of free-choice to decide how and when to create. It is part of the lesson of life to use the creative act with responsibility.

Q:   Can you tell us what was the spiritual purpose of our marriage and how will it proceed? Are we destined to form a community on the land that we have?

ZT:   People enter into marriage for many reasons, but evolved souls always know why they are marrying. Now that does not mean that they know the destiny of the marriage, the children they will have, the roles they will play and so on, but that they recognise the broad purpose of their marriage. They have an inner knowledge of why they have come together and of the creativity that they have come to ground. This is obviously a spiritual feeling and, as I have said many times, if you seek first the things of Spirit then all else is added unto you. If the marriage is based on sound spiritual principles then everything else of a lesser level falls into place. If you are in spiritual harmony then automatically you will be in harmony on the lower planes of life.

You must surely have recognised, when you married, that there was reason and purpose in your marriage, that you wished to create as one as opposed to creating individually. You could see that from your union there would come a greater creativity, a greater purpose. Associated with this, of course, is the destiny of the land that you own and your desire to form a community. It is obvious that until you as a unit are one, until you can create totally in harmony and balance, that you cannot create a community or anything of lasting value and purpose. Therefore what you both need is time, time to grow together as one, to recognise the oneness of your being and your purpose, time to seek the spiritual links which exist between you, time to create on the higher levels of life. It is in the nature of that search that you will discover what you are destined to do in this life.

The first years of any marriage are a period of exploration, of exploration of the other aspect of one's being, for by looking in the mirror that is marriage one comes to know oneself and from that

318

knowing comes great growth and evolution. Once the marriage partners have awakened the hidden aspects of their being and have become balanced, holistic beings then they can create on levels beyond their comprehension.

Q: Some of us who have been married for many years feel that it is too late to change the pattern now, that there isn't enough time left to bring about this transformation of which you speak.
ZT: Then let me give you a fresh perspective on time! If your physical incarnation is destined to last eighty years, then the first seventy nine years can be but a time of preparation and in the last year of your life, your eightieth year, you may achieve the real purpose of your incarnation, you may learn the lesson you have come to learn, you may ground the point of consciousness you have come to ground. Spiritual understanding can come in the twinkling of an eye. You all have the time to achieve whatever your heart desires.

Q: You make marriage sound like an initiation. It seems to me that only a great Master can achieve success!
ZT: Marriage is indeed an initiation and not just for the marriage partners but for all who witness that marriage. A good marriage is indeed like a Master. People who come into the presence of a good marriage, who experience the energy of a holistic union, can be compared to those who go to visit a great living Master or guru. It is a similar experience that touches the souls of all concerned.

Q: I have had three children and feel that that is all that I am destined to have in this life. I would therefore be prepared to give up the sexual act but don't because my husband still feels the need for sexual relations. So I use contraception. Are you therefore saying that this is wrong and that I should deny my husband?
ZT: Whether or not you choose to use contraception is something that you alone can decide. It is not a question of right or wrong. Your husband's consciousness and yours ultimately will decide how you will act. What is important, however, is the energy that you create on the higher levels of life as you perform the sexual act. You should dedicate every act of love to your Creator and should invoke a positive energy on your union. Moreover, even though you use contraception and your personality, as opposed to your soul, is denying the creation of a child, you should still be prepared to

319

accept a physical child should it manifest. Even though by using contraception you are expressing your desire not to have a child, you should be aware that if a child does come to you that that is your Creator's wish and should be accepted as such. A child cannot come to you unless you have invited it on a soul level. So perhaps you should view all contraception as 'God willing'!

Q:   What happens if my form of contraception is a vasectomy or a sterilisation?
ZT:   That is not contraception. That is mutilation of the physical body for the purpose of sexual pleasure. True 'contraception' takes place on a level far higher than the physical. True contraception is the result of an agreement reached on a soul level.

# THE WINTER SOLSTICE

It is the day of the winter solstice. It is the time which the ancient peoples of this land regarded as the holiest, the most sacred day of the year. Although, for the most part, Christians celebrate the Christ-Mass on December 25th, that day has no real spiritual significance. It is this day, this moment in time, the winter solstice, that symbolises the moment of birth which the Christian Churches recognise and celebrate with the birth of the Master Jesus. The birth of which I talk now, the birth which the World is really celebrating, is a birth far older than the birth of that Master, for you are celebrating a birth of Cosmic Consciousness, a time of Light descending into Darkness. In just the same way that the incarnation of the Master Jesus onto the plane of Earth was a symbol of that greater birth so, at this time, your celebration of the solstice is a recognition of the grounding of the divine light within you.

Astronomically, of course, for you in the Northern Hemisphere this is the time of the shortest day and the greatest darkness and, therefore, a time of growth, for all things grow in the dark. Light comes forth from Darkness just as a child comes forth from the darkness of the womb. Birth is the creation of Light. Consider, therefore, that this day celebrates the birth of Light. There has to be Darkness, that is a necessary part of the Divine Plan, but from that Darkness comes the Light. You are beings of Light on this plane of Darkness. You incarnate to give of your energy, your love, your creativity and to ground your being on this plane of Darkness, and so create Light.

As you look around the World at this time, as you witness all the conflict and the divisiveness on both an individual and an international level, so you are truly experiencing a time of great Darkness, a Darkness which would appear to threaten to submerge this world into primaeval chaos. But remember the promise of your Creator, the promise of this winter solstice, that the Light will come forth from the Darkness. When the sun no longer moves over this Earth, when the solstices can no longer be celebrated, when that promise has been withdrawn, then a new era will be manifesting upon the plane of Earth. But for as long as you can meet and celebrate this winter solstice, then remember that sacred promise of your Creator: the gift of Light to lead Humanity from the plane of Darkness.

Remember, therefore, at this time, that both Light and Darkness have purpose. Do not see the Darkness as evil but rather as an opportunity for birth. Do not think it is your duty or right to crush evil, for that is not the role of a Saviour. A Saviour is one who saves and in as much as you seek to imitate that last demonstration of the Christ Consciousness realise that you have come to save this Earth, to save those who walk upon it, to shine your Light so as to uplift those who are in Darkness. The real meaning of this day, therefore, is one of renewal, one of commitment. A promise is being renewed by your Creator. The Divine Plan is manifesting on the Earth. Have no fear. Light will come from Darkness. All that is being tested is your reaction to the Darkness. You can only be responsible for yourself, for your own manifestation, for the path that you walk, for what you think, say and create on this plane of Earth. You can come forth from your own darkness: that is the real meaning of this day. You can come forth from the Darkness and grow into Light. You can give of the inner part of your being and manifest Light. You have come to save not just yourselves but to be the saviours of this plane of Darkness.

Remember, therefore, at this time, that no matter what the Darkness, no matter what the apparent evil, no matter what the conflict, the suffering and the degradation that Humanity inflicts upon itself that there is Light, that there is a Divine Plan, that there is a God Who touches every aspect of Humanity and the plane of Earth on which Humanity dwells. The solstice is a symbol of hope, of the fact that there is a purpose to life, that there is a Divine Plan, that there is a Divine Spirit. The peoples of old used to meet on this solstice day to give thanks for the renewal of the commitment of their Creator to Light, to give thanks for the cycles and the seasons of the Earth on which they dwelt, the cycles of Darkness and Light. They recognised and gave thanks for the Darkness just as much as for the Light for they knew that out of the Darkness would come Light, would come a great cosmic principle: the Christ Principle. In similar fashion you today should give thanks for this Darkness and the Light that will come forth from it. Be aware of the Light growing within you in this period of Darkness. Recognise that seed of light as a mother recognises the seed growing within her womb. Recognise it as the seed of life and know that it is for you to bring forth that seed into creativity, into life, into Light. That is the purpose of your being on the plane of Earth.

This solstice, in particular, heralds a time of crisis for the Earth because great changes are coming in this next cycle. These changes will manifest not only within Humanity individually and collectively but on the plane of Earth as a whole. Recognise that these are not ordinary times and this is not ordinary Darkness. This is the beginning of Armageddon, the time when out of a great Darkness will come a great Light, will come a great Saviour. You are now preparing for that Light, for that Saviour. This demands sacrifice and surrender. You have to give wholly and completely of yourself in order to bring forward that Light. You have to give in order to receive. You have first to create on an inner level in order to create outer form.

Many people will be transformed during this period of Darkness. Some will emerge as different people, sounding a different note, manifesting a different way of life. So give thanks for the Darkness, for where there is the greatest Darkness, the greatest evil, there is also the greatest opportunity for growth and learning; for the power of Light is just as great as is the power of Darkness and can be created by the very reflection of a human mirror. There is, therefore, a great potential for Light on the Earth at this time, but that Light has to be shone into the Darkness. You have to lead that others may see and follow. You have to demonstrate. You have to be counted.

Remember, as did the Atlanteans and the Druids as they stood in their circles of stone, that what you are celebrating now is a celebration of Nature, of that which is natural. Humanity has no part in the solstice. Humanity has not created it. Humanity merely worships at the altar of Nature, of the God of the Sun and the Goddess of the Earth. So many human celebrations today are mental, intellectual ceremonies thereby reflecting the nature of religion and the Church, but you meet here on a holy day to celebrate the turning of the Earth in a natural process. Seek such a moment within your own beings, for there are natural cycles and events within you which so often you deny or seek to cover up with your emotions or your intellects. There is a part within you which reflects the true nature of your being. Be open to it on this holy day. Reveal your true nature to the glory of the Creator that gave it to you.

So join with us of the Spiritual Hierarchy in celebrating this natural event. Unite with the forces of Nature both visible and invisible. At this time of great animal slaughter link with the Animal Kingdom and seek to merge your consciousness with its consciousness. Recognise the nature of both your sacrifice and the animal sacrifice. See that all things are but one in the destiny of this Earth. As it says in the Christmas story and can be repeated for ever and ever: Glory to God on high and Peace on Earth amongst all people. There can be no greater invocation: Glory to God, that Being Who gave you Light and Darkness: Peace on Earth, the shining of your Light on the Darkness. Celebrate this event. Join in the communion of Nature and be at one with the Force of all Life.


## QUESTIONS AND ANSWERS


Q: This is our final gathering before we all separate for Christmas. Is there anything you would like to say to us before we go?

ZT: I think that it would be true to say that for many of you this has been a difficult year. It has not been a year of planetary upheaval, as some people prophesied, but rather, as I said at the beginning of the year, a year of resolution. Many of you have made important resolutions on both inner and outer levels. It has been a time for soul-searching, a time for looking inwards, not in a selfish manner but rather to see the obstacles in your being that are standing in the way of your spiritual purpose, your destiny. These inner obstacles, of course, manifest in external form as the problems you have to face, the physical aspects of life that demand your attention. There is always a link between the inner and the outer levels.

Next year, however, is going to be different. It is going to be significant for many of you because what you are going to see is change, change brought about by the resolutions you made last year. You are going to change in many ways, in many directions. Some of you will change countries, some life styles, some inner aspects of your being. Some of you will walk very different paths, some of you will discover aspects of yourselves that you never dreamed could exist within you. Therefore my plea to you is to be open to change. Do not consciously seek it but, when it comes, do not fight it. Remember that it is you that sows the seeds of change and if you have not sown them by now, then it is too late, for the solstice has come, the Earth has turned, the new pattern has begun. It is rather like the gardener who wishes to sow his seeds after spring has passed. It is too late. He should have got them in the ground at the right time. But to those of you who have sown your seeds I say "Watch", for as the darkness turns to light, as you proceed towards Easter and the seed begins to shoot so you will discover new aspects of yourself.

Q: Sometimes I feel very alone when I try to live as the Masters suggest. Is this me or is it something we must just accept?

ZT: You are never alone. Even in your darkest hour inside you is light, your spirit. That is the promise of your Creator. You are always linked. You are never alone. If you are alone then it is because you choose to be so. At this time of year you often feel sorry for the people who are alone, but very often those people have created their own loneliness because they will not give. The response to loneliness is to serve, because when you are serving you have no time for self-pity, for loneliness. So if you see someone who is lonely tell them to start serving, to serve others, to mix with the flow of Humanity and to be one with it.

Q: During a recent solstice channelling there was a very brief reference to an energy injection that was to be implanted into the ether in 1984. It reminded me of another channelling I heard many years ago which said that there had also been an energy injection in the late 1960's. I wondered if you would elaborate on these energy injections?

ZT: Creation on the Earth is a two-way business and I am not talking now of human reproduction but of cosmic creation. Human beings are like cosmic radio aerials: they both receive and transmit. On the one hand there are the thoughts, the desires, the little wills of Humanity going upwards and on the other hand

325

coming down there is the energy of your Creator, the impulse of your God radiating Its consciousness down onto the Earth to fulfil an evolutionary plan, a cosmic pattern, of which most human beings have no concept whatsoever. It is impossible for you to understand Creation at your point of consciousness, so let us just accept that the human pattern that is manifesting on the Earth is part of a great Cosmic Plan. Physical life on the Earth can be likened to a school that is designed to further the evolution of Humanity and, being a school, so the many classrooms are prepared in order to give you the most propitious environment in which to learn your lessons.

So cosmic impulses are sent down to Earth to initiate cycles of learning, and when I talk about cosmic impulses I am talking about surges of cosmic energy which descend into the aura of the Earth and touch the consciousness of all Humanity. Obviously these cosmic impulses touch some people more than others, but the impulses are sent down to prepare the classrooms of Earth for the lessons that are to be learnt. Now obviously there are major impulses which initiate cycles like the Piscean or the Aquarian Ages and there are lesser impulses which initiate events like the solstices, but the impulse that was referred to in that channelling was not just concerned with the solstice, it was concerned with the whole year of 1984. I do not want to get sidetracked now into numerology but as you know 1984 is a karmic year, signified by the numerology of 22 and this means that 1984 is a year when karma will have to be faced and transmuted. It is a time when Humanity has to come to terms with the seeds that it has sown.

If I was to describe the nature of the energy of the impulse that was sent down this year I would say resolution. It is the impulse of resolution that has been sent down so that how Humanity lives and faces the tests of this year will decide the nature of future events. How you live and face this year, how you demonstrate your life, how you respond to that guiding light within you, will determine the karma that you will have to transmute in the years to come. This pattern, of course, will be repeated all over the globe, in every field of human endeavour. This is a year of resolution when old attitudes and understandings must either transform or else die.

326

# A
# CHRISTMAS
# INVOCATION

As the Christ-Mass energy descends upon us, let us recognise not only the flow of energy between each one of us, the opening of our hearts, the giving of our love and energy, but also the downpouring of Spirit. Let us remember the story of the Christ-Mass and the descending of a great Light into a world of Darkness. Let us all unite in that downpouring. Let us unite with that Light and reflect it now and for evermore.

Let us be at one with the energy of the Christ-Mass. Let us resolve not to fight evil but to transmute it, not to oppose but to reflect, not to challenge but to stand. Let us join hands to form a circle of peace and then let us send that peace out to this troubled planet. Let us unite our energies, our light, and send it out to touch every aspect of Darkness on this planet and, as we do that, let us recognise that as we give so we are open to receive, to receive the joy of the Christ-Mass.

May we all go forth along our different paths to touch this planet and those who dwell upon it in our appointed and destined ways, knowing that we are a part of Light, joined to Light and serving Light.